RADICALS IN ROBES

ALSO BY CASS R. SUNSTEIN

Laws of Fear: Beyond the Precautionary Principle, 2005

The Second Bill of Rights, 2004

Animal Rights (editor, with Martha Nussbaum), 2004

Why Societies Need Dissent, 2003

Risk and Reason, 2002

The Cost-Benefit State, 2002

Designing Democracy, 2001

The Vote (co-editor, with Richard A. Epstein), 2001

Punitive Damages (with Reid Hastie, John Payne, David Schkade, and W. Kip Viscusi), 2002

Republic.com, 2001

Behavioral Law and Economics (editor), 2000

One Case at a Time, 1999

Administrative Law and Regulatory Policy (with Stephen Breyer, Richard B. Stewart, and Matthew Spitzer), 1999

The Cost of Rights (with Stephen Holmes), 1999

Clones and Clones (co-editor, with Martha Nussbaum), 1998

Legal Reasoning and Political Conflict, 1996

Free Markets and Social Justice, 1997

Democracy and the Problem of Free Speech, 1993

The Partial Constitution, 1993

After the Rights Revolution, 1990

The Bill of Rights and the Modern State (co-editor with Geoffey R. Stone and Richard A. Epstein), 1992

RADICALS IN ROBES

Why Extreme
Right-Wing Courts Are
Wrong for America

Cass R. Sunstein

BASIC
BOOKS

A Member of the Perseus Books Group
New York

Published by Basic Books,
A Member of the Perseus Books Group

Books published by Basic Books are available at special
discounts for bulk purchases in the United States by
corporations, institutions, and other organizations. For more
information, please contact the Special Markets Department at
the Perseus Books Group, 11 Cambridge Center, Cambridge,
MA 02142, or special.markets@perseusbooks.com.

Designed by Deborah Gayle

Library of Congress Cataloging-in-Publication Data
Sunstein, Cass R.
  Radicals in robes: why extreme right-wing courts are wrong
for America / Cass R. Sunstein.
      p. cm.
  ISBN-13: 978-0-465-08326-8 (hardcover) 1. Political ques-
tions and judicial power—United States. 2. Judicial
power—United States. 3. Judicial process—United States. 4.
Civil rights—United States. I. Title.
  KF5130.S86 2005
  347.73'12—dc22
                                           2005013765
ISBN 0–465–08326–9

05 06 07 08 / 10 9 8 7 6 5 4 3 2 1

For David A. Strauss

The spirit of liberty is that spirit which is not too sure that it is right.
Learned Hand

The dead have no rights.
Thomas Jefferson

Contents

Preface

EVERY DAY OF EVERY YEAR, we Americans are freer because of our Constitution. If we're allowed to say what we like, worship as we choose, proceed without fear of the police, and even govern ourselves, we owe a large debt to our founding document. But our freedom is more fragile than it appears. The meaning of the Constitution is often disputed, and the disputes are often settled by the Supreme Court of the United States. The rights of Americans depend on what the Court says, and the Court doesn't always say what it said before.

It is customary to describe battles over the Constitution as pitting "liberals" against "conservatives," but this description is hopelessly inadequate. While ideology matters, different judges follow radically different approaches to constitutional law, and these approaches go well beyond ideology. My first goal in this book is to describe the four approaches that have long dominated constitutional debates, and to show how these approaches apply to the constitutional questions that trouble us today.

Two of them are minority positions, claiming distinguished historical pedigrees but few supporters on the current federal courts. I will argue for a third, which continues to have strong representation on the judiciary and in the nation as a whole. The fourth, which is ascendant, threatens both our democracy and our rights.

The first position is favored by many American liberals. We may call it *perfectionism*. Perfectionists want to make the Constitution the best that it can be. They follow the document's text, but they are entirely willing to understand that text in a way that reflects their own deepest beliefs about freedom of speech, equal protection of the laws, the power of the President, and other fundamental questions. Perfectionism played a major role in the liberal decisions of the Supreme Court under Chief Justice Earl Warren—the court that, among many other things, banned racial segregation in America; required a rule of one person, one vote; prohibited compulsory school prayer; and provided broad protection to political dissent. Many American liberals are willing to ask the Supreme Court to recognize or create new rights of many different kinds. When liberal perfectionists are committed, in principle, to a right, they often want the Supreme Court to say that that right is part of the Constitution.

The second position is *majoritarianism*. Majoritarians want to reduce the role of the Supreme Court in American government by allowing the democratic process to work its will. Unless the Constitution has been plainly violated, majoritarians believe that the courts should defer to the judgments of elected representatives. This commitment to bipartisan restraint would both permit affirmative action programs and allow states to forbid same-sex sodomy. Oliver Wendell Holmes, perhaps the greatest figure in the history of American law, was a majoritarian, and majoritarianism has recently attracted significant support among lawyers and law professors. Remarkably, however, it is hard to find a consistent majoritarian on today's Supreme Court.

The third position is *minimalism*. Minimalists are skeptical about general theories of interpretation; they want to proceed one step at a time. They are willing to nudge the law in one or another direction, but they refuse to promote a broad agenda, and they are skeptical of "movement judges" of any kind. They insist that the Constitution is not frozen in the past. But they are nervous about the exercise of judicial power, and they disagree with those who want the Supreme Court to elaborate new rights and liberties lacking a clear foundation in our traditions and practices. Minimalists may be either conservative or liberal. Their distinguishing feature is that they believe in narrow, incremental decisions, not broad rulings that the nation may later have cause to regret. Justice Felix Frankfurter was a distinguished minimalist. In recent years, Justice Sandra Day O'Connor has been the Court's leading minimalist, and I argue for minimalism in this book.

The fourth position is *fundamentalism*. Fundamentalists believe that the Constitution must be interpreted according to the "original understanding." In their view, the founding document must be interpreted to mean exactly what it meant at the time it was ratified. If the Constitution did not originally ban the federal government from discriminating on the basis of race, then the federal government is permitted to discriminate on that basis. If the Constitution did not originally permit Congress to forbid child labor, then Congress cannot forbid child labor. If the Constitution did not originally give broad protection to political dissent, then courts cannot give broad protection to political dissent.

My second goal in this book is to explain what is wrong with the fundamentalist position.

As a constitutional creed, fundamentalism bears an obvious resemblance to religious fundamentalism. Religious fundamentalism usually represents an effort to restore the literal meaning of a sacred text. For fundamentalists, it is illegitimate to understand the words of those texts in a way that departs from the original meaning or that allows changes over time. "Strict construction" of the Constitution finds a parallel in literal interpretation of the Koran or the Bible. Some fundamentalists seem to approach the Constitution as if it were inspired directly by God. But since my topic is law, not religion, I do not mean to say anything about religious fundamentalism. It is in constitutional law that fundamentalism can be shown to be destructive and pernicious. Fundamentalism would make Americans much less free than they now are. It would constrict the right to free speech. It would eliminate the right of privacy. It might well allow states to establish official religions. It would do much more.

Fundamentalists often assert that theirs is the only legitimate approach to the Constitution. This is arrogant and wrong. Fundamentalists like to accuse their critics of bad faith. But some prominent fundamentalists have not hesitated to betray their commitment to the original understanding when the historical evidence points to results they dislike. Their willingness to do so suggests that some of the time, they are speaking for a partisan ideology rather than for law.

In extreme cases, the role of ideology is transparent—as in the disgraceful attack on an independent judiciary during the 2005 effort to ask federal judges to reinsert the feeding tube of Terri Schiavo, a brain-damaged woman in Florida. We live in an era in which some prominent politicians are demanding that the courts interpret the Constitution as if it conformed to positions of Republican party leaders—and threatening federal judges with reprisal if they refuse to do exactly as politicians want.

Their efforts should be rejected. My plea, in the end, is for minimalism—an approach to the Constitution that refuses to freeze the document in the eighteenth century, but that firmly recognizes the limited role of the federal judiciary and makes a large space for democratic self-government.

It is not at all pleasant to challenge, as wrong, dangerous, radical, and occasionally hypocritical, the many people of honor and good faith who have come to embrace fundamentalism. Fundamentalists are right to seek to cabin judicial power, and their democratic commitments are a good starting point for constitutional law. But I hope to show that the most appealing goals of fundamentalism can be accomplished in much better ways—and that many of fundamentalism's goals are not appealing at all.

RADICALS IN
ROBES

INTRODUCTION

The Constitution in Exile

It is some time in the future. You are reading a weekly
magazine, which explores how the Constitution has recently
changed as a result of decisions of the Supreme Court.

- *States can ban the purchase and sale of contraceptives. The
  Court has ruled that the Constitution contains no right of privacy. Having overturned Roe v. Wade and allowed states to
  criminalize abortions, the Court now concludes that the Constitution does not protect any right to sexual or reproductive
  freedom. In some states, doctors are subject to criminal punishment for performing abortions. In other states, those who
  use contraceptives or engage in certain heterosexual and
  homosexual acts are subject to fines or jail sentences.*

- *Key provisions of the Clean Air Act, the Federal Communications Act, and the Occupational Safety and Health Act are
  unconstitutional. Using a long-dead idea from the early twentieth century, the Supreme Court has ruled that Congress must
  narrowly confine the power of regulators. Many regulations,
  controlling air pollution, safety at work, and sexually explicit
  material on the airwaves, are invalid.*

1

- *The Federal Government can discriminate on the basis of race and sex. Employment discrimination in federal agencies, IRS audits targeted to specific groups, and sex discrimination in the military are all perfectly legitimate. Free to discriminate on the basis of race, the Department of Justice has eagerly embraced "racial profiling" in its continuing war on terror.*

- *States can establish official churches. The Establishment Clause of the First Amendment, which everybody thought prevented state-sanctioned churches, is now read to prohibit Congress from interfering with states' efforts to aid religion or even to create official religions. A large chunk of the Utah state budget now supports the Mormon Church, its schools, and its missionary programs.*

- *The President has broad power to detain suspected terrorists and those who are alleged to have assisted them. Because of the threat of terrorism, the Court has held that as Commander in Chief of the Armed Forces, the President can detain American citizens who are suspected of assisting terrorists.*

- *Important provisions of environmental laws, including the Endangered Species Act and the Clean Water Act, are beyond national power; some of the Civil Right Acts may be next. Having struck down the Violence Against Women Act in 2000, the Court has invalidated provisions of key laws protecting the environment. It has signaled that it may rethink its decisions upholding various civil rights laws, including the Civil Rights Act of 1964, which forbids employment discrimination.*

- *Even modest gun control laws are invalid. For the first time in the nation's history, the Court has ruled that the Second Amendment forbids both the national and state governments from imposing restrictions on individual gun ownership. The Court has struck down the most aggressive restrictions; it has also indicated that it is prepared to invalidate even the most moderate limitations on gun ownership.*

Do these changes seem radical? They are. But all of them have been urged by a new group of constitutional revisionists, on or off the federal bench; and these revisionists are having a growing influence on the development of the law.

Back to the Past

A few years ago, I found myself in a large audience at the University of Chicago Law School, preparing to hear a speech by Douglas H. Ginsburg, Chief Judge of the influential court of appeals in Washington, D.C. Judge Ginsburg is a graduate of the University of Chicago Law School, my home institution. I like and admire him. He's also an exceptionally able judge, unfailingly fair-minded, and a generous and kind person to boot. On the bench, he's neither an ideologue nor an extremist. But on this day, Judge Ginsburg spoke in terms of a constitutional revolution.[1]

Ginsburg contended that the real American Constitution has long been in exile, and it is time for the nation to restore it. The real Constitution, Ginsburg argued, was abandoned in the 1930s, when the Supreme Court capitulated to Franklin Delano Roosevelt and his New Deal. The Constitution was properly read in 1932, when the national government had sharply limited power and the system of constitutional rights was radically different from what it is today.

Ginsburg began by emphasizing that "ours is a written Constitution." He claimed that this observation is controversial in only one place: "the most elite law schools." In his view, the fact that the Constitution is written has major implications. If judges are to be faithful to the written Constitution, they must try "to illuminate the meaning of the text as the Framers understood it." (Remember that claim; I will spend a good deal of time on it.) Fortunately, judges were faithful to the real Constitution for most of the nation's history—from the founding through the first third of the twentieth century. But sometime in the 1930s, "the wheels began to come off." With the Great Depression and the determination of the Roosevelt Administration, the Supreme Court abandoned its commitment to the Constitution as written.

How did this happen? Judge Ginsburg's first example involved what may well be the most important power Congress has: the power to "regulate commerce . . . among the several states." In the twentieth century, the Commerce Clause has provided Congress with the power to protect civil rights, to combat crime, and to do much more. But Judge Ginsburg referred, with approval, to the old idea that under the Constitution, Congress lacked the power to ban child labor. He made his strongest complaint about the Supreme Court's decision, in 1937, to uphold the National Labor Relations Act, which protects the rights of Americans to organize and to join labor unions. In upholding the Act, the Court said that when labor-management strife occurs, interstate commerce is affected; a strike in Pennsylvania often has a big impact elsewhere. Judge Ginsburg objects that this is "loose reasoning" and "a stark break from the Court's precedent." The National Labor Relations Act, he implies, is unconstitutional.

His complaint goes much deeper. The Court's acceptance of the National Labor Relations Act is not merely "extreme" but also "illustrative." Ginsburg notes that the Supreme Court has upheld a key provision of the most important environmental law, the Clean Air Act, which, in his apparent view, violates the separation of powers by granting too much discretion to the Environmental Protection Agency. He thinks that with the rise of the modern regulatory state, the "structural constraints in the written Constitution have been disregarded."

This is a strong charge, but it is just the tip of the iceberg. Since the 1930s, the Court has "blinked away" crucial provisions of the Bill of Rights. Of these, Judge Ginsburg singles out the Constitution's Takings Clause, which says that government may take private property only for public use and upon the payment of "just compensation." Judge Ginsburg objects that the Takings Clause has been read to provide "no protection against a regulation that deprives" people of most of the economic value of their property. Properly read, Ginsburg argues, the Takings Clause provides far more protection to property than the Supreme Court has been willing to give.

In decisions involving property, the Court has "blinked away" individual rights. At other times, it has created new rights "of its own devising," acting as a "council of revision with a self-determined mandate." What does Judge Ginsburg have in mind? His chief objection is to the right of privacy. Evidently he rejects *Roe v. Wade* and believes that no constitutional right to privacy protects the right to choose abortion. But he goes much further than that. His real objection is to the Court's reasoning in its 1965 decision in *Griswold v. Connecticut,* in which it struck down a law forbidding married people to use contraceptives. A judge "devoted to the Constitution as written might conclude that the document says nothing about the privacy of" married couples.

The *Griswold* decision, he says, is "not an aberration." It is matched by recent decisions holding that the Constitution imposes limits on capital punishment, such as the 2002 decision striking down a death sentence imposed on a mentally retarded defendant. Here, too, the Court created rights out of whole cloth, defying the actual Constitution.

Judge Ginsburg concludes that until 1932 or so, the Court followed the nation's founding document. But at that point, it adopted the "freewheeling style" that it employs today. But he offers hope for the future. A small but growing group of scholars and judges has recently begun calling for more fidelity to the constitutional text, focusing on the original meaning. "Like archeologists, legal and historical researchers have been rediscovering neglected clauses, dusting them off, and in some instances even imagining how they might be returned to active service."

Judge Ginsburg's leading example is the Second Amendment to the Constitution, which protects the right "to keep and bear arms." He gives a strong signal that judges might well strike down gun control legislation. "And now let the litigation begin."

Judge Ginsburg is calling for a form of constitutional fundamentalism. He is speaking on behalf of what he has called the Constitution in Exile[2]—the "real" Constitution that he believes should be restored. What makes this argument so remarkable is that Judge Ginsburg is a modest and responsible person with a first-rate intellect. On the bench he is both excellent and restrained. If someone like this is calling for radical changes in constitutional understandings, we can be sure that many others are doing the same.

And so they are. All over the country, activists are trying to transform the Constitution, moving it much closer to the version that existed at a much earlier point in our history—or perhaps to the views of the most extreme elements of the Republican party. These reformers include a number of federal judges—radicals in robes, fundamentalists on the bench. Usually appointed by Ronald Reagan, George H. W. Bush, or George W. Bush, some of these judges do not hesitate to depart radically from longstanding understandings of constitutional meaning. Not only are they are eager to understand the Second Amendment to protect the personal right to keep and bear arms; they are also willing to impose severe restrictions on Congress's power and to strike down affirmative action programs, campaign finance regulation, environmental regulations, and much else.

"And now let the litigation begin."

Our Many Constitutions

Is the United States governed by a single Constitution? Almost everyone thinks so. But in a sense, they're wrong. As Judge Douglas Ginsburg suggests, our political disagreements produce fundamental changes in our founding document. With the election of a new president the Constitution's meaning can shift dramatically, altering our most basic rights and institutions.

As it was understood in 1915, the Constitution could not possibly have permitted a Social Security Act or a National Labor Relations Act, and it prohibited minimum-wage and maximum-hour laws. In the 1930s, President Roosevelt's New Deal included all these things. Roosevelt didn't change a word of the Constitution. But by 1937, the Supreme Court had upheld nearly everything he wanted. The Constitution, the Court agreed, did not stand in his way.

In 1945, nearly everyone thought that if the state and federal governments sought to separate people on grounds of race, the Constitution would not be violated. The Constitution did not protect the right to vote; it permitted official prayers in the public schools; and it failed to provide much protection to political dissent. By 1970, everyone agreed that the Constitution prohibited racial segregation, safeguarded the right to vote, banned official prayers in the public schools, and offered broad protection not only to political dissent but also to speech of all kinds. If American citizens in 1945 were placed in a time machine, they would have a hard time recognizing their Constitution of just twenty-five years later.

Richard Nixon and Ronald Reagan intensely disapproved of these rights-expanding efforts, and they set about to change them. By 2005, the Constitution was starting to look a bit more like it did in 1920. The powers of the national government were being limited, the rights of criminal defendants were scaled back, the Constitution offered less to members of minority groups, and the rights of private property owners were being expanded. In 2005, the Constitution did not look exactly as Richard Nixon or Ronald Reagan envisioned it. But it made major moves in their direction.

The meaning of our Constitution has been much debated during the last twenty years. There are continuing battles over abortion, the right to vote, the power of the President, the war on terror, sex discrimination, capital punishment, gun control, the end of life, and same-sex relationships. Important as they are, these battles obscure much larger questions about competing visions of the Constitution.

My purpose in this book is to explain the nature of these competing visions and their implications for concrete constitutional issues. I shall show that the visions are both identifiable and enduring, and that they help to illuminate our disagreements over our founding document. I shall also show that in the last decade, a new form of judicial activism has emerged from the nation's advocacy groups, law schools, and even courtrooms. The new activists claim that they are returning to the original Constitution. They purport to revere history, and sometimes they are faithful to it. But all too often, they read the Constitution as it embodies the views of a partisan political platform. Here I will identify their approach, explore its defects, and set out an alternative—one that rejects judicial arrogance in its many forms, liberal and conservative alike. The last point is worth emphasizing. While my main target is the new (and growing) activism of the extreme right, I shall be challenging the old activism as well, symbolized above all by *Roe v. Wade* and the aggressive liberal decisions of the Warren Court.

Back to the Present

Since the election of President Reagan, a disciplined, carefully orchestrated, and quite self-conscious effort by high-level Republican officials in the White House and the Senate has radically transformed the federal judiciary. For more than two decades, Republican leaders have had a clear agenda for the nation's courts, including the following major goals:

- to reduce the powers of the federal government, including Congress itself;

- to scale back the rights of those accused of crime;

- to strike down affirmative action programs;

- to eliminate campaign finance laws;

- to diminish privacy rights, above all the right to abortion;

- to invigorate the Constitution's Takings Clause in order to insulate property rights from democratic control;

- to forbid Congress from allowing citizens to bring suit to enforce environmental regulation;

- to protect commercial interests, including commercial advertisers, from government regulation.

Republican leaders have sought out judicial candidates who would interpret the Constitution and other federal statutes in a way that would promote this agenda. And their nominees have been appointed to the bench. The most radical goals have yet to be achieved; federal judges pay attention to the law, and they do not like to break radically from the past. But to a degree that has been insufficiently appreciated and is in some ways barely believable, the contemporary federal courts are fundamentally different from the federal courts of just two decades ago. What was then the center is now the left. What was then the far right is now the center. What was then on the left no longer exists.

Consider a few examples. Justices William Brennan and Thurgood Marshall were the prominent liberals on the Court in 1980; they did not hesitate to use the Constitution to protect the most disadvantaged members of society, including criminal defendants, African-Americans, and the poor. Brennan and Marshall have no successors on the current Court; their approach to the Constitution has entirely disappeared from the bench. For many years, William Rehnquist was the most conservative member of the Court. He was highly respected for his intelligence and well liked for his integrity and amiability; and as the Court was composed, he was far to the right of Chief Justice Warren Burger, also a prominent conservative. But Justices Antonin Scalia and Clarence Thomas are far to Rehnquist's right, converting him into a relative moderate by comparison.

In 1980, the Scalia/Thomas brand of conservatism had no defenders within the federal judiciary; their distinctive approach was restricted to a few professors at a few law schools. But it is extremely prominent on the federal bench today. Justice John Paul Stevens is a Republican moderate, appointed to the Court by President Gerald Ford. For a long period, Justice Stevens was well known as a maverick and a centrist—independent-minded, hardly liberal, and someone whose views could not be put into any predictable category. He is now considered part of the Court's "liberal wing." In most areas, Justice Stevens has changed little if at all; what has changed is the Court's center of gravity.

But what about the often-noticed fact that the Court is often divided 5–4 or 6–3? Don't the close divisions show a moderate court, divided between liberal and conservative wings? Actually the close divisions tell us very little. Whatever the Court's composition and orientation, it will often end up dividing 5–4 or 6–3, simply because people won't bring cases that they are bound to lose. If the Supreme Court shifted radically to the left, people would bring, and settle, different cases, and the cases that came to the Court would inevitably be the close ones for the particular justices who compose it. No less than any other, a left-wing court would soon find itself often divided, 5–4 or 6–3. So too if the Court shifts radically to the right. The existence of close votes should not mislead us; it is a simple fact that the Court is far more conservative now than it was a quarter-century ago.

Conservative constitutional thought itself has changed even more radically. In the 1960s and 1970s, many principled conservatives were committed to a restrained and cautious federal judiciary. Their targets included *Roe v. Wade,* which protected the right to abortion, and *Miranda v. Arizona,* which protected accused criminals; conservatives saw these rulings as unsupportable judicial interference with political choices. They wanted courts to back off. They asked judges to respect the decisions of Congress, the President, and state legislatures; they spoke in explicitly democratic terms. This is far less true today. Increasingly, the goal has been to promote "movement judges"—judges with no interest in judicial restraint and with a demonstrated willingness to strike down the acts of Congress and state government.

On the central issues of the day, some conservatives seem to think that the Constitution should be interpreted to overlap with the latest Republican Party platform. In its most extreme form, this view can be found in the suggestion that it is time to return to the Constitution in Exile, or some "lost Constitution."[3]

Of course legal thought is diverse, and the extreme view is hardly shared by all conservatives, the most principled of whom continue to reject it. We shall encounter several varieties of conservative thought, some far less ideological, and some with considerable appeal. Indeed, the approach that I shall be defending has its deepest roots in conservative thought, with its insistence on incremental change and its distrust of reform by reference to theories and abstractions. But the emergence of the extreme view, and its national influence, are unmistakable.

In fact it seems to have reached the White House itself. When President Bush speaks of "strict construction," he is speaking, in the view of many of his supporters, for the Constitution in Exile or the Lost Constitution. Mona Charen, a prominent conservative commentator, made the point entirely clear, stating that the President's idea of "strict construction" is understood, by those who listen, to mean that the Constitution means what it meant when it was ratified.[4] What Charen failed to acknowledge is that this position would lead to radical alterations in our institutions and our rights. On that point, advocates of "strict construction" have been all too obscure—even loose.

Of Presidents, Politicians, and Constitutional Change

In transforming the federal judiciary, Presidents Reagan, George H. W. Bush, and George W. Bush have hardly restored the Constitution to its meaning in 1932; but they have produced large changes in constitutional law. Their goal—of course shared by some of their Democratic predecessors, above all Franklin Delano Roosevelt—has been to populate the bench with young judges committed to their preferred view of the Constitution. On that count, they have mostly succeeded. A quarter-century after Reagan's election, many of his appointees are still active—and will remain so for years. But the effort to reshape the federal judiciary has not been limited to Republican presidents. Some Republican senators have been equally single-minded. Showing extraordinarily little respect for presidential prerogatives, aggressive Republican senators did a great deal to block President Bill Clinton's judicial nominees.

Sometimes the obstructionists justified their actions by labeling Clinton nominees (whatever the facts) as "liberal activists." Sometimes they offered no reasons at all and simply refused to schedule confirmation hearings. As a result, many moderate Clinton nominees received no serious consideration from the Republican-led

Senate Judiciary Committee. To take just one example, the current dean of the Harvard Law School, Elena Kagan, is no ideologue; she's an exceptionally qualified and universally respected person with centrist views. President Clinton nominated her for the United States Court of Appeals for the District of Columbia Circuit. But under the leadership of Senator Orrin Hatch, the Republican-led Senate Judiciary Committee failed to provide Kagan with a hearing.

Unlike their Republican counterparts, Democrats in the White House and the Senate have often been passive. Democrats have of course cared about the fate of *Roe v. Wade* and the right to abortion. But until quite recently, they have considered the composition of the federal judiciary a relatively low priority. President Clinton chose two centrist justices for the Supreme Court, Ruth Bader Ginsburg and Stephen Breyer. These are exceptionally distinguished choices, and I shall argue that their caution and moderation are entirely appropriate. But because of their centrism, they cannot be seen as ideological counterweights to Justices Antonin Scalia and Clarence Thomas. And with a few prominent exceptions—most prominently the Supreme Court nominations of Robert Bork and Clarence Thomas—Democratic senators have tended to defer to Republican presidents. Under Reagan and the first President Bush, several immoderate "movement" judges were confirmed to the lower courts without the slightest protest. Under George W. Bush, Senate Democrats were occasionally more aggressive, blocking a small group that included some of his most extreme appointees. But the overwhelming majority of President Bush's nominees have been confirmed. At most, Democrats have placed a finger in a dike, with predictably weak results.

The result of this generally one-sided political battle is that America now has an ideologically reconstructed federal judiciary, one that has frequently taken a strong stand against both Congress and the states. Some of the conservative reconstruction deserves to be enthusiastically welcomed, for it counteracted an unhealthy use of the federal courts, by liberal reformers, as an engine for social change that ought to have been debated in democratic arenas. Conservatives have long been correct to raise doubts about the courts' use of ambiguous constitutional provisions to invalidate the outcomes of democratic processes. But in many ways, a judiciary with a tendency toward left-wing activism has been replaced by one tending toward right-wing activism. Consider the fact that the Rehnquist Court has overturned more than three dozen federal enactments since 1995—a record of aggressiveness against the national legislature that is unequaled in the nation's history. In terms of sheer numbers of invalidations of acts of Congress, the Rehnquist Court qualifies as the all-time champion. Here are a few illustrations:

- The Rehnquist Court has thrown most affirmative action programs into extremely serious question, raising the possibility that public employers will not be able to operate such programs and that affirmative action will be acceptable only rarely and in narrow circumstances.

- The Rehnquist Court has used the First Amendment to invalidate many forms of campaign finance legislation— with Justices Scalia and Thomas suggesting that they would strike down almost all legislation limiting campaign contributions and expenditures.

- The Rehnquist Court has ruled that Congress lacks the power to give citizens and taxpayers as such the right to sue to ensure enforcement of environmental laws.

- The Rehnquist Court has interpreted regulatory protections extremely narrowly, sometimes choosing the interpretation that gives a minimal amount to victims of discrimination, pollution, and other misconduct.

- For the first time since the New Deal, the Rehnquist Court has reinvigorated the commerce clause as a serious limitation on congressional power. As a result of the Court's invalidation of the Violence Against Women Act, a large number of federal laws have been thrown into constitutional doubt. Several environmental statutes are in constitutional trouble.

- Departing from its own precedents, the Rehnquist Court has sharply limited congressional authority to enforce the Fourteenth Amendment. In the process, the Court has struck down key provisions of the Americans with Disabilities Act, the Religious Freedom Restoration Act, and the Violence Against Women Act, all of which received overwhelming bipartisan support in Congress.

- The Rehnquist Court has used the idea of state sovereign immunity to strike down a number of congressional enactments, including parts of the Age Discrimination in Employment Act and the Americans with Disabilities Act.

Of course the Rehnquist Court is not a radical court, and it has not done everything that extremists would like it to do. Judges generally follow precedent, even if they do not agree with it. The Court has not permitted mandatory school prayer or overruled *Roe v. Wade*. It has not entirely eliminated affirmative action programs. It has rejected President Bush's boldest claims of authority to detain suspected terrorists. It has struck down laws that criminalize same-sex relationships. In especially controversial decisions, it has invalidated the death penalty for mentally retarded people and for juveniles. But we should not lose the forest for the trees. Even if those who sought to reorient the Supreme Court have not received all that they wanted, they have succeeded in producing a body of constitutional law that is fundamentally different from what it was twenty years ago. Notably, many of the more cautious decisions were issued by a bare majority of 5–4 or a close vote of 6–3; with small changes in the Court's composition, the moderate decisions would not be moderate at all.

What is especially odd, and at first glance inexplicable, is that the federal judiciary has been under particular assault from the extreme right in a time in which judges have already gone so far in the directions that conservatives prefer. The Supreme Court has upheld voucher programs for public schools; it has pointedly refused an opportunity to strike down the use of the words "under God" in the Pledge of Allegiance; it has increasingly rejected the idea of a strict separation of church and state; it has not questioned laws forbidding same-sex marriages; it has firmly rejected the idea that affirmative action is constitutionally compelled; it has generally refused to use the Constitution to provide new protections for disabled people and aliens; it has upheld bans on physician-assisted suicide; it has mostly rejected attempts to broaden the right of privacy. Why are extremists complaining so bitterly about a federal judiciary that has been moving steadily to the right?

The New Path of the Law

Perhaps the answer is simple: Much larger changes can be imagined. We could easily foresee a situation in which federal judges shift far more abruptly in the directions in which they have been heading. They might not only invalidate all affirmative action programs, but also

- reduce or even eliminate the right of privacy;

- elevate commercial advertising to the same status as political speech, thus forbidding controls on commercials by tobacco companies (among others);

- strike down almost all campaign finance reform;

- reduce the power of Congress and the states to enact gun control legislation;

- further reduce congressional power under the Commerce Clause and the Fourteenth Amendment;

- limit democratic efforts to protect disabled people, women, and the elderly from various forms of discrimination;

- significantly extend the reach of the Takings Clause, thus limiting environmental and other regulatory legislation.

To many people, these results will seem appealing on political grounds. But even if so, they might want to hesitate before approving of Supreme Court decisions that move in this direction. If judicial decisions greatly overlap with the views of members of an identifiable political party, something is unquestionably amiss; and members of that very party are likely, before long, to regret the increase in judicial power. American history is full of examples.

Of course courts move slowly. Of course judicial appointees are disciplined by law, and they usually attempt to follow settled principles. But significant changes have been occurring, accompanied by large-scale shifts and a growing ambition in the commitments of the most extreme conservatives. As we shall see, conservative critics are entirely correct to object to some of the Court's liberal decisions, including *Roe v. Wade* itself. They are right to say that the Court should be reluctant to wield ambiguous constitutional provisions as a kind of all-purpose weapon against reasonable judgments from Congress and the states. But now, some Republican leaders are asking the Court to do exactly that.

Many right-wing extremists even appear to have convinced themselves that by a remarkable coincidence, there is a close fit between their own political commitments and the Constitution itself. This is of course a delusion. But in a way, they're right. By appointing judges who see things their way, they are making the fit closer every day.

PART ONE

The Great Divide

CHAPTER ONE

Fundamentalists and Minimalists, Perfectionists and Majoritarians

HERE'S MY PERSONAL CHOICE for the silliest moment in the presidential debates of 2004. The two candidates were asked whom they would appoint to the Supreme Court. President George W. Bush replied, "I would pick somebody who would not allow their personal opinion to get in the way of the law. I would pick somebody who would strictly interpret the Constitution of the United States." Senator John Kerry did not disagree. He said, "I don't believe we need a good conservative judge, and I don't believe we need a good liberal judge. . . . I want to make sure we have judges who interpret the Constitution of the United States according to the law."

The candidates were in complete agreement: Judges should interpret the law. This claim is at once correct and ludicrously unhelpful, in a way a sham. Everyone knew that Bush and Kerry would favor different sorts of judges. Consider President Bush's mention of, and criticism, in the same debate, of "the *Dred Scott* case, which is where judges years ago said that the Constitution allowed slavery because of personal property rights. That's a personal opinion; that's not what the Constitution says. So I would pick people that would be strict constructionists. Judges interpret the Constitution. No litmus tests except for how they interpret the Constitution."

One oddity here is that anti-abortion groups regularly equate *Roe v. Wade*, protecting the right to choose abortion, with *Dred Scott*; they think that the nation should be rid of *Roe* for the same reason that it has rid itself of *Dred Scott*. While saying that he would have no "litmus tests," President Bush was also taken, by many insiders, to be giving a subtle but clear signal that he would favor appointees who oppose *Roe v. Wade*.

Of course judges aren't politicians, and both candidates were right to say that the judicial task is to interpret the law. But in the controversial cases, judges often disagree. When they do, what are they disagreeing about?

It is standard to separate judges along two lines. The first involves ideology. Some judges lean to the left, others to the right. Maybe Democratic presidents tend to appoint liberal judges, whereas Republican presidents appoint conservative ones. The second involves interpretation. Some judges favor "strict construction," while others are much looser. Maybe some judges take the Constitution seriously as it was written, whereas other judges use the Constitution as the basis for imposing their own values and preferences.

The first division is certainly helpful. At least some of the time, ideology matters greatly in judicial decisions. Consider the usual suspects: affirmative action, campaign finance reform, abortion, capital punishment, disability discrimination, environmental protection, and sex discrimination. On all these issues, Republican appointees show more conservative voting patterns than Democratic appointees do.[1] Ideology isn't all there is to judging;

Republican and Democratic appointees often agree, simply because the law constrains them. But where the law leaves room for reasonable doubt, ideology can play an important role.

Of course some people deny this point—or deny, at least, that their favorite judges are influenced by ideology. But as a class, Republican appointees interpret the Constitution differently from Democratic appointees. The difference has a lot to do with ideology.

Are judges properly divided into "strict" and "loose" interpreters of the Constitution? Justice Antonin Scalia is often thought to be the leading practitioner of "strict construction." President Bush, a frequent supporter of strict construction, has singled out Justice Scalia as the type of person he would like to appoint to the Supreme Court. But Scalia deplores strict construction. "I am not a strict constructionist, and no one ought to be."[2] Scalia does not believe that the Constitution should be interpreted "strictly" or "broadly." He describes strict construction as a "degraded" idea that brings his "whole philosophy into disrepute."[3]

The distinction between strict and loose interpretation is unhelpful. But it does point toward something real. Some judges, including Scalia, insist on interpreting the text in accordance with its original meaning, and other judges do not. This difference, which Scalia himself describes as "the great divide,"[4] is important, and it helps explain some disputes about the meaning of the Constitution. It begins to illuminate the real divisions on constitutional interpretation.

Two Approaches: Of Nudges and Earthquakes

Consider two kinds of judges: *fundamentalists* and *minimalists*. Those who embrace the Lost Constitution or the Constitution in

Exile certainly count as fundamentalists, and Republican presidents have sought to appoint many fundamentalists to the federal bench. Justices Scalia and Thomas unquestionably fall into this category.

As I am understanding them here, fundamentalists think that constititutional interpretation requires an act of *rediscovery*. Their goal is to return to what they see as the essential source of constitutional meaning: the views of those who ratified the document. They believe that "originalism" is the proper approach for constitutional interpretation and that the Constitution should be read to fit with the original understanding of the founding generation. The central constitutional questions thus become historical ones. If the Constitution was not originally understood to ban sex discrimination, protect privacy, outlaw racial segregation, or forbid censorship of blasphemy, that's that. Judges have no authority to depart from the understanding of 1789, when the original Constitution was ratified, or 1791, when the Bill of Rights was ratified, or 1868, when the Fourteenth Amendment was ratified.

Fundamentalists have a broad and ambitious theory of constitutional interpretation, but they typically believe that their theory reflects the right kind of judicial modesty, simply because they are following the rules established by others. Fundamentalists know that current constitutional law does not reflect their own views, and they tend to feel angry and even embattled about that fact. For this reason, fundamentalists have radical inclinations; they seek to make large-scale changes in constitutional law. (Justice Thomas is the best example here; Justice Scalia, who often accepts precedent, is more cautious.) Many fundamentalists do not want to make these changes all at once, but they hope to make them sooner rather than later.

Fundamentalists do not want narrow rulings tailored to the facts of the particular cases. They don't believe, for example, that judges should say that this affirmative action plan is illegitimate because of its distinctive features, but that other affirmative action programs with other features might be valid. Such narrow rulings, they think, leave a great deal of unpredictability and also increase judicial discretion.[5] They insist that firm, clear rules, laid down in advance, are the best way of ensuring clarity for the future.

Clear rules have two major virtues for judges, who are after all, human. First, they constrain them by reducing their ability to shift with the political winds. Second, clear rules embolden judges by encouraging them to protect liberty when the stakes are highest.[6] Fundamentalists also believe that clear rules provide a highly visible background against which other branches of government can do their work. The characteristic feature of fundamentalism, then, is an effort to understand the American Constitution as it was originally understood, accompanied by skepticism about cautious, tailored decisions in favor of decisions that are broad and even sweeping.

———————

Fundamentalists are opposed by minimalists, who dislike ambitious theories, including originalism, and who do not want to do much more than is necessary to resolve cases.[7] As a matter of principle, minimalists do not want to take sides in large-scale social controversies. They favor shallow rulings over deep ones, in the sense that they seek to avoid taking stands on the biggest and most contested questions of constitutional law. They prefer outcomes and opinions that can attract support from people holding many different theoretical positions. Minimalist judges try to avoid the deepest questions about the role of religion in society, the meaning of the free speech guarantee, the extent of the Constitution's protection of "liberty," or the scope of the President's authority as Commander in Chief of the Armed Forces.

Above all, minimalists attempt to reach *incompletely theorized agreements* in which the most fundamental questions are left undecided. They believe that such agreements are a practical necessity in a diverse society. They also believe that such agreements allow people to show one another a large measure of mutual respect. Minimalists have no desire to revolutionize the law by reference to first principles. They know that such principles are contested and that it is hard for diverse people, and diverse judges, to agree on them. They think that law, and even social peace, are possible only when people are willing to set aside their deepest disagreements, and are able to decide what to do without agreeing on exactly why to do it.

Minimalists believe that a free society makes it *possible for people to agree when agreement is necessary, and unnecessary for people to agree when agreement is impossible.* For minimalists, constitutional law consists of a series of incompletely theorized agreements in which judges accept a certain approach to free speech, or equality, or religious freedom, without necessarily agreeing on the deepest foundations of that approach.

Minimalists celebrate the system of precedent in this spirit. Judges may not agree with how previous judges have ruled, but they can agree to respect those rulings—partly because respect for precedent promotes stability, and partly because such respect makes it unnecessary for judges to fight over the most fundamental questions whenever a new problem arises. For example, some liberal judges believe that affirmative action programs should almost always be upheld, and some conservative judges believe that such programs should almost always be struck down. But if judges respect precedent, they will not simply follow their own judgments; they must pay heed to what others have said before them. Many fundamentalists will not much hesitate to reject precedents that they believe to be wrong. Minimalists are far more cautious about undoing the fabric of existing law.

Minimalists also favor narrow rulings over wide ones. They like to decide cases one at a time. They prefer decisions that resolve the problem at hand without also resolving a series of other problems that might have relevant differences. Minimalist judges may say, for instance, that it is permissible to adopt some kinds of affirmative action plans but not others; everything depends on context. In general, minimalists try to avoid broad judgments that might turn out, on reflection, to be unwarranted.[8]

Of course minimalists know that narrow rulings can create big problems for lower courts, other branches of government, and ordinary citizens who want to know what the law is. But in the most controversial areas, they are willing to pay uncertainty's price, believing that it is even worse to set out law that might turn out to be badly wrong.

By itself, minimalism is a method and a constraint; it is not a program, and it does not dictate particular results. We can easily find liberal minimalists and conservative minimalists. Justice Ruth Bader Ginsburg's approach to the law is complex, but much of the time, she is a (somewhat) liberal minimalist. She likes to decide cases, rather than set out broad principles; and she is reluctant to embrace large-scale generalities about the foundations of the law. Conservative minimalism is nicely captured in the opinions of Justice Sandra Day O'Connor. O'Connor is no ideologue; she isn't a part of any movement. But much of the time, her votes are in a conservative direction. She has contributed a great deal to decisions cabining affirmative action and increasing government's power to protect fetal life; but she has refused to vote to forbid affirmative action in all circumstances or to overrule *Roe v. Wade*.

Minimalists are cautious by nature, and the minimalist camp is large and diverse. We can even imagine minimalists with fundamentalist leanings. Such judges would prefer narrow decisions but would nudge the law toward the views of those who ratified the relevant provision of the Constitution. The point is that all minimalists accept the following proposition: For judges, nudges are much better than earthquakes.

Politics

Modern constitutional disputes, I suggest, are best understood in terms of the division between fundamentalism and minimalism. That division dominates the most important debates within the Supreme Court itself. Justices Scalia and Thomas are emphatically fundamentalists. They are often opposed by O'Connor, the Court's leading minimalist. The same division has played a major role in the appointments of recent presidents. President Reagan sought to appoint many fundamentalists to the bench, believing that it was extremely important to reorient constitutional law by reference to the most basic principles. When President George W. Bush speaks of "strict construction," as he often does, he is taken by many to embrace fundamentalism. President Bill Clinton generally chose minimalists. But minimalism also has had its advocates under both Reagan and Bush, and some of their appointees have strong minimalist inclinations.

The debate between fundamentalism and minimalism lies at the heart of confirmation battles within the U.S. Senate. Over the past generation, Democratic senators have had no trouble with minimalists, even if these judges have been quite conservative. But these senators have given careful scrutiny to, and sometimes blocked, those they believe to be fundamentalists. Robert Bork, an exceptionally able, honorable, and distinguished judge, was rejected by the U.S. Senate in October 1987 above all because he appeared to be a fundamentalist seeking to make radical changes in the law. By contrast, Anthony Kennedy was confirmed in February 1988 on the ground that though unquestionably conservative, he was really a minimalist.

Several of President George W. Bush's lower court nominees expressed enthusiasm for the Constitution in Exile, and their fundamentalism got them into big trouble. For example, President Bush nominated Judge Janice Rodgers Brown to the influential United States Court of Appeals in Washington, D.C.; the nomination was resisted initially on the ground that Judge Brown described Franklin Delano Roosevelt's New Deal as "our own socialist revolution" and spoke favorably about wildly activist, and long-abandoned, Supreme Court decisions invalidating maximum-hour and minimum-wage laws.

Under President Bush, many Republicans accused the Democrats of "playing politics" with the judiciary. They were right; the ideological beliefs of the Bush appointees were sometimes the source of the difficulty. But the accusation neglects something important. Some appointees had controversial and even radical views about the Constitution, and they were chosen for exactly that reason.

Perfectionists

Fundamentalism and minimalism are the principal antagonists in contemporary constitutional law. But there is a third position with an enduring influence, which I shall call *perfectionism*.[9] Perfectionists agree that the Constitution is binding; it is, after all, what they want to perfect. But they believe that the continuing judicial task is to make the document as good as it can be by interpreting its broad terms in a way that casts its ideals in the best possible light. Under Chief Justice Earl Warren, the Court often followed the perfectionist path; Justices William Brennan, Thurgood Marshall, and William O. Douglas can all be described as perfectionists.

Of course conservatives can act as perfectionists, too. When they interpret the Equal Protection Clause to forbid affirmative action, they should probably be seen as trying to make the clause "the best it can be," rather than as following any original understanding. As we shall see, some conservatives are perfectionists in fundamentalist clothing; they invoke history, but they don't really care about it. What matters, for my purposes, is that fundamentalism, rather than perfectionism, has been the animating creed of the political right.

Ronald Dworkin, one of the leading legal philosophers of the twentieth century (and the twenty-first as well), does not use the term, but he sees perfectionism, as I am understanding it here, as an essential part of legal interpretation. In his view, legal interpretation is a matter of putting the existing legal materials "in their best constructive light," or of making them "the best they can be."[10] Dworkin agrees that judges are obliged to "fit" previous law; they must be faithful to it, and they cannot legitimately make up the law out of whole cloth. But if previous law leaves ambiguities or gaps, judges must try to make it better rather than worse. Suppose, for example, that courts are deciding whether the Constitution protects the right to physician-assisted suicide. Dworkin thinks that judges must identify the most attractive principle that can be brought forward to justify the Court's previous decisions on the content of "liberty," and ask whether that principle protects the right to physician-assisted suicide as well.

In the last few decades, perfectionists of various kinds have sought to use the Constitution to strike down bans on same-sex marriage, to create a right to welfare, and to give people a right to make medical decisions free from governmental constraint. On the current Supreme Court, perfectionists have been fairly quiet, simply because the perfectionists of the Warren Court have no successors on that Court. Perfectionism can easily be found in the major law schools, but it is rare on the federal courts. Hence fundamentalism is the real contemporary alternative to minimalism. Indeed, the major battle, within current constitutional law, is between fundamentalists and their minimalist adversaries. I shall attempt to demonstrate this point with many examples.

Some perfectionists claim to be fundamentalists. For example, the First Amendment says that Congress shall "make no law abridging the freedom of speech," and free speech advocates enlist fundamentalism on their behalf. They like to say that the framers of the Constitution gave us a simple and absolute free speech principle. The journalist Christopher Hitchens, writing in the *New York Times,* seems to favor such a principle and announces that "the authors of the Constitution were right the first time."[11] Hitchens is typical of the many free speech enthusiasts who believe that the authors of the First Amendment believed in broad protection of dissenters. But what does Hitchens think the authors were right *about?* By its literal terms, the First Amendment is limited to Congress; it does not forbid censorship by the President or the courts, who, as far as the text goes, can regulate speech however they wish.

In any case, real fundamentalists, interested in what the ratifiers wanted, will ask what they understood by the prohibition on
any "law abridging the freedom of speech." Free speech advocates
would be disturbed to find that some historians believe that as
originally understood, the First Amendment allowed subsequent
punishment of political dissent.[12] They would be even more disturbed to find that some historical evidence suggests that the free
speech principle was narrow rather than broad—and that it may
well have been compatible with laws punishing blasphemy, libel,
and even dissent that the government deemed dangerous.

On free speech, then, civil libertarians claim to be fundamentalists, but they're really perfectionists. They're speaking for themselves, not for those who ratified the Constitution. We'll see that
many people with different political views are no different. They
claim history's support for their constitutional positions on gun
control, commercial advertising, affirmative action, and property
rights. Don't be fooled; their game is perfectionist.

Agendas, Movements, and Threats

It is not possible to demonstrate, in the abstract, the superiority of
one or another approach to constitutional interpretation. We cannot say, once and for all time, that fundamentalism is inferior to
minimalism, or vice-versa. Nor can we rule out perfectionism. The
greatest figure in the history of American law was Chief Justice
John Marshall; Marshall's greatness comes from his many opinions establishing the authority of the national government in the
young United States. Marshall was a distinctive kind of perfectionist, one who insisted on ensuring that the United States be
genuinely united, rather than a collection of several states. We

might describe Chief Justice Marshall as a nation-building perfectionist. History's verdict is entirely in his favor.

Or consider the more recent example of South Africa, building a new constitutional tradition in the aftermath of apartheid. There, perfectionist judges, firmly committed to racial equality, might be very much in order. Many people continue to defend the Warren Court, to which I will turn shortly; they believe that the (liberal) perfectionism of that particular court served the nation well. But I have many doubts about the Warren Court. And for the contemporary United States, I believe, and I shall attempt to show, that minimalism is best and that both fundamentalism and perfectionism are dangerous. The reason they are dangerous is best captured in Judge Learned Hand's comment, made in the heat of World War II, that "the spirit of liberty is that spirit which is not too sure that it is right."[13] Hand's comment has strong implications for both elected representatives and citizens. It suggests that when we disagree with one another, even on the most fundamental issues, each of us ought to have a little voice in our heads, cautioning: *I might be wrong.*

Unelected judges, even more than most, should respect liberty's spirit. They lack a strong democratic pedigree; they do not stand for reelection. In addition, they have no particular expertise in ethics or political theory. They're sometimes unable to foresee the consequences of their own decisions. For these reasons, they should be reluctant to endorse controversial views about politics or morality, and to use those views in ambitious rulings against their fellow citizens. Their judgments may be erroneous; judges lack special access to moral and political truth. Even when they are right, their decisions may be futile or counterproductive. If, for example, federal judges ruled that states must recognize same-sex marriages, they might well set back the very cause that they are attempting to promote. In the 1960s and 1970s, conservatives invoked arguments of this kind as the basis for powerful attacks on perfectionism. They convincingly argued that judges should back off. In my view, federal courts do best, in the most controversial areas, when they rule narrowly and proceed incrementally.

Of course countless people disagree. Many perfectionists, and most fundamentalists, despise minimalism. I have noted that under the leadership of Chief Justice Earl Warren, the Supreme Court often ruled ambitiously. It struck down racial segregation in the schools and elsewhere. It created a right to privacy, saying that married people have a right to use contraceptives. It gave broad protection to political dissent, saying that the government cannot regulate speech unless it can show a clear and present danger. It prohibited official prayer in the public schools. It required the police to give the *Miranda* warnings to those in custody; it said that evidence obtained in violation of the Constitution could not be used to obtain a criminal conviction. It imposed a rule of one person, one vote in state elections. It struck down poll taxes. It did much more.

To say the least, the Warren Court did not limit its rulings to the facts of particular cases. After Earl Warren left the Court, the Court sometimes continued in his path, above all by vindicating the right to choose abortion and by striking down sex discrimination. Perfectionism has left a large mark on the law, which is one reason that many fundamentalists see minimalism as a form of capitulation to illegitimate law. And indeed, we will see that perfectionism, or at least its traces, plays a role in many areas of contemporary constitutional law.

Why is minimalism so controversial? The answer is simple. If you have no doubt that your own theory is right, as fundamentalists and perfectionists tend to, then minimalism will seem a dodge or even a form of cowardice. Those who believe in the Lost Constitution or the Constitution in Exile are exceedingly confident about their views. They are quite sure of themselves; they do not hesitate to accuse others of bad faith. They know what the Constitution means, and they know that the Supreme Court has abandoned it. They think that current law has been built, in steps small and large, in an illegitimate way, producing an illegitimate structure. Why, they ask, should contemporary judges perpetuate error rather than correcting it?

Fundamentalists have a clear agenda for the federal judiciary. Many of them consider themselves part of a movement with identifiable goals, which include the overruling of *Roe v. Wade,* the elimination of affirmative action, and decisions in the direction of the Constitution of 1789. Because Justices Scalia and Thomas are plainly committed to fundamentalism, they can aptly be described as "movement judges." They endorse originalism and hence want to interpret the Constitution in accordance with its original meaning. To their great and enduring credit, they usually follow their own preferred method. They take the historical materials very seriously.

On the other hand, there are a number of important areas in which fundamentalists follow their own partisan convictions rather than the original understanding. To take just one example, fundamentalists (including Scalia and Thomas) have voted in favor of striking down affirmative action programs without even bothering to investigate the question whether such programs are inconsistent with the original understanding of the Fourteenth

Amendment. (They aren't.) Here we can see false fundamentalism, hiding behind the Constitution to impose judges' own political values. Unfortunately, false fundamentalism is not hard to find.

Theories

Fundamentalists have an official theory, originalism, which I take up in Chapter 3. But what is the theory behind perfectionism? It's certainly harder to describe, which is one reason fundamentalists have had a major advantage in public debate. It is much easier to defend the claim that judges should "follow the Constitution as it was originally understood" than the claim that judges should "interpret the Constitution to make it the best that it can be." (Try defending the latter claim before a jury of your peers.) And because perfectionism is more a ghost than an active participant in current controversies, its own foundations might be thought to be a historical curiosity. But some ghosts continue to haunt. Because much of current law is rooted in perfectionism, we had better try to understand what it is all about.

Some perfectionists invoke the Constitution itself to justify their approach; they speak as if the document, fairly read, necessarily generates the results they seek. But this is implausible. More candid perfectionists appeal to what they see as the requirements of democracy. Call them *democratic perfectionists*. These people believe that where the Constitution is ambiguous, judges should interpret it to promote democracy rather than to compromise it. Democratic perfectionists insist that the Supreme Court should act most aggressively when the requirements of democracy are themselves at risk.[14] They believe, for example, that the right to free speech needs to be protected because the people's sovereignty is compromised without it. They justify the Court's invalidation of poll taxes, and its insistence on one person, one vote, by reference to democratic principles.

Extending their democratic claims, they also insist that the Court should protect those groups that are least able to protect themselves in democratic arenas. For this reason, they believe that the Constitution's Equal Protection Clause should be interpreted to prevent discrimination against African-Americans, women, illegitimate children, disabled people, and (more recently) gays and lesbians. Perfectionists contend that members of the relevant groups lack the political power to protect themselves—and that a strong judicial role is therefore necessary to "perfect" democracy itself.

But many perfectionists also believe in a strong constitutional right to privacy, and they cannot easily justify that protection with reference to democracy. Why can't a self-governing people decide to interfere with privacy if it likes? Some perfectionists insist that the Constitution should be read to protect the essentials of human dignity, including a right to make the most fundamental choices free from the constraining arm of the government. Call such people *rights perfectionists*. For them, the right to make fundamental choices includes sexual and reproductive liberty, which, they believe, the Constitution should be read to safeguard. Hence perfectionists seek to carve out a realm of freedom into which the state cannot intervene.

Is perfectionism a plausible approach to the Constitution? Recall Judge Douglas Ginsburg's emphasis on the fact that the document is written—a fact that, in his view, *requires* it to be interpreted as it was originally understood. Perfectionists think this is a fraud. Any theory of interpretation, they insist, must be defended, not merely announced. Of course the Constitution is

binding and it has to be interpreted as "written." But perfectionists contend that its written words are best understood to offer
general principles that are capable of change over time. Often they
argue that a perfectionist approach is invited by the very generality of the document's key phrases: freedom of speech, equal protection of the laws, due process of law. Sometimes perfectionists
contend that their approach to the document makes the constitutional system work best. In their view, any approach has to be
defended on just that ground.

Fundamentalism seems to have major advantages over perfectionism. It doesn't allow federal judges to "perfect" the document
by their own lights. It promises to create a solid and unchanging
Constitution, whose meaning does not evolve with new circumstances. If judges are bound by the original understanding of the
Constitution, then they cannot interpret the document to favor
the values and liberties that they prefer. Hence fundamentalism
can claim the virtues associated with the rule of law. Perfectionists
often respond that "we" should not be bound by understandings
of decades or centuries ago. But their fundamentalist antagonists
respond that any interpretation will be done by a "they," not an
"us"—and federal judges are the relevant "they." A big problem
with perfectionism is that it gives the judges enormous power to
pick and choose—to select the values they deem crucial to democracy, or dignity, and to understand the Constitution so as to promote those values.

But we should be careful about favoring fundamentalism over
perfectionism on these grounds. Is it so clear that the Constitution
should be interpreted so as to be solid and static? Perhaps it is better if the Constitution's meaning shows some movement over
time, even if judges are helping to produce the movement. Still

more important, fundamentalism represents a *choice*—one that has to be justified against alternatives. Suppose that we are asked to agree that the Constitution should be interpreted in accordance with its original meaning. Should we? Why? If that approach would lead to a an inferior system of individual rights, there's at least a problem.

In the end, I believe that fundamentalism must be defended in ways perfectionists would understand. Fundamentalists must suggest, for example, that judges who pursue perfection will make things worse rather than better—and that judges who follow fundamentalism will really improve the system as a whole. Candid fundamentalists know that they must say, in the end, that their approach will make constitutional law better, all things considered. I am not attempting to defend perfectionism. Ultimately I shall reject it. But it is important to understand the nature of the debate.

Activism and Restraint

Current debates about constitutional interpretation, I have said, are best understood in terms of the division between fundamentalism and minimalism. But many people will think that this opposition misses the central point. They will contend that some judges are "activists," whereas others are "restrained." Of course the opposition between activism and restraint has played a pivotal role in recent debates over the federal judiciary. Liberal judges are often excoriated for their activism; members of the Rehnquist Court are often criticized as activists too.

But what is judicial activism? Does *Brown v. Board of Education,* invalidating racial segregation, count as an activist decision? Does *Roe v. Wade,* because it extended the right to privacy to include a woman's right to an abortion? Would it be activist for the current court to overrule *Roe*?

There are, broadly speaking, two accounts of judicial activism. Some people label a decision "activist" when they think that the court has departed from the correct approach to the Constitution. On this view, the word "activist" isn't merely a description. It is also and always an insult. When people criticize judges as activist, they mean just this: *The court is not following the right understanding of the Constitution.* To label a decision "activist" is to label it wrong.

On a different account, the word "activist" is purely descriptive, and a decision that is activist is not necessarily wrong. A court that rejects its own precedents might be considered activist. No one believes that this form of activism is never justified. Of course some courts should reject some precedents if they are ludicrously mistaken or hopelessly outdated. A court that is activist, in the sense that it rejects precedent, might be entirely right. Or a court might be described as activist if it strikes down the actions of other branches of government. No one thinks that a court should uphold all actions of the other branches. A court should not allow governments to lock people up because of their skin color. A court that is activist, in the sense that it invalidates some decisions of the political branches, will often be something to celebrate.

People are free to use the term "activist" however they wish, so long as listeners understand what they mean. But the risk of misunderstanding is very high, and it is especially confusing if people describe a decision as "activist" when and because they disagree with it. To reduce that risk and to prevent confusion, I suggest that it is best to measure judicial activism by seeing how often a court strikes down the actions of other parts of government, especially those of Congress. Such decisions preempt the democratic process. They take decisions out of the hands of voters. They are activist in that important sense. This is a value-neutral definition of acitivism. It doesn't say whether activism is good or bad.

By this definition, *Roe v. Wade* is an activist decision, whereas the much-despised *Plessy v. Ferguson,* upholding racial segregation, is not. *Bowers v. Hardwick,* the 1986 decision upholding bans on homosexual sodomy (overruled in 2003), is restrained in the same sense as *Plessy.* For clarity's sake, let us simply stipulate that a court that frequently invalidates federal and state statutes is activist, while a court that rarely does so is restrained. I am proposing this approach simply as a way of being clear on what we are saying. To reiterate: I don't mean to suggest that an activist court, so defined, is always wrong, or that a restrained court, so defined, is always right.

On this understanding, both fundamentalists and minimalists are capable of activism; indeed, there is no good answer to the question whether one or another camp is "more" activist. A quick glance at the Constitution in Exile should be enough to show that many fundamentalists are activists with a vengeance, because they are eager to embark on a large-scale project of invalidating acts of Congress and state governments. It is easy to find fundamentalists who are highly activist with respect to affirmative action programs, the powers of Congress under the Commerce Clause, campaign finance reform, and the protection of private property. But fundamentalists also favor restraint—in the sense of respect for democratic prerogatives—with respect to abortion, discrimination on the basis of sexual orientation, and protection of criminal defendants. Liberal perfectionists are restrained where their fundamentalist counterparts are activist, and vice-versa.

Minimalists are much harder to categorize. But because of their defining creed, they are not systematic believers in restraint. Justice O'Connor, for example, is entirely willing to strike down some affirmative action programs. She just doesn't want to adopt a general rule against such programs. She has also voted to invalidate acts of Congress under the commerce clause and to protect property rights against state regulation. But she favors narrow and cautious rulings. Under my definition, minimalists are willing to be activists too.

Does Nonpartisan Restraint Exist?

Does *anyone* have a principled commitment to judicial restraint? We can certainly identify an alternative to fundamentalism, minimalism, and perfectionism: *nonpartisan restraint*. Let us describe its advocates as *majoritarians*.

Majoritarians are willing to give the benefit of every doubt to other branches of government—to uphold the actions of those branches unless they clearly violate the Constitution. Where fundamentalists would strike down federal and state legislation, majoritarians want courts to stand aside. Where perfectionists would protect equality and dignity, majoritarians say that the elected branches should usually be allowed to do as they like. Majoritarians would permit the government to ban same-sex sodomy, or for that matter opposite-sex sodomy. They would also permit the government to create affirmative action programs, or even racial quotas designed to increase the number of African-Americans in colleges and graduate programs.

No member of the current Supreme Court is a committed majoritarian. But this approach was embraced in one of the most important essays in the entire history of constitutional law, written by Harvard law professor James Bradley Thayer in 1893.[15] Fundamentalists and minimalists alike have to come to terms with him. Thayer argued that because the American Constitution is often ambiguous, those who decide on its meaning must inevitably exercise discretion. Laws that "will seem unconstitutional to one man, or body of men, may reasonably not seem so to another; . . . the constitution often admits of different interpretations; . . . there is often a range of choice and judgement." In Thayer's view, "whatever choice is rational is constitutional."

Thayer's argument, in brief, was that courts should strike down laws only "when those who have the right to make laws have not merely made a mistake, but have made a very clear one,—so clear that it is not open to rational question." The question for courts "is not one of the mere and simple preponderance of reasons for or against, but of what is very plain and clear, clear beyond a reasonable doubt." Most people are familiar with the "beyond a reasonable doubt" requirement in criminal law, which means that people cannot be convicted unless prosecutors are able to meet that demanding standard. Thayer believed that courts should follow the same standard in reviewing the work of legislators; judges should strike down legislation only in the clearest cases of constitutional violation.

In asking for restraint, Thayer was emphasizing two points. The first is the fallibility of federal judges. When judges conclude that a law is unconstitutional, they are of course relying on their own interpretation, and they might be wrong. Judges are learned in the law, certainly. But should we conclude that judicial interpretations are necessarily correct? Thayer was not questioning the judges' power to strike down unconstitutional laws. He was saying only that in exercising that power, judges should not be (too) sure that they are right.

Thayer's second point was that a strong judiciary might harm democracy itself. Constitutional disputes tend to be entangled with the deepest questions about what is fair and just. He feared that if judges become too aggressive, the moral responsibilities of elected officials might weaken. Those officials might ask, *Will the judges allow it?* instead of, *Is it really constitutional or even morally acceptable?* If the latter question is not asked, democracy itself is at risk.

Writing over a century ago, Thayer lamented that "our doctrine of constitutional law has had a tendency to drive out questions of justice and right, and to fill the minds of legislators with thoughts of mere legality, of what the constitution allows." Indeed things have often been worse, for "even in the matter of legality, they have felt little responsibility; if we are wrong, they say, the courts will correct it." Thayer sought to place the responsibility for justice on democracy, where it belongs. "Under no system can the power of courts go far to save a people from ruin; our chief protection lies elsewhere."

Thayer's concerns have a lot of contemporary relevance. Consider the war on terrorism. Is America permitted to torture suspected terrorists in order to obtain valuable information that might save American lives? In discussing that question, the Bush administration has often focused on the question of whether courts will stand in its way. Its lawyers have failed to devote enough attention to another question, which is how the President of the United States should interpret laws that appear to forbid acts of torture against people who have not been convicted of any crime. Democrats are hardly immune from the tendency against which Thayer warned. In extending the power of the federal government, they have often asked whether courts will permit Congress to do as it likes. They have rarely asked whether the Constitution is properly understood to limit the authority of the national legislature. This is a situation that Thayer would deplore.

Thayer has no followers on the Supreme Court. No national leader, Republican or Democrat, is arguing for his position. But Thayer had a strong influence on one of America's greatest jurists, Oliver Wendell Holmes; in fact Holmes was Thayer's protégé.

Holmes stated his commitment to nonpartisan restraint most influentially in dissenting from the infamous decision in *Lochner v. New York*,[16] where the Supreme Court invalidated restrictions on maximum-hour regulation. In the Court's view, maximum-hour laws deprived both employees and employers of liberty without due process of law. In one of the most celebrated opinions in the history of the Supreme Court, Holmes disagreed. He explained that "a constitution is not intended to embody a particular economic theory. . . . It is made for people of fundamentally differing views, and the accident of our finding certain opinions natural and familiar or novel and even shocking ought not to conclude our judgment on whether statutes embodying them conflict with the Constitution of the United States." Accusing the Court of imposing its own views on the country, Holmes announced that the "Fourteenth Amendment does not enact Mr. Herbert Spencer's Social Statics." In his most crucial passage, Holmes argued that the constitutional protection of liberty does not "prevent the natural outcome of a dominant opinion, unless it can be said that a rational and fair man necessarily would admit that the statute proposed would infringe fundamental principles as they have been understood by the traditions of our people and our law."

Holmes's majoritarianism is far more ambitious than Thayer's, because it reflects Holmes's distinctive vision of the Constitution. In Holmes's view, the founding document recognizes America's extraordinary diversity—its diversity at any one time, and its diversity across time. In a free nation like ours, many ideas will emerge and new social commitments are inevitable. Over the years, some previously honored values will lose out, while others, previously ignored or even despised, will come to the fore. What judges think—what any of us thinks—should not be regarded as sacrosanct. If we have a firm belief, it may simply be because of fortuities of our lives and circumstances. Hence Holmes's remarkable suggestion that the "*accident* of our finding certain opinions *natural* and familiar or novel and even shocking" is beside the constitutional point.

Holmes meant exactly what he said. With few exceptions, he believed that courts should respect the outcomes of democratic processes.[17] Holmes wrote the shocking opinion for the Court in *Buck v. Bell,* in which the Court upheld a law calling for the compulsory sterilization of people with a low IQ. In his short and cavalier opinion, Holmes wrote, "three generations of imbeciles are enough."[18] This is Holmes's majoritarianism with a vengeance.

In the history of American legal thought, majoritarianism has occasionally attracted significant support. During the New Deal period, many supporters of President Franklin Delano Roosevelt argued for a much weaker judicial role. Justice Felix Frankfurter, the great conservative on the liberal Warren Court, was generally committed to judicial restraint, with the presumption that democratic processes should be allowed to do as they like. More recently, Professor Mark Tushnet, a distinguished scholar of constitutional law, has gone so far as to argue that the Constitution should be "taken away from the courts"—that judges should be deprived of the power to strike down the acts of other branches of government.[19] Constitutional interpretation, in Tushnet's view, should be undertaken by Congress, the President, and state governments.

While Tushnet's own politics are left of center, his skepticism about judicial power cuts across partisan lines. Judge Robert Bork, a vigorous critic of the Warren Court, has argued for steps that would make it possible for Congress to "overrule" Supreme Court decisions.[20] Stanford Law School Dean Larry Kramer has argued against judicial supremacy and for "popular constitutionalism."[21] Under that approach, all branches of government, and above all We the People, would be involved in constitutional interpretation. Kramer does not say that the Court should be deprived of power to strike down legislation; but he would not allow the judges to have the final word.

Thayer, Holmes, and their followers are great critics of both fundamentalism and perfectionism. They want something like a wide principle: Courts should uphold legislation unless it is clearly beyond constitutional boundaries. Taken seriously, this principle would have dramatic consequences. It would rule out the Constitution in Exile, simply because the Constitution does not unambiguously call for it. Majoritarians would certainly eliminate the right to choose abortion; indeed, they would eliminate the right of privacy altogether. Majoritarians would permit governments to discriminate on the basis of sex and would certainly allow the national government to discriminate on the basis of race. (The

Equal Protection Clause, the main source of the constitutional ban on racial discrimination, does not even apply to the national government.) They would probably permit state and federal governments to ban commercial advertising, libelous speech, sexually explicit speech, and possibly even blasphemy.

Majoritarians can defend their position with an ambitious theory about democratic self-government. Following Thayer, they can urge that when the Constitution is vague, We the People and our elected representatives should be entitled to interpret it. This idea has received considerable elaboration in Dean Kramer's plea for popular constitutionalism. But as I have emphasized, majoritarianism has no defenders on the federal bench. Minimalists are skeptical about it, simply because it embraces a large theory that would call for major revisions in current practices. For judges who prefer to decide one case at a time, nonpartisan restraint is simply too radical.

But nonpartisan restraint does have something important in common with minimalism: It asks courts to avoid resolving the most fundamental questions on their merits, and it expects ordinary citizens and their representatives to play a large role in resolving those questions. Those who endorse nonpartisan restraint are not too sure that they are right. And some minimalists have at least a degree of sympathy for nonpartisan restraint. Most of the time, they believe that judges should give the benefit of the doubt to the elected branches.

The Players

Four tendencies organize contemporary constitutional thought: fundamentalism, perfectionism, majoritarianism, and minimalism. It is easy to imagine interesting debates among them. Each position is vulnerable to coalitions of the other three.

Are fundamentalists trapped in the past? Do they engage in ancestor worship? Perfectionists, minimalists, and majoritarians think so. In their view, time machines aren't a good way to do constitutional law. To their critics, fundamentalists are engaged in a project that would ultimately endanger American constitutionalism itself.

Are minimalists spineless? Does minimalism violate the rule of law? Fundamentalists, perfectionists, and majoritarians think so. In their view, minimalists are wrong to favor narrow, cautious rulings. Such rulings make the law far too unpredictable—a matter of seat-of-the-pants decisions by unelected judges.

Do majoritarians fail to take the Constitution seriously? Fundamentalists, minimalists, and perfectionists think so. In their view, majoritarians convert the Constitution into a program for majority rule, even majority oppression—a real irony in light of the fact that the Constitution limits what majorities can do. For fundamentalists, minimalists, and perfectionists, majoritarianism refuses to use the founding document to protect rights that are central to self-government and even to citizenship itself.

Are perfectionists arrogant? Do they cede too much power to unelected judges? Fundamentalists, minimalists, and majoritarians think so. They contend that perfectionists do not respect democracy and that they ignore the fallibility of the judiciary. In their view, perfectionists adapt the Constitution to their own preferences, allowing it to serve as a kind of all-purpose clay for judicial molding.

I will deal with many of these debates. But for the foreseeable future, the real battle is between fundamentalism and minimalism. To understand this battle, and its intensity, we need to venture directly into the heart of contemporary fundamentalism.

CHAPTER TWO

History's Dead Hand

Originalism seems to me more compatible with the nature and purpose of a Constitution in a democratic system. A democratic society does not, by and large, need constitutional guarantees to insure that its laws will reflect "current values." Elections take care of that quite well. The purpose of constitutional guarantees—and in particular those constitutional guarantees of individual rights that are at the center of this controversy—is precisely to prevent the law from reflecting certain changes in original values that the society adopting the Constitution thinks fundamentally undesirable. Or, more precisely, to require the society to devote to the subject the long and hard consideration required for a constitutional amendment before those particular values can be cast aside.

—Antonin Scalia[1]

Some men look at constitutions with sanctimonious reverence, and deem them like the arc of the covenant, too sacred to be touched. They ascribe to the men of the preceding age a wisdom more than human, and suppose what they did to be beyond amendment. I knew that age well; I belonged to it, and labored with it. It deserved well of its country. It was very like the present,

but without the experience of the present; and forty years of expe-
rience in government is worth a century of book-reading; and this
they would say themselves, were they to rise from the dead. . . . Let
us no[t] weakly believe that one generation is not as capable as
another of taking care of itself, and of ordering its own affairs.

—Thomas Jefferson[2]

FUNDAMENTALISTS ENDORSE AN "ORIGINALIST" APPROACH to
constitutional interpretation. In their view, the meaning of the
Constitution is settled by discovering the original understanding
of those who ratified the document. In defending the Constitution
in Exile, Judge Douglas Ginsburg seems to think that originalism
is self-evident—that it follows from the very fact that the Constitution is written. He writes as if those who reject originalism
reject the Constitution itself. They're lawless. Far from following
the Constitution, they make it up.

This stance is entirely typical. Fundamentalists often think
that their approach is the only way to ensure that the Constitution
is really law. They think that those who reject fundamentalism are
wrongly substituting their own views for those enshrined in the
Constitution. Federal judges might believe that the phrase "equal
protection of the laws" bans government from discriminating
against women. But why should their own thoughts matter? What
matters is what We the People thought when the Constitution was
ratified.

Judge Robert Bork, for example, has argued that fundamentalist judges are neutral. Judges who reject fundamentalism, on
the other hand, participate in "a major heresy," because they deny
"that judges are bound by law."[3] This heresy is perpetrated by
perfectionists and minimalists alike. The line between heretics and

real judges depends on whether one considers oneself "bound by the only thing that can be called law, the principles of the text . . . as generally understood at the time of enactment." In Judge Bork's view, no one who disagrees with this view "should be nominated or confirmed."

Here, then, is a straightforward claim that the Supreme Court should consist *solely* of fundamentalists. Many fundamentalists make this claim, demonstrating their belief that theirs is the only legitimate approach to constitutional interpretation.

Justice Scalia seems to agree. He believes that if judges depart from the original understanding, they are imposing their own values, and hence making up the Constitution rather than following it. With Judge Bork, he thinks that the only way for judges to be "neutral" is to follow the original understanding.

Of course the whole idea of a Lost Constitution, or a Constitution in Exile, is based squarely on fundamentalism. It assumes that those who ratified the Constitution created a particular kind of document, which the Supreme Court has long betrayed. Fundamentalists think that constitutional law requires rediscovery—a revival of the document that they believe was given to us by the Founding Fathers.

Two (Important) Technicalities

Understood in this light, fundamentalism has two features that are easily overlooked. First, fundamentalists are interested in what the Constitution meant to the *ratifiers,* not the framers. Only the ratifiers of the Constitution and its amendments—"We the People"—have the authority to make and change the Constitution. Those who write constitutional provisions have no such authority. In this way, fundamentalists claim that their view is highly democratic, simply because it holds judges to the judgments of the citizenry.

Second, sophisticated fundamentalists do not ask about anyone's "original intent." They know that it can be extremely difficult to discern intentions, which are inside people's heads, where they cannot easily be explored. Most fundamentalists prefer to ask not about original intentions but instead original *meaning,* which is a more objective idea. For example, the Equal Protection Clause was not originally understood to forbid discrimination against women—that was not its meaning. Case closed. But as I originally understood, the Second Amendment may well have guaranteed an individual the right to bear arms. Case open. "And now let the litigation begin."

Why Fundamentalism?

Why do intelligent and honorable people support fundamentalism? As I have suggested, a key reason involves democracy itself. The Constitution is an expression of the public's will, perhaps the deepest expression of that will. Because the Constitution was ratified by We the People through a process that is supposed to ensure a consensus on its behalf, it stands above ordinary legislation that reflects the view of elected representatives. On this view, the original understanding is binding for the same reason that the Constitution itself is binding. Here, then, is an explanation for Judge Ginsburg's confidence that fundamentalism follows from the very fact that the Constitution is written: Oughtn't judges to follow the will of the people, rather than understanding the Constitution as they think best?

Fundamentalists like to emphasize that the Constitution contains broad and general terms, which different people might like to specify in different ways. It protects "freedom of speech" and "the free exercise of religion." It forbids "cruel and unusual punishments." It bans governments from depriving people of "life, liberty, or property without due process of law." Suppose that judges are asked, in the abstract, about the meaning of these provisions. Some judges will believe that the free speech principle forbids campaign finance regulations. (How can free speech exist if people are banned from using their money on ideas and candidates that they favor?) Other judges will believe that the same principle requires campaign finance regulations. (How can free speech exist if wealthy people are allowed to dominate campaigns?) Some judges believe that affirmative action programs violate the Equal Protection Clause; others believe that that very clause requires such programs.

Perfectionists, in short, disagree about what it means for the Constitution to be perfect. But if judges consult the original understanding, they will avoid abstract disputes about basic values. Judges need not ask what freedom or equality means; they will be following the judgments of We the People.

Fundamentalism also seems to have a justification in ordinary thinking about interpretation. If your best friend asks you to do something, you're likely to try to understand the original meaning of his words; you won't select the interpretation that you deem best. Suppose that he says: "For my birthday, I'd like some really good music." You might think Barbra Streisand's singing is terrible, but if your friend likes Streisand, you might get him some of her recordings. Fundamentalists believe courts should think in the same way, as agents of the people, implementing their commands. Consider here the words of Oliver Wendell Holmes: "If my fellow citizens want to go to Hell I'll help them. It's my job."[4] Fundamen-

talists argue that perfectionist approaches, having abandoned the
original meaning, do not involve interpretation at all.

There is a further point, involving the rule of law itself. If we
want the law to be a system of rules, and not to change with the
prevailing political winds, we might embrace fundamentalism for
that reason alone. Many people do like the idea of a "Living Constitution," capable of change over time. But that very capacity for
life might mean nothing better than lawlessness—and hence a
kind of death. Justice Scalia has emphasized this point above all.
He wants a "rock-solid, unchanging Constitution." He deplores
the fact that the "American people have been converted to belief
in The Living Constitution, a 'morphing' document that means,
from age to age, what it ought to mean." He thinks that by "trying to make the Constitution do everything that needs doing from
age to age, we shall have caused it to do nothing at all."[5]

Scalia's form of fundamentalism opposes those who argue
that the Constitution should be given content by judges who are
attuned, or think that they are attuned, to changing social values. The "Great Divide," in his view, is between those who focus
on the original meaning and those who rely on the Constitution's current meaning.[6] Of course perfectionists, and minimalists as well, think that the Living Constitution is necessary to
promote flexibility over time. To this fundamentalists respond
that the Living Constitution approach actually reduces our
democracy's capacity for experimentation—by, for example, forbidding the invocation of God at public school graduations and
banning the use of evidence obtained by unconstitutional
searches.

Against the view that the Living Constitution is necessary to
protect an ample category of rights, fundamentalists argue that in

many cases, their approach offers a more rather than less expansive understanding of rights. Consider the right to bear arms, recognized in the Second Amendment. Justice Scalia thinks there "will be few tears shed if and when the Second Amendment is held to guarantee nothing more than the state National Guard. But this just shows that the Founders were right when they feared that some (in their view misguided) future generation might wish to abandon liberties that they considered essential, and so sought to protect those liberties in a Bill of Rights."[7]

Suppose that judges refuse to be controlled by the original understanding. Where shall they look to decide on the evolving meaning of the Constitution? Justice Scalia thinks that "there is no agreement, and no chance of agreement, upon what is to be the guiding principle of the evolution."[8] Of course, fundamentalists also disagree among themselves. History can be ambiguous, and there are hard questions—to which I shall return—about how to apply the original meaning to new and unforeseen phenomena such as wiretapping, television, and the Internet. But fundamentalists insist that these are tiny problems compared to those raised when believers in a Living Constitution take it to mean what it should, and hence authorize judges to understand it to be whatever the Supreme Court's majority wants.

It's an appealing argument.

Of Legitimacy and Morality

Many fundamentalists add a general point about legitimacy. Judge Bork thinks courts can claim legitimate authority only if they can trace their decisions to the views of those who ratified the Constitution. "Why should the Court, a committee of nine lawyers, be the sole agent for overriding democratic outcomes?

The man who prefers results to processes has no reason to say that the Court is more legitimate than any other institution capable of wielding power. If the Court will not agree with him, why not argue his case to some other group, say the Joint Chiefs of Staff, a body with rather better means for enforcing its decisions. No answer exists."[9]

Like Scalia, Bork believes that judges who abandon the historical understanding must make moral choices that are intolerably divisive. If judges try to ascertain the abstract meaning of freedom of speech, for example, they will have "to make a major moral decision." Unfortunately, people cannot "all agree to a single moral system."[10] Thus Judge Bork argues that diverse people, unable to achieve moral consensus on the most controversial issues, can converge on the law itself. Perfectionists, by contrast, end up in a kind of moral soup: "Why is sexual gratification more worthy than moral gratification? Why is the gratification of low-cost electricity or higher income more worthy than the pleasure of clean air?"[11]

Chief Justice William H. Rehnquist also rejects the idea of a Living Constitution on the ground that it requires judges to make moral judgments.[12] "There is no conceivable way in which I can logically demonstrate to you that the judgments of my conscience are superior to the judgments of your conscience, or vice versa."[13] It follows that judicial decisions ought not to be based on the supposed dictates of morality; and perfectionists cannot avoid basing law on exactly that. Rehnquist enlists Oliver Wendell Holmes on behalf of his claim: "We have been cocksure of many things that were not so. . . . But while one's experience thus makes certain preferences dogmatic for oneself, recognition of how they came to be so leaves one able to see that others, poor souls, may be equally dogmatic about something else."[14] Rehnquist's suggestion is that in a heterogeneous society, full of different moral positions, judges ought not to determine the law by consulting their consciences.

Recall that in Chapter 1, I said that minimalists like incompletely theorized agreements—agreements that can be shared by people who disagree on theoretical issues, or are not sure what they think. Some fundamentalists are, in their way, attracted to exactly those agreements. They hope to achieve a kind of incompletely theorized agreement in favor of fundamentalism, in which people with diverse views about morality are willing to put their moral judgments aside in order to ask judges to follow the constitutional text as originally understood. By seeking incompletely theorized agreements on fundamentalism, some fundamentalists are, in a way, turning the minimalists' own method against them.

How do fundamentalists understand judicial activism? That's an easy one. They believe that judges are restrained when they follow the original understanding, and activist when they do not. It follows that a fundamentalist judge who votes to strike down countless acts of Congress and the state legislatures counts as restrained, whereas a judge who departs from the original understanding, in order to uphold acts of elected representatives, counts as activist.

The Radicalism of Fundamentalism

In the abstract, there is no decisive argument against fundamentalism. It is a theory of interpretation, no more and no less, and we could imagine times and places in which it would be the best approach of all.

Let's try a little science fiction. Imagine a society whose founders were all-knowing and all-seeing, even godlike. Imagine that their judgments about both rights and institutions were infallible—right then, right for all time. Now suppose that this society's judges are very good at reconstructing history but very bad at moral and political argument. Imagine that the democratic process works extremely well in that society, so that democratic decisions that do not violate the original understanding are rarely unjust. In such a society, shouldn't everyone accept fundamentalism? Many fundamentalists believe that our society isn't so terribly far from this one; maybe they're right.

In the first few decades of the young United States, there was certainly a strong argument for fundamentalism. (Note, however, that Chief Justice John Marshall was a perfectionist, attempting to understand the Constitution, whenever possible, in a way that would ensure the unity of the young United States.) For any fledgling country, fundamentalism has a real claim to judicial attention. But even in fledgling countries, there is no consensus in favor of fundamentalism. In the past few decades, there has been an explosion of constitution-making all over the world, in nations as diverse as Russia, South Africa, Ukraine, Hungary, Poland, Lithuania, and Iraq. Ask judges interpreting their new constitutions whether they are committed to fundamentalism; you'll frequently find a great deal of skepticism. Indeed, I have spoken to several judges who are now being asked to interpret the very constitutions that they helped to write. Often they ridicule the idea that they should follow the original meaning. The real task, they say, is to interpret the words, not to travel in a time machine to ascertain the meaning from years gone by. They tend to be perfectionists. It's not clear that they're right, but it's not clear that they're wrong. Recall here Jefferson's words from the epigraph to this chapter, suggesting that the founding generation was "very like the present, but without the experience of the present; and forty years of experience in government is worth a century of book-reading; and this they would say themselves, were they to rise from the dead."

Suppose the Supreme Court of the United States suddenly adopted fundamentalism, and understood the Constitution in accordance with specific views of those who ratified its provisions. What would happen? The consequences would be extremely radical. For example:

- Discrimination by states on the basis of sex would be entirely acceptable. If a state chose to forbid women to be lawyers or doctors or engineers, the Constitution would not stand in the way.

- The national government would be permitted to discriminate on the basis of race. The Equal Protection Clause of the Fourteenth Amendment is the Constitution's prohibition on racial discrimination—and by its clear language, it applies only to state governments, not to the federal one. Honest fundamentalists have to admit that according to their method, the national government can segregate the armed forces, the public schools, or anything it chooses. In fact the national government could discriminate against African-Americans, Hispanics, and Asian-Americans whenever it wanted.

- The national government could certainly discriminate against women. If it wanted to ban women from the U.S. Civil Service, or to restrict them to clerical positions, the Constitution would not be offended.

• State governments would probably be permitted to impose racial segregation. As a matter of history, the Fourteenth Amendment was not understood to ban segregation on the basis of race. Of course the Supreme Court struck down racial segregation in its great 1954 decision in *Brown v. Board of Education*. But this decision was almost certainly wrong on fundamentalist grounds.[15] If *Brown v. Board of Education* is right, it is either because perfectionism deserves to have its day(s), or because minimalism justified the Court's decision.

• State governments would be permitted to impose poll taxes on state and local elections; they could also violate the one-person, one-vote principle. On fundamentalist grounds, these interferences with the right to vote, and many more, would be entirely acceptable. In fact state governments could do a great deal to give some people more political power than others. Certainly *Bush v. Gore* would be seen as an abuse of judicial authority, because the Court's decision, involving the Fourteenth Amendment, had no roots in the original understanding.

• The entire Bill of Rights might apply only to the national government, not to the states. Very possibly, states could censor speech of which they disapproved, impose cruel and unusual punishment, or search people's homes without a warrant. There is a reasonable argument that on fundamentalist grounds, the Court has been wrong to read the Fourteenth Amendment to apply the Bill of Rights to state governments.

• Almost certainly, states could establish official churches. Justice Thomas has specifically argued that they can.[16]

• The Constitution would provide far less protection than it now does to free speech. There is a plausible argument that on the original understanding, the federal government could punish speech that it deemed dangerous or unacceptable, so long as it did not ban such speech in advance. Even if this view is too extreme, as I believe that it is, there is a legitimate argument that on the original understanding, the government could regulate libelous speech, blasphemous speech, and commercial advertising.

• Compulsory sterilization of criminals would not offend the Constitution. The government could ban contraceptives or sodomy. There would be no right of privacy.

This is an extraordinary agenda for constitutional law; and it provides only a glimpse of what fundamentalism, taken seriously, would require. Should we really adopt it? To answer this question, we need to ask some deeper questions about fundamentalism.

Is Fundamentalism Self-Defeating?

Fundamentalists want the Constitution to be interpreted to fit with the original understanding of those who ratified it. But let's ponder this claim. The more we do so, the harder it is to understand what it means.

Consider the constitutional provision that forbids states from denying any person "the equal protection of the laws." Let us suppose that we went into a time machine and asked the ratifiers this question: *Does the Equal Protection Clause ban sex discrimination?* If that is the question, the answer would certainly be no. Discrimination on the basis of sex was generally thought to be reasonable, and not to offend the equal protection principle. A better, and certainly prior, question would be this: *Do you mean to set out a general principle that prevents states from denying people "equal protection"—a principle that changes over time— or do you mean to freeze your current understandings of what "equal protection" means?*

The ratifiers of the Equal Protection Clause might find this question puzzling. But they might not. Suppose the current generation amended the United States Constitution to require a balanced budget, to protect the right to housing, or to ban discrimination on the basis of disability. We might reasonably be asked whether we seek, with such provisions, to set out a general principle whose meaning is not fixed, or instead to establish a specific rule whose meaning will be given content by reference to our current understandings. That's a pretty straightforward question. It's not entirely clear how we would answer it.

Maybe the ratifiers of many constitutional provisions sought a general commitment whose particular content would change as new social understandings emerged over time. There is nothing weird about this suggestion. Suppose a new nation, for example Iraq, forbids "cruel and unusual punishment" in its Constitution. Those who ratified this provision might well believe that the important question, for future interpreters, is whether a practice really *does* constitute cruel and unusual punishment—not whether the ratifiers of that provision *believed* that it did. And in fact, the very generality of many provisions of the American Constitution seems to suggest that broad principles, rather than specific understandings, are involved. If the ratifiers wanted to entrench their specific understandings, why didn't they do that? Why did they choose instead to use general terms like "equal protection" and "freedom of speech"?

Perfectionism Triumphant?

Perfectionists often take these questions as a decisive objection to fundamentalism. They think that fundamentalism turns out to be self-defeating—that it can easily be hoisted by its own petard. Here's the reason: *The text of the Constitution provides strong evidence that the original understanding is that the original understanding is not binding.* Ironically, fundamentalism must be rejected on fundamentalist grounds.

The argument is clever, but perfectionists shouldn't feel so triumphant. Their argument against fundamentalism is purely historical, and it must stand or fall on historical grounds. The question is whether those who ratified a constitutional provision really believed its meaning would change over time.

True, the text uses some generalities. But it doesn't follow that the ratifiers meant to allow posterity—in the form of federal judges!—to infuse the text with new meaning. Maybe those who ratified the text meant to cabin the judges rather than to license them. Maybe they believed that the Constitution would be understood in accordance not with the judges' views about its meaning, but with their own. Perfectionists need to do a lot of historical work to show that the ratifiers rejected fundamentalism. At this point, all we can conclude is that fundamentalists cannot be so confident that their theory of interpretation is consistent with the original understanding. They have to investigate it.

I will not rehearse the history here, simply because it is so complicated.[17] The simple lesson is that it doesn't answer the question that we're asking because it offers no clear lessons about the ratifiers' views on interpretation. It doesn't unambiguously say whether judges were to be bound by the original understanding or to take the text as the basis for general principles that change over time. A point for fundamentalists: A great deal of historical evidence supports the view that the ratifiers wanted judges to interpret the Constitution as it was originally understood. Of course there is counterevidence. But the claim that fundamentalism is self-defeating is a historical conjecture—and no more.

Is Fundamentalism Coherent?

Even if the fundamentalist project is not self-defeating, it may be incoherent, especially over long periods of time. It may well require interpreters to ask meaningless questions.

To see the problem, consider the Fourth Amendment, ratified in 1791, which forbids "unreasonable searches and seizures." Suppose that the national government decides to put a wiretap in everyone's home. Does the Fourth Amendment ban universal government wiretapping? If we put this question to the ratifiers of the Fourth Amendment, they would not have an easy time answering it. In fact they would be hopelessly confused, simply because they would not know what wiretapping is (and might well not believe us if we told them about it). If we asked them whether they meant to ban government wiretapping, they would have to answer no. But is this the end of the constitutional question? No sensible person thinks so. The Fourth Amendment's ban on unreasonable searches and seizures applies to all means of searching and seizing, and hence it applies to methods that the ratifiers could not possibly have imagined.

Where does this leave fundamentalism? Perhaps fundamentalists could respond that if the ratifiers were really informed of the nature of wiretapping, they would certainly have thought that the Fourth Amendment banned universal wiretapping. That's reasonable enough—but it's a bit more complicated than it seems. Imagine explaining "wiretapping" to James Madison and Alexander Hamilton. What would they have to know, and who would they have to be, to make a judgment about the relationship between wiretapping and the ban on unreasonable searches and seizures?

Maybe it isn't so hard to suppose that if duly informed, the ratifiers would take a stand against universal wiretapping, and maybe that supposition is enough to resolve the constitutional question. But now turn to a somewhat harder question, involving racial segregation in public schools. The Equal Protection Clause was ratified in 1868. In 1869, it would certainly have been possible to ask the ratifiers whether they meant to forbid school segregation on the basis of race; and the answer would likely have been no. But now suppose it is 1969, not 1869, and we are asking the ratifiers whether they meant to eliminate school segregation on the basis of race. What kind of question is that? What do we have to tell the ratifiers in order to help them to answer it?

Even if the ratifiers did not believe that they prohibited school segregation in 1869, perhaps they would believe that the provision they ratified prohibited it in 1969—at least once they were informed of the new role of public education, the changing relationships between African-Americans and whites, and the consequences of school segregation for those relationships and for the nation as a whole. As with wiretapping, so too, perhaps, with segregation: To produce a sensible answer from long-dead ratifiers, we have to tell them what we know, which means we have to tell them what our world is like. Suppose we do that. Will they still be the ratifiers of 1869? Or will they be something else, simply because they know so much more? Will they turn out to be us?

Fundamentalists are right to say that the constitutional text makes some things clear. The President has to be at least thirty-five years of age, and must be born in the United States, and it is not possible to respect the text and to say that a twenty-five-year-old, or someone born in Germany, can be president. Fundamentalists are also right to insist that there is often a simple answer to the question of what the ratifiers meant by a constitutional provision—certainly if the question is asked shortly after ratification. But after many decades have passed, it is not clear whether the fundamentalists' question—*What did you mean to do?*—remains coherent.

If the segregation problem is difficult, many other problems will turn out to be difficult, too. It is standard, and correct, to say that the ratifiers of the Equal Protection Clause did not mean to ban discrimination on the basis of sex. But did they mean to ban sex discrimination a century and a half later, when relations between men and women have changed so radically? It is not clear that this is a purely historical question at all; and if it is not a historical question, it is not clear what kind of question it is. The Due Process Clause says that no person may be deprived of liberty or property without due process of law. In 1792, it would be puzzling to argue that someone receiving national welfare benefits had a right to a hearing before being taken off the welfare rolls. But how do we understand the ratifiers' views with respect to the elimination of disability benefits, or social security benefits, in 2005? What must we tell the ratifiers in order to enable them to answer such questions?

Fundamentalists have said very little about these problems. They tend to ask about the narrow goals of those who ratified constitutional provisions—as if an understanding of those goals, a month or a year after ratification, provides appropriate answers to interpretive questions posed decades or even centuries later. I think that fundamentalists proceed in this way for identifiable reasons: They want to freeze the meaning of the Constitution, so as to ensure that it is hard and unchanging, and they seek to minimize the discretion of federal judges. But these are reasons of their own, not of the ratifiers, and they must be evaluated as such.

Let us move, then, from the historical and conceptual problems with the fundamentalist project, and take that project as the fundamentalists understand it.

Why Fundamentalism Is Indefensible

Suppose the Constitution's ratifiers were committed to fundamentalism and that the fundamentalists' questions have coherent answers. Does it follow that we must be fundamentalists? Actually it doesn't. It is up to *us* to decide whether to accept fundamentalism. We can't say that fundamentalism is right simply because the framers believed that it is right; that would be circular reasoning.

To his credit, Judge Bork is aware of the point. In a key passage, he writes, "It has been argued . . . that the claim of proponents of original understanding to political neutrality is a pretense since the choice of that philosophy is itself a political decision. It certainly is, but the political content of that choice is not made by the judge; it was made long ago by those who designed and enacted the Constitution."[18] If we put the conceptual problems to one side, Judge Bork is right to say that the political content of the key choices was made long ago. But should judges be bound by those choices? Don't answer "yes" so quickly. As we have seen, a fundamentalist approach would radically alter constitutional law for the worse. Why should we adopt an approach that turns constitutional law into a far inferior version of what it is today?

During the controversy over the nomination of Judge Bork to the Supreme Court, Judge Richard Posner, a Reagan appointee, produced an ingenious little paper called "Bork and Beethoven."[19] Posner noticed that the conservative magazine *Commentary* had published an essay celebrating Bork's fundamentalism in the same issue in which another essay sharply criticized the "authentic-performance movement" in music, in which musicians play great composers on the original instruments. Posner observes that the "two articles take opposite positions on the issue of 'originalism'—that is, interpretive fidelity to a text's understanding by its author." While one essay endorses Bork's fidelity to the views of people in 1787, the other despises the authentic-performance movement on the grounds that the music sounds awful. If originalism makes bad music, Posner asks, "why *should* the people listen to it?" Posner thinks Bork offers a "summons to holy war," which is no argument on its behalf.

Fundamentalists get a lot of rhetorical mileage out of the claim that their approach is neutral while other approaches are simply a matter of "politics." But there is nothing neutral in fundamentalism. It is a political choice, which must be defended on political grounds. If it produces a far worse system of constitutional law, that must count as a strong point against it. Liberals and conservatives disagree on many things, but they agree that the Constitution is best taken to forbid racial segregation by the federal government and to protect a robust free speech principle. Is it unacceptably "result-oriented" to object to fundamentalism on the ground that it would lead to intolerable consequences? Actually it isn't. Any approach to interpretation has to be defended, not just celebrated, and if an approach would produce intolerable results, it is hard to defend.

Some more science fiction: Imagine a society in which a very old constitution has a good text; imagine too that if that text is interpreted to conform with the ratifiers' original understanding, it wouldn't be any good at all. Suppose that the original understanding would permit a lot of censorship as well as racial segregation. Suppose that in our imaginary society, courts could be trusted, most of the time, to give the right content to constitutional text, in a way that would balance sound moral judgment with the demands of modesty and with respect for reasonable disagreement. Suppose finally that in such a society, the democratic process could not always be trusted, because majorities, sometimes panicked and sometimes prejudiced, produce, on occasion, intolerably unjust results—which courts often forbid under the society's constitution.

Fundamentalism would make no sense in such a society. I don't mean to say that this imaginary society is our own. But if an approach to interpretation would produce a much inferior system of constitutional law, that is certainly a big point against it. The most sensible fundamentalists agree. They argue that their approach would indeed produce the best results overall. The problem is that this is an utterly implausible position.

Democracy, Legitimacy, and Rules

Fundamentalists often justify their approach through the claim that it is highly democratic, far more so than allowing unelected judges to give meaning to the constitutional text. But there is a major gap in their argument. Why should living people be governed by the decisions of those who died many generations ago?

Most of the relevant understandings come from 1789, when the Constitution was ratified, or 1791, when the Bill of Rights was ratified. If democracy is our lodestar, it is hardly clear that we should be controlled by those decisions today. Why should we be governed by people long dead? In any case the group that ratified the Constitution included just a small subset of the society; it excluded all women, the vast majority of African-Americans, many of those without property, and numerous others who were not permitted to vote. Does the ideal of democracy strongly argue in favor of binding current generations to the understandings of a small portion of the population from centuries ago? That would be a puzzling conclusion.

This is not an argument that the Constitution itself should not be taken as binding. Of course it should. The Constitution is binding because it is good to take it as binding. It is good to take it as binding because it is an exceedingly good constitution, all things considered, and because many bad things, including relative chaos, would ensue if we abandoned it. We're much better off with it than without it. But no abstract concept, like "democracy," is enough to explain why we must follow the Constitution; and invoking that concept is a hopelessly inadequate way to justify fundamentalism.

Many fundamentalists appeal to the idea of consent as a basis for legitimacy. In their view, we are bound by the Constitution because we agreed to it; we are not bound by the Constitution of Italy or any model constitution that might be drafted by today's best and brightest. It's true that we're not bound by those constitutions, but it's false to say that we're bound by the Constitution because "we" agreed to it. None of us did. Of course we benefit greatly from its existence, and most of us do not try to change it; but it is fanciful to say that we've agreed to it. The legitimacy of the Constitution does not lie in consent. It is legitimate because it provides an excellent framework for democratic self-government and promotes other goals as well, including liberty and also economic prosperity (as witnessed by well over two hundred years of history).

The fundamentalists' arguments about legitimacy beg all the important questions. Judge Bork, for example, implies that the Constitution's legitimacy comes from the fact that (a subset of) We the People ratified it a long time ago. But ancient ratification is not enough to make the Constitution legitimate. We follow the Constitution because it is good for us to follow the Constitution. Is it good for us to follow the original understanding? Actually it would be terrible.

Justice Scalia emphasizes the stability that comes from fundamentalism, which, in his view, can produce a "rock-hard" Constitution. True, fundamentalism might lead to greater stability in our constitutional understandings than we have now. Historians, with all their fallibility and internal disputes, would become royalty in the fundamentalists' new order. Unless readings of history change, and if the problem of incoherence can be solved, the Constitution would mean the same thing thirty years from now as it means today. But fundamentalism would produce stability only by radically destabilizing the system of rights that we have come to know (and generally love, or at least like). Even worse, fundamentalism would destabilize not only our rights but our institutions as well. The idea of a Constitution in Exile is enough to establish the point. In a way fundamentalism might promote values associated with the rule of law—but only after defeating established expectations and upsetting longstanding practices by reference to an abstract theory.

In any case, stability is only one value, and for good societies it is not the most important one. If an approach to the Constitution would lead to a little less stability but a lot more democracy, there is good reason to adopt it. Since 1950, our constitutional system has not been entirely stable; the document has been reinterpreted to ban racial segregation, to protect the right to vote, to forbid sex discrimination, and to contain a robust principle of free speech. Should we really have sought more stability?

Of Faint Hearts

Justice Scalia, the leading defender of fundamentalism, is entirely aware of this point. He believes in fundamentalism, but as a judge committed to law, he believes in precedent too, and he is often willing to stick with precedent even though it departs from the original understanding. This is why he describes himself as a "faint-hearted originalist." His faintness of heart is a frank recognition that taken seriously, fundamentalism would lead in intolerable directions. Justice Scalia might move toward the Lost Constitution, and he's willing to support some fairly radical changes, but he doesn't want to uproot current law root and branch. In these ways, he's a true conservative.

On this count, Scalia is very different from Justice Thomas, who is not so faint of heart. Scalia has said that Thomas "doesn't believe in *stare decisis* [respecting precedent], period. . . . if a constitutional authority is wrong, [Thomas] would say, 'Let's get it right.' I wouldn't do that."[20] Fundamentalists who reject precedents are far more radical than those who don't. And indeed, a number of constitutional scholars have recently argued that in constitutional law, the idea of stare decisis has no place. In the words of Northwestern University's Stephen Presser, "For us, and for Clarence Thomas, it's more important to get it right than to maintain continuity."[21]

This is an extreme position. In my view, faint-hearted fundamentalism is the only plausible form of fundamentalism. It ensures that the existing fabric of constitutional law will not be undone, and it means that judges will refer to the original understanding only when they can do so without doing undue violence to settled principles.

Of course this formulation leaves a lot of vagueness. Because of that vagueness, faint-hearted fundamentalists cannot easily show that their approach promotes their goal of binding judges through clear rules. It is therefore worth asking whether faint-hearted fundamentalism is superior to the most reasonable alternative, which is minimalism. This question cannot be answered in the abstract. It is time to investigate some details.

A clarifying note before embarking: We shall be exploring a number of areas, in a way that will show concrete disagreements among fundamentalists, minimalists, and perfectionists (majoritarians, who are not much on the current scene, will make cameo appearances). Most of the key debates will pit fundamentalists against minimalists. But there is an important difference between those areas in which fundamentalists are faithful to their own creed and those in which they are not.

On fundamentalist grounds, it is quite right to say that there is no right of privacy, and the right to marry should be rejected as well. We are going to begin with areas in which fundamentalists are most principled and most plausible. But even in those areas, their views would lead to radical changes in constitutional law—changes that would make constitutional law worse rather than better.

Worse still, fundamentalism fails to justify many of the fundamentalists' favorite positions—including their attack on affirmative action, their insistence on the President's power to protect national security, their solicitude for commercial advertising, their effort to revive property rights, and their claim that the separation of powers raises questions about the Clean Air Act, the Federal Communications Act, and the Occupational Safety and Health Act. On gun control and federalism, the evidence is better for them, but it suggests that fundamentalists should be more tentative than they now are.

I shall begin with those cases in which fundamentalists are following their own principles, and then turn to those in which fundamentalists are abandoning their principles in favor of what seems to be a partisan program.

PART TWO

Great Divisions

CHAPTER THREE

Is There a Right to Privacy?

*[T]here is no right to "liberty" under the Due Process Clause. . . .
The Fourteenth Amendment expressly allows states to deprive
their citizens of "liberty," so long as "due process of law" is provided.*

—Antonin Scalia[1]

FUNDAMENTALISTS DON'T BELIEVE that the Constitution protects the right to privacy. In their view, government has no
general duty to respect people's choices about how to conduct
their private lives. Fundamentalists freely acknowledge that the
government is prohibited from conducting unreasonable searches
and seizures; the Fourth Amendment is explicit on that point, and
it protects a form of privacy. But fundamentalists reject the
Supreme Court's protection of privacy through the Fourteenth
Amendment's Due Process Clause, which forbids states from
depriving people of "life, liberty, or property, without due process
of law."

Theirs is a fully plausible reading of the Constitution. But it
would wreak havoc with established law. It would eliminate constitutional protections where the nation has come to rely on them—
by, for example, allowing states to ban use of contraceptives by

married couples. Some perfectionists want to build on the right
of privacy, extending it to include a right to physician-assisted
suicide, to ride motorcycles without helmets, and even to be,
and to employ, a prostitute. But here as elsewhere, perfectionists
overreach. Rejecting the radicalism of fundamentalists, and the
ambition of perfectionists, minimalists have a much better
approach.

Beginnings

It all began, of course, with *Roe v. Wade*.[2] In 1973, the Supreme
Court ruled that the Constitution protects the right to choose
abortion. The case was brought by Jane Roe, a single woman living in Texas. ("Jane Roe" was a pseudonym; her real name, which
she disclosed years later, was Norma McCorvey.) Roe alleged that
she was unmarried and pregnant, that she could not afford to
travel to another state to obtain a safe and legal abortion, and that
under Texas law, she was forbidden from doing what she wanted
to do. A parallel lawsuit, also decided in *Roe v. Wade,* was
brought by a married couple. The wife of the pair, suffering from
a "neural-chemical" disorder, had been advised by her doctor to
discontinue use of birth control pills. She contended that if she
became pregnant, she would want, for medical reasons, to terminate her pregnancy under safe, clinical conditions.

The Supreme Court acknowledged that the Constitution
"does not explicitly mention a right of personal privacy." But the
Court said that the Due Process Clause's guarantee of liberty is
best read to "encompass a woman's decision whether or not to
terminate her pregnancy." The Court agreed that the privacy
right, so understood, is not absolute. It said that the state could
protect the fetus after the point when it had become viable. It

added that the state could regulate the woman's choice in a way that would be reasonably related to the protection of her health. But protection of the fetus was not, by itself, enough to overcome the woman's right to choose. The Court's anti-minimalist decision in *Roe v. Wade* seemed to come out of nowhere. Exemplifying perfectionism at its most extreme, it raised grave doubts about the Court's use of the Constitution to solve divisive social controversies.

Actually, though, it didn't all begin with *Roe v. Wade*. It all began with *Griswold v. Connecticut*,[3] which created the modern right to privacy. There the Court struck down a Connecticut law that prohibited married couples from using contraceptives. This was a singularly odd law. By 1965, Connecticut's prohibition was practically unenforced, because the citizens of Connecticut, many of whom used contraceptives, did not want to see people criminally punished for that behavior. The case was brought not by married couples, who had nothing to fear, but by the executive director of the Planned Parenthood League of Connecticut and its medical director. The Court really wanted to invalidate the law; but it struggled to find a constitutionally legitimate basis for doing so. The Court's opinion was written by Justice William O. Douglas, perhaps the Court's most unabashed perfectionist.

The Court failed to identify a provision of the document that the Connecticut law violated. Instead it spoke vaguely of the "penumbras" and "emanations" of the Bill of Rights, in language that continues to turn the stomach of fundamentalists (and many others). The Court stressed "the zone of privacy created by several fundamental constitutional guarantees." And while *Griswold* itself involved behavior within marriage, the Court built on its decision in short order—ruling that all people, married or single,

had a right to use contraceptives, and even to have access to them
on the market.[4] Dissenting from the Court's decision in *Griswold*,
Justice Potter Stewart said that although the Connecticut law was
"uncommonly silly," it was not unconstitutional. In his view, our
founding document creates no "general right of privacy," first recognized in *Griswold* itself.

But actually it didn't all begin with *Griswold v. Connecticut*.
It began not in 1965 but in 1923, with the Court's decision in
Meyer v. Nebraska.[5] In that case, the Court was confronted with
a state law that banned the teaching of any language other than
English in any public or private grammar school. Giving a broad
reading to the Due Process Clause, the Court said that liberty,
under that clause, included "the right of the individual to contract, to engage in any of the common occupations of life, to
acquire useful knowledge, to marry, establish a home and bring
up children, to worship God according to the dictates of his own
conscience, and generally to enjoy those privileges long recognized at common law as essential to the orderly pursuit of happiness by free men." A law that prohibited the teaching of
foreign languages was a clear violation of the right to liberty.
The Court built on its decision in *Meyer* two years later, when it
struck down an Oregon statute requiring students to attend public rather than private schools.[6] With *Meyer v. Nebraska*, the
Court started the process of freeing private choices from the
constraining arm of the state.

But it didn't really begin with *Meyer v. Nebraska*. It began
nearly twenty years earlier, in 1905, with *Lochner v. New York*,[7]
when the Court invalidated a law fixing maximum hours for
bakers. The Court said that freedom of contract is part of
human liberty. It insisted that the state must produce a strong

justification for any intrusion on "the general right of an individual to be free in his person . . ." The roots of constitutional protection of liberty under the Due Process Clause lie in the *Lochner* case, and a direct line can be traced to the protection of "privacy" in *Roe v. Wade* from the protection of "liberty" in *Lochner,* where it was born.

Actually, though, it wasn't born there. It really began with *Dred Scott v. Sandford,* which helped to precipitate the Civil War.[8] In *Dred Scott,* the Supreme Court held that under the Constitution, slaves and their descendents could never count as "citizens" of the United States. Not incidentally, this much-reviled decision was a self-conscious exercise in fundamentalism. The Court spoke explicitly in fundamentalist terms: "It is not the province of the court to decide upon the justice or injustice, the policy or impolicy, of these laws. . . . The duty of the court is, to interpret the instrument [the Constitution's authors] have framed, with the best lights we can obtain on the subject, and to administer it as we find it, according to its true intent when it was adopted." It is not implausible to describe *Dred Scott v. Sandford* as the first prominent appearance of "originalism" in American constitutional law.

While this decision is famous for entrenching slavery, the Court also offered an important ruling about the meaning of the Due Process Clause of the Fifth Amendment. It would be unconstitutional, the Court said, for the national government to deprive people of their right of ownership in a slave. In the key passage, the Court announced that an "act of Congress which deprives a citizen of the United States of his liberty or property . . . could hardly be dignified with the name of due process of law." This was the Court's first recognition that the

Due Process Clause forbids government to interfere with people's liberty or property unless it has an extremely good reason for doing so.

And that really is where it all began.

Dilemmas of Due Process

As the law now stands, the right of privacy is part of the Constitution's protection of "liberty" under the Due Process Clause. Or so the Supreme Court tells us. But fundamentalists are right to point out that the Constitution doesn't provide any general protection of liberty. It doesn't say that the government needs a good reason to intrude on people's choices. It merely says that government cannot deprive people of "liberty . . . without due process of law." To understand the debate over privacy, we need to spend some time with this phrase.

Fundamentalists raise two questions about the Due Process Clause. First, what are the limits of "liberty"? If we are fundamentalists, we might think that the term includes only one thing: freedom from imprisonment or bodily restraint. History suggests that this may in fact be the correct interpretation. Charles Warren, writing in 1926, said that "freedom" under English law meant only an absence of "physical restraint"; he concluded that when the Constitution originally used that phrase in the Fifth Amendment, it "took it with the meaning" it had in England at that time.[9] If this is right, and if the Due Process Clause has the same meaning in the Fourteenth as in the Fifth Amendment, then the decisions in all the cases just described—from *Dred Scott* to *Roe v. Wade*—are wrong. In all of them, the Court interpreted "liberty" to include a general freedom with respect to personal decisions—an idea that extends well beyond freedom from imprisonment. It is one thing to say that government must respect your right not to be locked up, and quite another to say that it must respect your right to use contraceptives, choose abortion, send children to the schools of your choice, or work as many hours as you like.

Fundamentalists also raise questions about the phrase "without due process of law." They are tempted to think that the Due Process Clause says, very simply, that when the state takes your life, liberty, or property, it has to provide you with a hearing ("due process of law"). This is the idea of *procedural due process:* a right to procedural protection, in the form of a hearing, if the government is taking something away from you. During the hearing, you can argue that you haven't done what the government accuses you of doing. As we will see in Chapter 7, procedural due process is an extremely important idea. Much of human liberty consists of protection against arbitrary acts by the government, and if you have a right to a hearing, you have a right to challenge government's decisions as arbitrary. When national security is threatened, the right to a hearing clearly ranks as one of the most important of all. But it is also exceedingly important for our daily lives.

Nonetheless, this right is sharply limited. It does not deprive the state of power to ban the use of contraceptives, to impose maximum-hour laws, or to forbid women from having abortions. It simply says that people accused of violating the law cannot be denied a hearing. Fundamentalists are drawn to the view that under the Due Process Clause, governments can invade liberty however they like—so long as they give people a chance to contest the factual basis of any accusations against them. As a matter of text and history, this position is more than plausible.

On the other hand, the history is ambiguous, and parts of it can be understood to support the more ambitious idea of *substantive due process,* which underlies all of the decisions discussed above.[10] According to that idea, it isn't enough for government to give people hearings; government must also give a good explanation for any intrusion on liberty. But even if the text is read in this way, which isn't so easy, it is a struggle to argue that as originally understood, the Due Process Clause protects the right to use contraceptives or to have an abortion or to have sex with someone of the same gender. Nothing in the historical materials supports the Supreme Court's modern privacy decisions.

Thus far, then, there is nothing irresponsible, on fundamentalist grounds, about the fundamentalists' reading of the Due Process Clause. (This is a striking contrast, as we shall see, to the fundamentalists' attacks on affirmative action, on regulation of property, and on the grant of discretionary power to the Environmental Protection Agency.) But the fundamentalist reading would have truly remarkable implications. It would undo a great deal of the fabric of existing constitutional law, with consequences that most Americans would abhor. It would allow government to invade bedrooms, marital and otherwise. Minimalists don't like to insist on anything, but they insist that this is at least a problem.

Liberty Unleashed and the Price of Perfection

In the decades after *Roe v. Wade,* the Constitution's protection of privacy and liberty was greatly disputed. To put it bluntly, the law became a mess.[11] Is there a constitutional right to ride motorcycles without a helmet? No. Does the Constitution protect the right of a grandparent to live with her grandchildren? Yes. Can states forbid unrelated people to live together? Yes. Do police officers have a constitutional right to wear their hair as they like? No. Can a state deprive a genetic father of his rights to his child, by presuming that a child born to a married woman, living with her husband, is the child of the marriage? Yes. Is there a constitutional right to withdraw life-saving equipment? Yes.

Try to make sense of these rulings, if you would.

Perfectionists frequently argue for an ever-expanding list of privacy rights. They like *Griswold v. Connecticut* and *Roe v. Wade* and want to build on these decisions to recognize broad rights of personal autonomy. Some perfectionists suggest that government cannot legitimately interfere with people's choices unless those choices cause some kind of harm to others. In this way, they borrow from John Stuart Mill's *On Liberty,* contending that the Constitution should be interpreted to include some version of Mill's "harm principle." Other perfectionists try to isolate a list of particularly important choices, such as those involved in sex and reproduction, and contend that such choices deserve constitutional protection by virtue of their importance.

The problem with these arguments should not be obscure. If accepted, they would require federal judges to make difficult and delicate judgments about what people are entitled to do. Should the Constitution permit people to refuse to wear seatbelts? Should it allow them access to medicines deemed unsafe by the Food and Drug Administration? If accepted, the perfectionist arguments would authorize courts to invalidate the judgments of countless democratic institutions, judgments that many citizens believe to be correct on principle. Shouldn't judges hesitate before going that far? At least when the constitutional text and history, fairly interpreted, do not seem to grant judges the power to take such steps?

Traditionalism: The Fundamentalist Trump Card

Faced with these questions, the Supreme Court has attempted to discipline itself through a particular route, greatly appealing to fundamentalists. The route is called *traditionalism.* The basic idea is that privacy and liberty rights do not count as such unless they have been recognized by longstanding traditions. It should be clear that traditionalism could stop the protection of liberty or privacy rights in its tracks.

In judge-made constitutional law in the United States, tradition has been an extraordinarily important source of rights, especially in the understanding of the Due Process Clause. Dissenting from the Court's interpretation of that clause in *Lochner v. New York,* Justice Holmes said that a law should be held to violate that clause only if it "would infringe fundamental principles as they have been understood by the traditions of our people and our law."[12] Some of the modern privacy cases try to build directly on the foundation laid by tradition. In *Griswold v. Connecticut,* the Court relied heavily on what it saw as the "tradition" of marital privacy. A number of recent justices, especially those with fundamentalist inclinations, have attempted to revive traditionalism as a way of disciplining the Court's decisions.

Tradition initially reemerged as a way of limiting the right to privacy in the 1986 case of *Bowers v. Hardwick,*[13] where the Court upheld a ban on same-sex sodomy. There the Court emphasized that sodomy was a criminal offense at common law and that in 1868, when the Fourteenth Amendment was ratified, sodomy was illegal in thirty-two of the thirty-seven states.

"Against this background, to claim that a right to engage in such conduct is 'deeply rooted in this Nation's history and tradition' or 'implicit in the concept of ordered liberty' is, at best, facetious."

One of the most important uses of tradition can be found in *Michael H. v. Gerald D.,*[14] in which the Court denied an adulterous father's claim of a constitutional right to visit his child, who had been conceived by a woman who was married to someone else. Justice Scalia, writing for the plurality in 1989, relied heavily on the absence of any such right in tradition. He emphasized "the historic respect—indeed, sanctity would not be too strong a term—traditionally accorded to the relationships that develop within the unitary family." In a much-discussed footnote, Scalia explained why he relied on "historical traditions specifically relating to the rights of an adulterous natural father, rather than inquiring more generally 'whether parenthood is an interest that traditionally has received our attention and protection.'" Justice Scalia wrote:

> Why should the relevant category not be even more general — perhaps "family relationships"; or "personal relationships"; or even "emotional attachments in general"? . . . We refer to the most specific level at which a relevant tradition protecting, or denying protection to, the asserted right can be identified. . . . Because general traditions provide such imprecise guidance, they permit judges to dictate rather than discern the society's views. Although assuredly having the virtue (if it be that) of leaving judges free to decide as they think best when the unanticipated occurs, a rule of law that binds neither by text nor by any particular, identifiable tradition, is no rule of law at all.

Tradition was also a key issue in cases involving the patient's right to withdraw life-saving medical equipment and the right to die. Suicide has been banned by tradition. Should this count decisively against the alleged right to die? So Justice Scalia argued, in a separate opinion in 1990, concluding that the Constitution does not constrain the state's power over individual choice in this area.[15] He and Justice Thomas have increasingly insisted that where the constitutional text is unclear, judicial decisions about liberty or privacy should be made by reference to longstanding traditions.[16] The Court endorsed this view in 2001, rejecting the view that the Constitution creates a right to physician-assisted suicide.[17]

Between 1984 and 2003, traditionalism usually triumphed, and so did fundamentalists. In that period, the Court was extremely reluctant to use the idea of substantive due process to strike down legislation. Its refusal to overrule *Roe v. Wade* seemed to reflect not enthusiastic approval of that decision, and much less a willingness to extend its logic, but simple respect for precedent. Fundamentalists despise *Roe,* of course, and would prefer to see it overruled, but if that proves impossible, they think a tradition-centered view of the Due Process Clause is a pretty good foundation for the future.

Are they right? If traditions contain injustice and confusion, then they might not be the best source of constitutional law. At the very least, we might want courts to ask whether traditions are rational—about whether they draw arbitrary lines. In any case traditionalism was thrown into doubt in 2003 by the Court's decision in *Lawrence v. Texas,* which casts a new light on privacy and sexual freedom and which is despised by fundamentalists for that reason. To understand current debates, and possible future developments, it is necessary to understand what *Lawrence* did. As we shall see, the Court explicitly rejected the fundamentalist effort to limit the reach of constitutional privacy. But the meaning of its decision remains obscure.

The Birth of Sexual Freedom?

The stated facts of *Lawrence* were simple. Police officers in Houston responded to a private report of a weapons disturbance in a private residence. On entering the residence, owned by John Geddes Lawrence, they did not see any weapons. But they did see Lawrence engaging in a sexual act with Tyron Garner. The two were arrested, held in custody, convicted of "deviate sexual intercourse, namely anal sex, with a member of the same sex (man)," and fined $200 each. Deviate sexual intercourse was defined under Texas law to include "any contact between any part of the genitals of one person and the mouth or anus of another person" or "the penetration of the genitals or the anus of another person with an object."

The heart of the Court's opinion began with a dramatic reading of precedent, stating, for the first time in the Court's history, that the Constitution recognizes a right to make sexual choices free from state control. Writing for the majority, Justice William Kennedy announced that "the right to make certain decisions regarding sexual conduct extends beyond the marital relationship." Regarding homosexual activity in particular, Justice Kennedy said that the government was seeking "to control a personal relationship that, whether or not entitled to formal recognition in the law, is within the liberty of persons to choose without being punished as criminals." Thus the Court suggested that the state could not intrude on sexual liberty "absent injury to a person or abuse of an institution the law protects."

The Court then turned from its precedents to traditionalism and in particular to the suggestion that prohibitions on same-sex sodomy "have ancient roots." Emphasizing the complexity of American traditions, the Court doubted the suggestion that there has been an unbroken path of hostility to same-sex sodomy. But the Court freely conceded that there is no history of accepting that practice; it did not contend that traditions affirmatively support a constitutional right to sexual freedom in that domain. On the contrary, the Court said that longstanding traditions were not decisive. Current convictions, not old ones, were important. Here is the key sentence: "[W]e think that our laws and traditions in the past half century are of most relevance here." Hence the Court stressed an "emerging recognition that liberty gives substantial protection to adult persons in deciding how to conduct their private lives in matters pertaining to sex."

The emerging recognition could be seen in many places. Fewer than half the states (twenty-four) outlawed sodomy even in 1986, and in those states the prohibitions went largely unenforced. The practices of Western nations have been increasingly opposed to the criminal punishment of homosexual conduct. Britain repealed its law forbidding homosexual conduct in 1967, and in 1981 the European Court of Human Rights concluded that laws banning consensual homosexual conduct are invalid under the European Convention on Human Rights. In 2003, only thirteen states forbade such conduct, and of these just four had laws that discriminated only against homosexual conduct. "In those states where sodomy is still proscribed, whether for same-sex or heterosexual conduct, there is a pattern of nonenforcement with respect to consenting adults acting in private."

The Court was aware of the potential breadth of its ruling, and in good minimalist fashion, it took steps to clarify its scope.

"The present case does not involve minors. It does not involve persons who might be injured or coerced or who are situated in relationships where consent might not easily be refused. It does not involve public conduct or prostitution. It does not involve whether the government must give formal recognition to any relationship that homosexual persons seek to enter." What was involved was "full and mutual consent" to engage in "sexual practices common to a homosexual lifestyle. . . . The State cannot demean their existence or control their destiny by making their private sexual conduct a crime." In a closing word, the Court wrote that the Texas law "furthers no legitimate state interest which can justify its intrusion into the personal and private life of the individual."

Was this a version of perfectionism, creating an ambitious new right to sexual privacy? Writing in dissent, Justice Scalia argued it was. "State laws against bigamy, same-sex marriage, adult incest, prostitution, masturbation, adultery, fornication, bestiality, and obscenity" were all "called into question by today's decision." The Court's decision therefore entails "a massive disruption of the current social order." Justice Scalia went so far as to contend that the Court's opinion "dismantles the structure of constitutional law that has permitted a distinction to be made between heterosexual and homosexual unions, insofar as formal recognition in marriage is concerned."

This, in Scalia's view, was a ludicrous and dangerous understanding of the Constitution. He emphasized that the real issue is whether the relevant rights are "deeply rooted in this Nation's history and tradition." He questioned the existence of an "emerging awareness" that consensual homosexual activity should be protected; but his more basic objection was that any emerging awareness, just like decisions in other nations, should be irrelevant to the Court's decision. "Constitutional entitlements do not spring into existence because some States choose to lessen or eliminate criminal sanctions on certain behavior."

Scalia saw the majority opinion as holding that the moral views underlying the Texas statute did not provide a legitimate basis for it. Here his objection was exceedingly simple: "This effectively decrees the end of all morals legislation."

Perfectionism or Minimalism?

Lawrence squarely rejects fundamentalism, and so the Court as a whole has rejected the fundamentalist approach to privacy and sex—at least for the moment. The Court has been narrowly divided on these subjects, and it would not be surprising to see a return to a tradition-focused approach, certainly if the Court's composition changes.

But what does *Lawrence* accept? Perfectionists like to argue that the right to engage in consensual sex counts, as a matter of principle, as part of the liberty protected by the Due Process Clause. They hope that in *Lawrence* the Court accepted, to some extent, John Stuart Mill's view in *On Liberty*—holding that the government may not interfere with (certain) private choices unless there is harm to others. Harvard professor Laurence Tribe argues that the Court has protected "the relationships and self-governing commitments out of which" sexual acts arise, and hence "the network of human connection over time that makes genuine freedom possible."[18]

Minimalists reject this position. They are not sure what *Lawrence* means, and the ruling makes them nervous. They do not want fallible judges to puzzle over what "makes genuine freedom possible." They are skeptical about the idea that the Constitution protects "self-governing commitments." Minimalists think that if there is a constitutional right to privacy, courts should build on it slowly and narrowly. Minimalists are confident that *Lawrence* does not require states to allow prostitution. If *Lawrence* is best taken to protect sexual privacy as such, minimalists want the Court to tread lightly. It is one thing to say that states may not criminalize consensual, noncommercial activity between adults, and quite another to rule that in the domain of sexual relations, the state and federal governments have no legitimate role.

Minimalists insist that the real problem in *Lawrence*, and in many other cases involving sexual privacy, was *procedural*. In the last decades, sodomy prosecutions have been rare and unpredictable, simply because the public would not stand for many of them. Emphasizing this point, minimalists contend that *Lawrence*, and many of the Court's privacy decisions, should be understood as an American variation on the old English idea of *desuetude*.[19] According to that idea, laws lapse, and can no longer be enforced, when their enforcement has already become exceedingly rare because the principle behind them has become hopelessly out of step with people's convictions.

Minimalists are drawn to a simple line of argument. If an old law is founded on a judgment that no longer has much support, we should expect it to be enforced little or not at all. It is therefore a tool for harassment, and not an ordinary law at all—in fact a violation of the rule of law itself. The rare enforcement occasions might well involve arbitrary or discriminatory factors. They might result from a police officer's mood, or personal animus, or bias of some kind. On this view, prosecution would be unconstitutional for procedural reasons having to do with the rule of law. The state may not enforce a law unsupported by public judgments—and no longer taken seriously as a law—in a few, randomly selected cases.

Griswold v. Connecticut can also be understood in this way.
The ban on contraception within marriage was not enforced by
prosecutors, and the people of Connecticut would not stand for
use of the criminal law against married couples. The ban served
principally to deter clinics from dispensing contraceptives to poor
people. The problem was not that the ban was unsupported by
old traditions but that it had no basis in modern convictions. Few
people believed that sex within marriage was legitimate only if it
was for purposes of procreation, and those people could not possibly have commanded a legislative majority or made it possible
to bring many prosecutions against married couples.

Notably, Connecticut's lawyers did not defend the statute on
the ground that surely motivated it: a religious or quasi-religious
judgment about when sexual activity is appropriate. They argued
instead that it was a means of preventing extramarital relations.
So defended, the law made little sense, for it remained to be
explained why the prohibition applied to *use* of contraceptives by
married people, and not just to their distribution. Because of the
absence of real enforcement, and its lack of foundation in anything like common public sentiment, the law offended a form of
procedural due process, not substantive due process.

Minimalists believe that *Griswold* should have decided on this
basis, which is narrower, more plausible as a matter of constitutional text, and more democratic. The statutory ban on the use of
contraceptives was a recipe for arbitrary and even discriminatory
action, in a way that did violence to democratic ideals and the rule
of law. It did violence to democratic ideals because a law plainly
lacking public support was nonetheless invoked to regulate private conduct. It violated the rule of law because it lacked the kind
of generality and predictability on which the rule of law depends.

It is worthwhile to underline the democratic nature of this idea. The ban on use of laws that are rarely enforced is designed to ensure that if enforcement is going to take place at all, there must be public support for it.

Minimalists believe *Lawrence* should be read in just this way. Although the Court spoke in terms of personal autonomy, a broad autonomy reading would have consequences that the Court likely did not intend. It would be remarkable if *Lawrence* were understood to forbid states from criminalizing prostitution or bestiality. In any case, a broad autonomy reading would ignore the Court's emphasis on society's "emerging awareness." It appears that the Court was responding to, and requiring, an evolution in public opinion—something like a broad consensus that the practice at issue should not be punished.

If anything, a ban on sodomy is even worse than the Connecticut law struck down in *Griswold*. Such a ban is used not for frequent arrests or convictions, but for rare and unpredictable harassment by the police. Minimalists insist on this point, and believe that the Court's protection of sexual privacy has been greatly informed by the risk of arbitrary enforcement. And they think that if sexual privacy is to be protected, it must be a result of narrow, cautious rulings, in which courts solve one problem at a time and show a reluctance to reject widely held moral beliefs. They insist that when the Court has struck down legislation, as in *Griswold* and *Lawrence,* it was acting in a way that fit closely with, and did not defy, the moral commitments of the nation as a whole.

Alternatives

To many perfectionists, this interpretation reads the right of privacy far too narrowly and fails to give enough protection to sexual liberty. Many perfectionists believe that John Stuart Mill had it exactly right: The state should not be allowed to interfere with private choices unless there is harm to others. Some perfectionists believe that the Supreme Court should adopt Mill's claim as part of constitutional law. But minimalists believe that this would be a grave mistake. They raise two objections to the perfectionist program.

The first objection involves the simple risk of judicial error. There is no reason to think that judges are going to be reliable when they consult their consciences to give content to ideas like "liberty" and "privacy." Unmoored from public convictions, the Court's conception of liberty might be confused or indefensible. (Recall *Dred Scott* and *Lochner.*) In any case, one of the rights people have is the right to democratic self-government. Suppose people believe, on principle, that laws should forbid prostitution, bigamy, obscenity, or bestiality. They may believe that these practices have corrosive effects on social norms or that participants in such practices are themselves harmed. Minimalists ask: If the Constitution does not speak clearly, shouldn't judges be cautious about imposing their own commitments on citizens who disagree?

The second objection is the danger of unintended bad consequences. Even if the Court has the right conception of liberty, it may not do much good by insisting on it when the nation strongly disagrees. Imagine the Court had held, in 1990, that the Due Process Clause requires states to recognize same-sex marriages. Suppose too in doing so, it was responding to the right conception of liberty. Such a ruling would undoubtedly have produced a large-scale social backlash, and very likely a constitutional amendment that might have made same-sex marriage impossible and set back the cause of gay rights for decades. The simple point is that judicial impositions may do little good and considerable harm, even from the standpoint of the causes that the Court hopes to promote. Note, for instance, that ten years after the Court's decision in *Brown v. Board of Education,* only about 2 percent of African-American children in the South were attending desegregated schools.[20] In countless domains, the Court's efforts to produce social reform have been far less effective in the real world than they promise on paper.

These are cautionary points and no more. But at the very least, they suggest that a minimalist ruling, building on existing precedent and on widespread convictions, has considerable advantages over a ruling that is based on the Court's interpretation of words like "liberty."

But perhaps the Court would have done better, in *Lawrence,* to continue on the path urged by fundamentalists—to uphold any intrusion on liberty that does not run afoul of Anglo-American traditions. Due process traditionalism might be supported on the ground that federal judges are not especially good at evaluating our practices, and that if a practice has endured there is probably good reason for it, if only because many people have endorsed it, or at least not seen fit to change it. Justice Scalia likes constitutional traditionalism because it reduces the discretion of federal judges to make up new rights, and because traditions are likely to carry with them a sensible understanding of what rights are. Constitutional traditionalism therefore simplifies constitutional decisions at the same time that it makes them less likely to go wrong.

Minimalists sympathize with this point but disagree. They respond that protection of privacy can be done in a modest way, one that protects liberty without compromising democracy. As we have seen, a statute like that invalidated in *Lawrence* is a recipe for arbitrary enforcement. The Court's refusal to permit criminal convictions under these circumstances is not radically inconsistent with democratic ideals. In a sense, it helps to vindicate them. Federal judges should not embark on a large-scale program for the protection of privacy. But there is nothing wrong with narrow rulings that forbid states from criminalizing conduct that is no longer viewed as a fit basis for fines or jail sentences.

The Future of Sex

In the aftermath of the *Lawrence* decision, it is tempting to join Justice Scalia in wondering about the constitutionality of laws forbidding prostitution, adultery, fornication, obscenity, polygamy, and incest. But Scalia's fears are wildly overstated.

Lawrence does not raise questions about laws forbidding incest and sexual harassment simply because it allows government to prohibit coercion. The Court has also made clear that prostitution and others forms of commercial sex receive far less protection than noncommercial sex. Why? Part of the answer is there is no pattern of nonenforcement against prostitution. Arrests and prosecutions are common. In any case, prostitution has a harmful effect on the lives of many prostitutes; the risk of exploitation (and worse) is real and serious. One need not take a position on the disputed question whether and how prostitution should be outlawed to see the legal point: Under the Court's privacy cases, restrictions on prostitution are easily defensible.

More difficult cases involve laws forbidding adultery.[21] It is not hard to imagine actual adultery prosecutions, or cases in which government discharges or refuses to employ people who have been involved in adulterous relationships. Many perfectionists would argue that adultery is a consensual relationship with which the state may not interfere on purely moral grounds. On the other hand, it is possible to justify prohibitions on adultery on the ground that it harms others, such as children and the betrayed spouse. Adultery laws are an effort to protect marital and parental relationships. Marriage can be and usually is understood as an exchange of commitments, and these have both individual and social value. A prohibition on adultery, moral and legal, operates in the service of those commitments. For these reasons, there is a good argument that adultery falls outside of the domain of constitutional protection.

One difficulty here is that criminal prosecutions for adultery are at least as rare as those for sodomy. There is a good argument that criminal prosecutions, in the context of adultery, are inconsistent with current social values. This is not because adultery is thought to be morally acceptable; it is not. It is because adultery is not considered a proper basis for the use of the criminal law. On this count, it is not so easy to distinguish an adultery prosecution from the sodomy prosecution forbidden in *Lawrence*.

My purpose here is not, however, to resolve the hardest questions; minimalists are content to leave those questions undecided. With respect to privacy and sex, the advantages of minimalism over perfectionism should now be clear. Minimalists respect democratic prerogatives. They do not require courts to take a large stand on the nature of freedom. They ask judges to hesitate before seizing on ambiguous constitutional provisions to forbid governments from embodying reasonable moral judgments in law. But they do not want to abandon privacy altogether. They insist that constitutional protection of privacy, as part of liberty, is firmly engrained in constitutional law, and that protection of that right, developed in minimalist fashion, does far more good than harm.

Fundamentalists believe that minimalists want to do too much. But would the nation really be better off if the Supreme Court rejected four decades of precedent and entirely eliminated privacy as a constitutional principle? Would it really be better if states could fine or imprison people who used contraceptives or engaged in certain sexual acts? Why?

Roe *and Its Ironies*

Thus far, we might seem to have been playing Hamlet without the prince. When most court watchers think about constitutional privacy, they think about one thing: *Roe v. Wade* and the future of the right to choose abortion.

The ruling in *Roe,* one of the most controversial in the nation's entire history, has long dominated debates over the future direction of the Supreme Court. In every recent presidential election, the question, *What will be the future of the Supreme Court?* is often taken, by liberals and conservatives alike, to be code for, *What will happen to the right to choose abortion?* Among liberals, preservation of *Roe* has probably been the most pressing issue in thinking about Supreme Court appointments. In recent years, conservatives have been a bit quieter. But for many of them, overruling *Roe* has been a high priority. There is no question that legal fundamentalists have long had *Roe* in their sights —and that in many ways it stands as the fundamentalists' Public Enemy Number One.

As a political matter, there are three major ironies here, and they are all relevant to thinking about the role of the Supreme Court in American life. The first irony: *Roe* was decided in 1973, at a time when the nation was rapidly moving in the direction of easing up restrictions on abortion. The society's moral trend-line was clear. For better or for worse, it was pro-choice, not pro-life. In 1973, the Court seemed to be ratifying a trend that was well underway. But in a few years, the Court's decision helped to create the pro-life movement—and thus gave a lot of new energy and organization to people who had been relatively quiet on the abortion question. In short, the Court fueled its own opposition. (Perfectionists and liberal activists take note.)

The second irony: *Roe* is a crucial decision for women's groups, many of whose members have long seen the ruling as central to women's equality. But from the standpoint of equality, the Court's decision has been a mixed blessing. The decision in *Roe* almost certainly contributed to the defeat the Equal Rights Amendment.[22] It also helped to demobilize the women's movement and at the same time to activate the strongest opponents of that movement.

The third irony: Democrats have made preservation of *Roe* a central issue in presidential elections, and many Republican leaders have made it clear that they would like the Court to overrule the decision. But if *Roe* were overruled, Democrats would almost certainly be helped and Republicans would almost certainly be hurt. Everyone knows that if abortion really becomes an active issue again—if abortion might actually be a crime—then countless Americans will vote for pro-choice candidates. A judicial decision to overrule *Roe* would immediately create a major crisis for the Republican Party. Some red states would undoubtedly turn blue or at least purple.

Choice Then and Choice Now

But my topic here is law, not politics. To understand the constitutional issue, we have to distinguish between two questions. The first is whether the Court should have done what it did in 1973. The second is what the Court should do now.

Minimalists are greatly embarrassed by *Roe,* and rightly so. This was the Court's first encounter with the abortion question, and the Court badly overreached, deciding many issues unnecessarily. Not only did the Court announce a broad right to choose abortion; it also developed a complex and rigid trimester system, in which it specified what states may do in each three-month period of a pregnancy. By saying so much, the Court ignored the minimalists' most fervent plea: In the most controversial cases, judges should proceed narrowly rather than broadly. With its ambitious ruling, not at all firmly rooted in precedent, the Court allowed pro-life citizens to think that they had been treated with contempt—as if their own moral commitments could be simply brushed aside by federal judges.

Perhaps the Court's ambitious ruling in *Roe* could be justified if the Constitution plainly banned states from outlawing abortion. But the Constitution does not plainly do that. Even if the Due Process Clause recognizes a right to privacy, many people think that the protection of fetal life is extremely important. As a matter of constitutional law, protecting fetal life may well be a constitutionally sufficient reason to intrude on the right to choose.

It is no wonder, in this light, that fundamentalists want the Court to overrule *Roe v. Wade* and to allow states to regulate abortion as they like. Justice Scalia's words nicely summarize the fundamentalist position: "We should get out of this area, where we have no right to be, and where we do neither ourselves nor the country any good by remaining."[23] In fact *Roe* can easily be seen as a case study in the pitfalls of perfectionism. Not only did the split the country; it also ignored one of the most remarkable virtues of a federal system, which is to allow different resolutions in different states, with their different mixes of moral values.

It is not at all silly to say that *Roe* was simply wrong—that the Court would have done better to stay out of the abortion controversy. But there is a reasonable alternative position. In dealing with the abortion question, the Court could have proceeded much more slowly. The Texas law challenged in *Roe* was exceedingly severe. It banned abortion even in cases in which the mother would face serious health problems from bringing the child to term, even in cases in which the pregnancy resulted from rape, and even in cases in which the pregnancy was a product of incest. The Court could have emphasized these points so as to rule quite narrowly. It could have said that even if states may protect fetal life, they may not require women to carry children to term when they have been raped and when childbirth would seriously endanger their health. The Court also dealt, in *Roe,* with a Georgia law that created a host of peculiar obstacles and burdens, going far beyond what was necessary to protect the state's legitimate interests. The Court might have struck down severe restrictions of this kind without deciding the most controversial questions about how to balance the rights of women and the protection of fetal life.

Justice Ruth Bader Ginsburg is one of the leading advocates for women's equality in the history of American law. But she is also a minimalist. She has herself argued that *Roe v. Wade* was a mistake, simply because it overreached—and that the Court would have done much better if it had proceeded in a narrow fashion.[24] One of the major advantages of this way of proceeding is that the Court would not have dictated a solution of its own. It would have participated in a dialogue about the abortion question, listening to what other institutions, and citizens, had to say.

What about *Roe* today? Fundamentalists insist that *Roe* was wrong and should be immediately overruled. But it is not senseless to think that, although *Roe* was wrong, and a big mistake, the Court should not now overrule it. Much of constitutional law is built on decisions with which current judges disagree. Our system works because it is based on respect for precedent; if judges overruled precedents simply because they disagree with them, constitutional law would be hopelessly unstable. Many fundamentalists believe that in constitutional law, judges should not much respect precedent. But this is arrogant. To be sure, precedents are not set in stone; the Court has overruled many of its decisions, including those permitting segregation and invalidating maximum-hour and minimum-wage laws. But when a decision has become an established part of American life, judges should have a strong presumption in its favor. Minimalists do not like radical shifts, and overruling *Roe* would certainly count as that.

Minimalists are willing to agree that the Constitution permits reasonable restrictions on the right to choose abortion. If states want to ensure that the choice of abortion is adequately informed, or to require a serious consultation with doctors before abortions are chosen, the Constitution should not stand in the way. Minimalists think that the Court might well have been wrong to forbid bans on what is sometimes called "partial birth abortion." Most important, minimalists respect *Roe*'s critics. They agree that *Roe* has shaky constitutional foundations. They know that countless citizens of good faith believe that abortion is a morally troublesome act; many minimalists share that belief. As a matter of constitutional law, minimalists are far from sure that *Roe* was right. But they are willing to accept it, not in spite of but because of their essential conservatism.

In rejecting *Roe,* and in attempting to eliminate the right of privacy, fundamentalists are attacking many decades of American law. That kind of attack is entirely characteristic of the fundamentalist program.

CHAPTER FOUR

Who May Marry?

The freedom to marry has long been recognized as one of the vital personal rights essential to the orderly pursuit of happiness by free men. . . . Marriage is one of the basic civil rights of man, fundamental to our very existence and survival.

—*Loving v. Virginia*[1]

Why should the state privilege some adult dyads but not others? Why should the state privilege only dyads? Why not triads? In other words, what business does the state have in deciding which adult personal relationships are deserving of legal protection and benefits and which are not?

—Patricia Cain[2]

IS THERE A CONSTITUTIONAL RIGHT TO MARRY? Fundamentalists think not. The Supreme Court thinks so. The Court's recognition of such a right has made many people wonder whether states must recognize same-sex marriages. As a matter of constitutional law, who is entitled to get married? Will federal courts strike down bans on same-sex marriages? Should they? What about polygamous marriages, or incestuous ones?

Fundamentalists, perfectionists, and minimalists give quite different answers to these questions. Fundamentalists would like to reject the idea that the Constitution contains any right to marry; they would permit states to ban prisoners, or poor people, from marrying. Many perfectionists would like to expand the right, certainly to same-sex couples. Minimalists accept the right to marry, but they want the Supreme Court to proceed with great caution. They think the future of marriage should be settled democratically, not by federal judges.

To understand these points, we have to begin with a basic question: What is the right to marry, anyway?

Marriage and the Supreme Court

Fundamentalists don't like it, but the Supreme Court has been circling around a constitutional right to marry for a long time. In 1888, the Court did not quite establish that right, but it did describe marriage as "the most important relation in life."[3] Indeed it went even further, saying that marriage is "the foundation of the family and of society, without which there would be neither civilization nor progress."

In its 1923 decision in *Meyer v. Nebraska*,[4] invalidating a law forbidding the teaching of any language other than English, the Court said that the Due Process Clause protected the right "to marry, establish a home and bring up children." Striking down a compulsory sterilization law in *Skinner v. Oklahoma*,[5] the Court described marriage as "fundamental to the very existence and survival of the race." *Griswold v. Connecticut*[6] held that states could not ban married couples from using contraceptives. The Court emphasized that it was dealing with "a right of privacy older than the Bill of Rights—older than our political parties, older than our school system. Marriage is a coming together for better or for worse, hopefully enduring, and intimate to the degree of being sacred." (The words "hopefully enduring" were written by the evidently hopeful Justice William O. Douglas, who was married four times.) In most of these cases, the Court was speaking in perfectionist terms, offering ambitious talk about the place of marriage in society.

None of these cases, however, explicitly protected the right to marry as such. In its modern form, the right to marry is a product of three important, messy, and confusing cases, combining perfectionist and minimalist features. The first was the 1969 decision, *Loving v. Virginia*,[7] where the Court struck down a ban on interracial marriage. Most of Chief Justice Earl Warren's majority opinion spoke in terms of the Equal Protection Clause, emphasizing the illegitimacy of racial discrimination. Warren could easily have stopped there, and minimalists wish he had. But in a separate ruling, set off in a puzzlingly perfectionist section, Warren also held that the ban violated the Due Process Clause. In his words, "the freedom to marry has long been recognized as one of the vital personal rights essential to the orderly pursuit of happiness by free men." He added that "[m]arriage is one of the 'basic civil rights of man,' fundamental to our very existence and survival."

What does this mean? Apparently the Court believed that procreation and the raising of children are inextricably linked to the institution of marriage. Later cases confirm that the right to marry counts as fundamental for constitutional purposes—and is sufficient by itself to make courts look askance at any restrictions on that right.

The key decision is *Zablocki v. Redhail*.[8] In that case, decided in 1978, the Court invoked the Equal Protection Clause to strike down a Wisconsin law forbidding people under child support

obligations to remarry unless they obtained a judicial determination
that they had met those obligations and that their children were not
likely to become public charges. The Court announced that "the
right to marry is of fundamental importance for all individuals" and
added that "the decision to marry has been placed on the same level
of importance as decisions relating to procreation, childbirth, child
rearing, and family relationships."

The opinion's author, Justice Thurgood Marshall, did not give
a clear explanation of this remarkable conclusion. He noted that
women have a right to seek an abortion and to give birth to an
illegitimate child, and insisted that "a decision to marry and raise
the child in a traditional family setting must receive equivalent
protection." He added that if the "right to procreate means anything at all, it must imply some right to enter the only relationship
in which" the state "allows sexual relations legally to take place."
Apparently, the right to marry has constitutional status because
the status of marriage is a legal precondition for sexual relations.
But in the modern era, in which the Constitution is seen to protect sexual relations outside of marriage, this suggestion loses its
foundation.

In *Turner v. Safley,* decided in 1987,[9] the Court followed and
extended *Zablocki,* striking down a prison regulation that prohibited inmates from marrying unless there were "compelling
reasons" for them to do so. "Compelling reasons" were understood to include pregnancy or the birth of an illegitimate child.
In an opinion by Justice O'Connor, the Court acknowledged
that the prison setting is distinctive and usually calls for a measure of judicial deference. But it concluded that *Zablocki* applies
in that setting, at least in such a way as to invalidate the prison
regulation.

In fact Justice O'Connor went far beyond previous decisions to spell out some of the foundations of the right to marry. She said that marriages, by inmates as by others, "are expressions of emotional support and public commitment." She emphasized that these are "important and significant aspects of the marital relationship." She added that marriages are often recognized as having spiritual significance—and that "marital status often is a prerequisite for" a number of material benefits, including property rights, government benefits, and less tangible advantages. These conclusions underlay the Court's conclusion that even in prison, the right to marry must be respected unless the state can produce compelling reasons for interfering with it.

In short, we have a paradox: persistent acknowledgment, over more than a century, of a right to marry, alongside confusing and sometimes implausible explanations of the basis for that right.

But What Is Marriage?

Suppose, then, there is a right to marry. What exactly does this mean? The Supreme Court has done precious little to specify either the nature or the limits of the right to marry.

To make any progress, we have to know what benefits the status of marriage confers. Some are material; others are wholly symbolic. Many of the battles over the right to marry, including those involving same-sex marriage, have nothing to do with material benefits and everything to do with symbols and hence legitimacy.

Of course state law varies, but the material benefits fall into six major categories.[10]

1. **Tax benefits (and burdens).** While a great deal of public attention is paid to the "marriage penalty," the tax system rewards

many couples when they marry—at least if one spouse earns a great deal more than the other. Hence there is a marriage "bonus" for couples in traditional relationships, in which the man is the breadwinner and the woman stays at home. (The marriage penalty can be significant if both spouses earn big incomes.) Married couples can file joint returns. Members of such couples are allowed to transfer property to one another without being subject to gain-loss valuation; this can be a substantial advantage.

2. **Entitlements.** Federal law benefits married couples through a number of entitlement programs. Under the Family and Medical Leave Act, employers must allow unpaid leave to workers who need to care for a spouse but need not do so for "partners." Veterans' benefits provide a range of economic programs (involving medical care, housing, and educational assistance) to the spouses, but not the partners, of veterans. Those who are married to federal employees can also claim benefits unavailable to those who are unmarried. Under state law, the entitlement to consortium protects spouses; the status of members of unmarried couples is unclear.

3. **Inheritance and other death benefits.** A member of a married couple obtains numerous benefits at the time of death. The law favors wives and husbands of those who die without a will, and many states forbid people to refuse to leave money to the person to whom they are married. Under the Uniform Probate Code, those who die intestate give much of their estate to their spouse, even if they have children. In wrongful death actions, spouses automatically qualify for benefits; the status of unmarried couples is far less clear.

4. **Ownership benefits.** Under both state and federal law, spouses often have automatic ownership rights that non-spouses lack. In community property states, people have automatic rights to the holdings of their spouses, and they cannot contract around the legal rules. Even in states that do not follow community property rules, states may presume joint ownership of property acquired after marriage and before legal separation.

5. **Surrogate decision-making.** Members of married couples are given the right to make surrogate decisions of various sorts in the event of incapacitation. When an emergency arises, a spouse is permitted to make judgments on behalf of an incapacitated partner. More generally, a spouse might be appointed formal guardian, entitled to make decisions about care, residence, and money, as well as about particular medical options.

6. **Evidentiary privileges.** Federal courts, and a number of state courts, recognize marital privileges, including a right to keep marital communications confidential and to exclude adverse spousal testimony.

This is a large set of benefits, and they help to make marriage attractive to many people. But in recognizing the right to marry, the Supreme Court almost certainly did not mean to say that the state is constitutionally required to provide them. Suppose California altered its laws to place married people on the same plane as unmarried couples or single people. It defies belief to suggest that the alteration would be an unconstitutional violation of the "right to marry." Indeed, in acknowledging a marriage right the

Court has been at pains to emphasize that it did not mean to cast constitutional doubt on measures that merely affect people's incentives to marry.[11]

What else, then, does marriage entail? The only possible answer is *symbolic*—a kind of official endorsement or recognition of the marital relationship as such. The Court has been entirely aware of this point. Recall that in *Turner,* Justice O'Connor stressed that marriages are "expressions of emotional support and public commitment." If a state says that people are "married," then they are in fact married, and not only for purposes of financial and other benefits. They are married in the sense that the relationship is taken, by everyone who knows about it, to have a particular quality. The official institution of marriage entails a certain public legitimacy and endorsement.

Debates over same-sex marriages have everything to do with this point. Many of those who oppose such marriages, including President George W. Bush, appear willing to give material benefits to same-sex couples. What they reject is the formal status of "marriage." And many advocates of same-sex marriage are not satisfied by the idea of civil unions carrying the material benefits of marriage. They are even insulted by that idea, because it withholds the legitimacy granted to marriage.

Minimalists think that when the Supreme Court speaks of the right to marry, it means to recognize *an individual right of access to the official institution of marriage, with the material and symbolic benefits that accompany that institution.* This reading does not require states to recognize any particular set of benefits, or even to have a system of marriage licenses at all. All that is required is access to whatever benefits are now in place.

The best analogy is to the right to vote. As the Constitution is now understood, states are not required to provide elections for state offices.[12] But when elections are held, the right to vote qualifies as fundamental, and state laws that deprive people of that right will usually be struck down. Marriage is understood the same way: the state is not required to create the practice in the first instance, but so long as the practice exists, the state must make it available to everyone. (Of course the state may not forbid religious institutions from performing marriages and even from defining marriage as they choose; my topic here is official licensing.)

Fundamentalists are extremely skeptical about the right to vote, and they reject the right to marry. For decades, fundamentalists argued vociferously against the rule of one person, one vote, and they even contended that the poll tax is constitutionally acceptable. On fundamentalist grounds, they're right. If fundamentalists had their way, the right to vote would not receive constitutional protection at all. (Put aside *Bush v. Gore* as a case in which many fundamentalists were willing and even happy to build on precedents they despised.) Even minimalists think some of the Warren Court's decisions on voting proceeded far too aggressively. But would it really be better if the Court had refused to give special protection to the right to vote?

It isn't clear, however, that the right to marry has the same status as the right to vote. Family life has traditionally been within the power of the states. Dissenting in *Zablocki v. Redhail,* Justice Rehnquist, not yet Chief Justice, said that the restriction on marriage should be viewed "in light of the traditional presumption" that state laws are valid, and hence he would acknowledge "the State's power to regulate family life and to assure the support of minor children." Here too we will be tempted to agree with him if we accept the fundamentalist view that no ratifiers of any constitutional provision meant to protect the right to marry.

Should we really accept fundamentalism here? For decades, the Supreme Court has said that the state must give a powerful justification for any effort to deny people the right of access to the institution of marriage. But Justice Rehnquist asks a legitimate question: *Why* does the right to marry qualify for constitutional protection?

With the right to vote, we can argue that equal access is internal to the right itself: The right to vote, to count as such, must be provided equally to all. Perhaps political equality and the right to vote should be taken to entail one another. If some people are not permitted to vote, or if some people's votes count more than others, then the idea of political equality is undermined; and that idea is integral to voting itself. Minimalists are not sure this argument is ultimately convincing, but they are willing to entertain the possibility that *if* the right to vote qualifies as fundamental for constitutional purposes, it is because something in that right, by its very nature, calls for equality in its distribution.

The same cannot be said of the right to marry. There is nothing internal to that right that calls for its equal distribution. If the right to marry qualifies as fundamental for equal protection purposes, it must be simply by virtue of its *importance*. Suppose this answer is accepted. It remains to ask what, in particular, it is about the right to marry that makes it important in a constitutionally relevant sense. The first answer, a tempting one, would point to the material benefits of marriage. But on reflection, these material benefits cannot be the basis for the view that marriage counts as a fundamental right. Material benefits of crucial sorts are part of many programs involving welfare, housing, and subsistence; and under current law they do not qualify as fundamental for constitutional purposes.[13] Hence it would be extremely odd to say that the marital benefits of marriage are by themselves enough to qualify the right to marry for the status of a fundamental right.

All this leaves only one possibility: The right to marry counts as fundamental for constitutional purposes because of the symbolic benefits that come from official, state-licensed marriage. And I believe this point does, in fact, underlie the Court's decisions. The Court is alert to the extraordinary importance that people place on the status of marriage—and to the value of that status both for participants in marriages and for those who know them. This too, however, is a somewhat puzzling conclusion. In no other context is a purely or even largely symbolic reason enough to give special constitutional protection to an interest. And the symbolic benefits of marriage are hardly inevitable; everything depends on how people read symbols. In a different society, for example, the symbolic benefits might be much lower. All I am suggesting is that the right to marry must be understood with reference to the fundamental importance of the symbolic interests at stake—and that those interests lie at the very heart of the Court's decisions recognizing the right to marry.

Enter Stage Right

The minimalist conclusion, then, is that the right to marry is a right of access to the material and symbolic benefits that accompany the marital relationship. But—to turn to the most controversial question—*Who may enter into that relationship?*

Begin with a narrow understanding. By finding a constitutional right to marry, the Court did not mean to suggest that it would strike down *any* law that departed from the traditional idea that a marriage is between (one) woman and (one) man. It meant only to say that when a man and a woman seek to marry,

the state must have exceedingly good reasons for putting significant barriers in their path. Thus the narrow understanding of the
right to marry says that *without very good reason, states may not
deny an adult man and an adult woman access to the institution
of marriage.* This rationale fits with the Court's decisions in *Loving, Zablocki,* and *Turner.* It has the further advantage of not
drawing into question bans on polygamous marriages or marriages between people and cats.

What might be said in favor of the narrow understanding of
the right to marry? The initial answer, much approved by fundamentalists, would be rooted in constitutional traditionalism. For
fundamentalists, the first choice is to eliminate the right to marry
altogether. But the second choice would be to discipline and limit
that right by understanding it to cover no more than what American traditions cover. If the right to marry is defined by reference
to those traditions, then it is clear that gays and lesbians cannot
marry. Indeed, the answer to *Who may marry?* is almost always
easy: One man may marry one woman, unless the marriage is
incestuous or otherwise inconsistent with American traditions.

Fundamentalists like this approach, for they insist that the Due
Process Clause, the basic source of liberty rights, is backward-
looking; it requires the state to justify any departure from longstanding views about individual rights.[14] As we saw in Chapter 3,
this view can find its foundation in Justice Holmes's famous dissenting opinion in the *Lochner* case, where he urged the Court to
use the Due Process Clause to strike down legislation only in cases
involving departures from longstanding traditions.[15] As we have
also seen, the discipline imposed by tradition is far from arbitrary.
Suppose we believe, with the great conservative theorist
Edmund Burke,[16] that traditions are likely to be wise simply
because they represent the judgment not of a single person but

of countless people over a long period of time. If so, then traditions have some of the advantages of free markets, reflecting as they do the assessments of the many rather than the few.

To say this is not to say that longstanding practices are always justified, any more than free markets are. Traditions might reflect prejudice or confusion rather than wisdom. But perhaps practices are likely to be longstanding only if they serve important social interests; if so, fundamentalists think there should be a presumption in their favor. It is certainly not nonsensical to say that if American states have generally refused to recognize certain marriages, the refusal might well have some sense behind it.

In any case the question is not whether longstanding practices always deserve support, measured against the best answer to that question in principle. The question is instead a comparative one: For judges interpreting the Due Process Clause, is constitutional traditionalism preferable to an alternative approach — in which, for example, judges pay close attention to their own judgments about liberty, or judgments of an evolving public? If we believe judges are likely to blunder, an effort to root the right to marry in traditions might well be better than any alternative. And even if we believe that judicial decisions have some advantages, we might agree that in the face of doubt, democratic judgments, especially in a federal system, deserve a measure of respect, in part because self-government is one of the rights to which people are entitled.

Of course traditions are not self-defining; they do not come prepackaged for easy identification. Why should we not consider bans on interracial marriage "traditional" as well? It is tempting to object, as perfectionists do, that constitutional traditionalism is a fraud, in which the key value judgment—How should the tradition be defined?—ends up doing all the work.[17] But the objection is overstated; there are no easy victories here for perfectionists. I have discussed Justice Scalia's claim that we should understand traditions at the lowest possible level of abstraction[18]; and if we accept his claim, then the use of traditions does impose a real limitation on judicial discretion. We should be able to agree, for example, that in the United States, there is no tradition of respect for incestuous marriages, or homosexual marriages, or marriages that involve more than two people. The emphasis on tradition, thus understood, might be defended on the ground that it reduces the burdens of judicial judgment and turns constitutional principles into something much closer to a system of rules.

For all of these reasons, due process traditionalism is far from irrational or arbitrary, even if it produces results that can seem so in particular cases. And if we are due process traditionalists, we might insist that if there is a right to marry, it includes only the time-honored form: one man and one woman. To repeat, fundamentalists would like to say that there is no right to marry at all; but so long as the Supreme Court has recognized that right, fundamentalists are likely to insist on traditionalism as a kind of second-best. And on this count, minimalists harbor a lot of sympathy for their argument.

Here, then, is an area where fundamentalists, big losers on the question of whether the right to marry exists, can make common cause with minimalists in opposition to a potentially aggressive judicial role.

Enter Stage Left

What might be wrong with this position? To put the issue more concretely, do bans on same-sex marriage violate the Constitution? Many perfectionists think so. They believe that too much of the time, traditions are rooted in power and prejudice. They believe that under the Constitution, it is entirely appropriate for judges to ask whether an abridgment of liberty is justified by principle, or whether any form of discrimination, including discrimination against gays and lesbians, can survive critical scrutiny.

To evaluate the perfectionist position, we have to distinguish the question of constitutional principle from the question of appropriate judicial decisions. In principle, it not so easy to defend the ban on same-sex marriage in constitutionally acceptable terms. What sorts of social harms would follow from recognizing marriages between people of the same sex? It is conventional to argue that the refusal to recognize same-sex marriage is a way of protecting the marital institution itself. If same-sex marriages were permitted, perhaps marriage itself would be endangered, at least in its traditional form. But aside from simple semantic arguments, this is very puzzling; how do same-sex marriages threaten the institution of marriage? Extending the right to enter into marriage would not endanger traditional marriages—unless it were thought that significant numbers of heterosexuals would forgo traditional marriages if gay and lesbian marriages were permitted (a difficult causal argument, to say the least).

Perhaps same-sex marriages would harm children—an empirical claim on which there is much dispute. Many people think that the risk to children is sufficient to justify the ban; perhaps the state should not play dice with the most vulnerable members of society.[19] But do we really have enough evidence of harm? Perfectionists are skeptical, and the available studies are not clear enough to eliminate their skepticism.[20] Even if the evidence is unclear, we might nonetheless conclude that risks should not be taken with children. But should people really be denied access to the institution of marriage simply because of speculation? Marriage licenses are not, and cannot constitutionally be, denied to people who have criminal records, or records of domestic abuse, or records of alcoholism, drug addiction, or general incompetence—even though people in all such groups pose risks to children. Why should gays and lesbians be treated differently, and worse?

Some people believe that the state can legitimately reserve marriage to men and women for symbolic reasons. Perhaps the state can argue that it does not want to give the same symbolic support to same-sex unions as to opposite-sex unions. Perhaps the state does not want to "endorse" such unions or to suggest that they are appropriate or legitimate, or have a standing similar to that of traditional marriage. But why not? On what basis may states refuse to endorse such unions? Consider the case of adultery, where the symbolic condemnation is far easier to understand. Compared to a ban on same-sex marriages, a prohibition on adultery seems simple to justify. As any divorce lawyer can tell you, adultery poses a far more direct and prevalent threat to marriage (or at least to marriages) than same-sex unions are ever likely to do. Such a prohibition is likely in many cases to protect one or even both spouses, and to protect children besides. If, as seems clear, the Court's decision in *Lawrence v. Texas* throws prohibitions on adultery into at least some doubt, it is much harder to invoke symbolic condemnation in support of banning same-sex marriage, which poses a much less serious threat to traditional marriages.

Minimalism and Marriage

Minimalists reject the fundamentalist challenge to the right to marry. They know that this right is firmly established, and they don't think courts should eliminate it. They also know that traditions are often senseless, and they do not want to commit themselves to any kind of traditionalism. But they are extremely skeptical of the perfectionist claim that when judges believe the law of marriage draws arbitrary lines, they should feel free to renovate it. Minimalists argue that the key issues should not be resolved by federal courts, and they favor exceedingly small steps in this controversial domain.

The overriding problem is institutional. It involves the need for judicial modesty in the face of strong public convictions and in particular the distinctive judicial virtue of prudence. This point is highly relevant to constitutional law, especially in the area of social reform. Minimalists insist that some constitutional rights are systematically "underenforced" by the judiciary, and for excellent reasons.[21] Those reasons have to do with the courts' limited fact-finding capacities, their weak democratic pedigree, their limited legitimacy, and their frequent ineffectiveness as instigators of social reform. There are particularly strong reasons for federal courts to hesitate in the context of same-sex marriage, not least because the issue of same-sex marriage is under intense discussion at the local, state, and national levels—and there are many possibilities, ranging from diverse forms of civil unions to ordinary marriage. In the area of gay rights, minimalists believe that federal courts can act as catalysts, striking down the most indefensible laws, while also leaving the democratic process considerable room to maneuver.

Consider the remarkable 2003 decision of the Supreme Judicial Court of Massachusetts in the *Goodridge* case, in which it interpreted the state constitution to require recognition of same-sex marriages.[22] The Supreme Judicial Court built on state precedents to develop a broader understanding of liberty and equality than the Supreme Court has established under the federal constitution. While the decision was ambitiously perfectionist, *Goodridge* is also a tribute to federalism. Massachusetts has long allowed an aggressive role for its Supreme Judicial Court, and its rulings can be overturned by amending the state constitution, a far less cumbersome process than amending the national constitution.

Nonetheless, the decision produced a firestorm of protest, in Massachusetts and elsewhere. It inspired constitutional amendments against same-sex marriage in a number of other states and led many officials, including the President, to propose a change to the national constitution to forbid these marriages. It also gave rise to a fear that Massachusetts would effectively ensure that all states would have to recognize such marriages, simply because same-sex couples could go to Massachusetts, marry there, and require other states to recognize their marriages under the Full Faith and Credit Clause. The fear was probably baseless, because as the law now stands, states do not have to recognize marriages that offend their own policies. But the fear attested to the widespread belief that the Massachusetts court had overstepped its bounds. Because of that court's distinctive traditions, it is not clear that minimalism was mandatory or even appropriate for it. Nonetheless, everyone should be able to agree that if same-sex marriage is to be permitted, it would be far better if this step had been taken by the elected representatives and voters of Massachusetts rather than the judges. *Goodridge* offers a powerful cautionary note about the actions of federal courts in this context.

It would be most unfortunate if, as it did with abortion, the Supreme Court were to attempt to settle the issue at this early stage. Some platitudes are worth repeating: A central advantage of a federal system is that it permits a wide range of experiments; a central disadvantage of centralized rules is that they foreclose such experiments. In many areas, minimalist decisions ultimately build constitutional law on a much more solid foundation than a perfectionist approach that tries to produce social reform in a single leap. In the area of sexual equality, the minimalist method eventually produced a broad prohibition on discrimination; so too with the long series of cases that led the Supreme Court to strike down racial segregation in *Brown v. Board of Education.*

The minimalist objection to an aggressive judicial ruling in favor of same-sex marriage has everything to do with the limited role of courts in the constitutional structure—and with the minimalist insistence that when society is divided, judges ought not to be too sure that they are right. Minimalists strongly disagree with the fundamentalist claim that there is no right to marry at all. Fundamentalists are wrong, and extreme, to want to abandon that right altogether. But on same-sex marriage, the central questions are for democratic arenas, not federal judges.

CHAPTER FIVE

Race and Affirmative Action

When blacks take positions in the highest places of government, industry, or academia, it is an open question today whether their skin color played a role in their advancement. The question itself is the stigma . . .

—Clarence Thomas[1]

THE CONSTITUTION'S PROHIBITION ON DISCRIMINATION can be found in the Equal Protection Clause of the Fourteenth Amendment.[2] That clause says, very simply, that no state may "deny to any person within its jurisdiction the equal protection of the laws." No provision of the Constitution, remarkably, forbids the national government from denying people "equal protection." Indeed it is very hard to identify any constitutional provision that would forbid the national government to discriminate on the basis of race, sex, or any other ground.

Would the Constitution in Exile, then, allow the national government to segregate schools by race, exclude women from federal employment, or place Americans of Middle Eastern descent in internment camps? Fundamentalists don't have an easy time in explaining why not; they're oddly silent here. But they do have a lot to say about the Constitution and equality. For decades, they've been attacking affirmative action with a vengeance. Unfortunately, their own method of interpretation doesn't give them much support.

Two Principles

On issues of race, fundamentalists and perfectionists sort themselves into two camps. Fundamentalists follow a simple principle: color-blindness. In their view, the Equal Protection Clause means that the government may not take account of race, period. It follows that any affirmative action program must be struck down by federal courts. It also follows that there is no constitutional problem if an official practice, not itself based on race, ends up hurting African-Americans more than it hurts whites. Suppose, for example, that a test for government employment is passed by most whites but failed by most African-Americans. Fundamentalists think that the employer doesn't have to show that the test is a good or even decent predictor of job performance. In short, they believe that the Equal Protection Clause requires a strict policy of racial neutrality. Just as the government cannot discriminate against African-Americans, so it cannot discriminate in their favor.

Many perfectionists have a strikingly different view. They think the Equal Protection Clause reflects what they call an "anti-subordination principle."[3] On this view, the core meaning of the clause is that African-Americans cannot be subordinated to whites. Perfectionists see the equality problem as involving the second-class citizenship of African-Americans. They believe the Equal Protection Clause is designed not to require color-blindness but to respond to that second-class citizenship. Above all, perfectionists believe governments may not seize on the characteristic of race to place one group of people below another. The United

States should not have a caste system, they insist, and the Constitution is directed against any such system.

For constitutional law, perfectionists draw two concrete lessons that contrast sharply with the views of fundamentalists. First, affirmative action is constitutionally acceptable. The Equal Protection Clause is not neutral between equality and inequality—and affirmative action programs promote equality because they counteract the subordination of African-Americans. Perfectionists conclude that the constitutional attack on affirmative action is a disgrace. Second, perfectionists think that properly read, the Equal Protection Clause raises doubts about some "neutral" government practices that impose disproportionate harms on African-Americans. They believe the state should have to produce a strong justification for practices that have an especially harmful effect on traditionally subordinated groups.

Thus the battle lines are drawn. Who are the activists here? On affirmative action, at least, fundamentalists favor activism while perfectionists counsel restraint. Indeed, fundamentalists want the courts to strike down programs that have been endorsed by every branch of government and by countless institutions at the national, state, and local levels. They are asking federal judges to assume an extraordinary role—one that would in many ways make *Roe v. Wade* look like a paragon of judicial self-abnegation.

False Fundamentalists

Fundamentalists are concerned above all with text and history. Do text and history support their attack on affirmative action? Actually they don't. On this subject, fundamentalists have abandoned their own favorite principles of interpretation. Astonishingly, the Court's most enthusiastic fundamentalists, Justices Scalia and

Thomas, have voted to strike down affirmative action programs without devoting so much as a sentence to the original understanding of the Equal Protection Clause. Both justices usually pay a great deal of attention to history, particularly when they are voting to invalidate the actions of other branches of government. But on affirmative action their judgments do not depend on history at all. They don't seem to care about it.

As we shall soon see, the history strongly suggests that affirmative action programs are constitutionally legitimate. This is an area—and there are others—in which self-proclaimed fundamentalists are false to their own defining creed. Here, at least, they are *false fundamentalists*. It is worth keeping that category in mind.

Fundamentalists might argue, in their own defense, that this claim misses the point. Maybe history, here, is unnecessary; maybe the text of the Constitution is sufficient, all by itself, to doom affirmative action programs. The founding document does call for "equal" protection of the laws. Isn't it necessarily "unequal" if discrimination against whites is permitted? How can it possibly be "equal" to ban discrimination against one group while allowing discrimination against another?

Many fundamentalists think these questions are decisive. They act as if those who disagree with them are ignoring the Constitution's plain text. But their arguments are almost comically weak. Whether affirmative action programs violate a requirement of equality cannot be settled by the text alone. We can stare at the word "equal" all we like without learning what the Equal Protection Clause really means. The question is whether affirmative action programs are consistent with the Constitution's equality principle, and the word by itself doesn't answer that. One could imagine an understanding of "equal" that forbids affirmative action programs, as the principle of race-neutrality does. One might as easily imagine an understanding that permits them, as the antisubordination principle does—and as we shall see, the ratifiers of the Fourteenth Amendment probably shared some such understanding.

Everyone agrees, for example, that the admissions office of a state university may favor students who have done well in high school. It can treat such students better than those who have flunked out or been suspended for abuse of drugs and alcohol. This form of favoritism does not violate equality. Reasonable classifications, of the kind that governments use every day, are unobjectionable. By their very nature, laws and practices classify. Whether they violate a requirement of "equality" depends on how we specify that contested ideal.

In fact the very principles that underlie the Equal Protection Clause inevitably classify. Suppose we think, as the Supreme Court now does, that under that Clause, race discrimination is unacceptable but age discrimination is just fine—that it is constitutionally acceptable, for instance, to enforce a mandatory retirement age. Does this inequality violate equal protection? Or suppose we think, as fundamentalists usually do, that race neutrality is required but that sex neutrality is not—that under the original understanding, government can discriminate against women but not against African-Americans. Does this inequality violate equal protection? The underlying point is that any imaginable system of constitutional law will treat some groups differently from others. Thus it does not offend the Equal Protection Clause if courts are more skeptical of race-based classifications than of age-based ones. The real question is what the word "equal" requires in this context. Language lessons are unhelpful

here. The claim that race neutrality is the only possible understanding of the words "equal protection" is a fraud.

But fundamentalists have another argument from the Constitution's text. They rightly insist that the Constitution speaks in
terms of individuals rather than groups. Recall the relevant language: "nor shall any state deny any person the equal protection of
the laws." Perhaps the key phrase here is "any person." Because
the document does not forbid discrimination against "groups,"
perhaps any affirmative action program is unacceptable, because it
denies equal protection to some individual "person."

The Supreme Court itself, in an important opinion by Justice
O'Connor, accepted exactly this argument in the 1989 case of
City of Richmond v. Croson.[4] Italicizing the words *"any person,"*
O'Connor wrote that the relevant rights are "guaranteed to the
individual. The rights established are personal rights." Those personal rights, she said, are violated whenever the state takes race
into account. Hence the Court moved dramatically in the direction favored by fundamentalists.

O'Connor's argument contains some truth, but it is badly misleading, and her conclusion does not follow. To be sure, "any person" may complain that a classification is constitutionally
unacceptable. If you are denied a job or a welfare check, you can
always claim that you have been denied the equal protection of the
laws. But on what grounds can you, or "any person," seek special
judicial assistance? If you're complaining that you've been denied
a government benefit as a result of unconstitutional discrimination,
you must usually show that it was because of your membership in
some *group.* Successful claims of discrimination are rarely based
on individual characteristics; the victims almost always belong to
some disfavored group. Thus, "any person" who complains of

unconstitutional discrimination is typically complaining about the government's use of some characteristic that is shared by some number of group members. The issue is whether the Constitution forbids the use of the characteristic in question.

Suppose Marilyn Jones has been denied a government job. As a "person," she certainly has a right to make a complaint under the Equal Protection Clause. But whether her complaint has any force depends on the characteristic on which government has allegedly seized in denying her the job. If the government has decided that Jones is incompetent, there is no problem, since discrimination against incompetent people raises no constitutional issue. But if the government denies jobs to Hispanics and Jones is Hispanic, the Equal Protection Clause is certainly implicated.

In short, any literal reading of the Constitution is utterly uninformative about the affirmative action problem. From the text alone, race neutrality might be constitutionally required, but it might not be. From the text alone, an antisubordination principle might be required, but it might not be.

I have not belabored these textual points to suggest that affirmative action is morally justified or even a good idea. But fundamentalists cannot invoke the Constitution's text on their own behalf. To pretend otherwise is just to pretend. What's really going on here is this: Being personally opposed to affirmative action, many fundamentalists read the text of the Constitution as if it were opposed to affirmative action too.

History

If the Constitution's text does not support the fundamentalists, then what of its history? It should be unnecessary to point out that fundamentalists insist that this question is crucially important (notwithstanding the stunning silence of Justices Scalia and Thomas on history here). Many fundamentalists say, loudly and with great confidence, that the lesson of the Civil War is that all racial classifications are unacceptable. They tend to think that if the Fourteenth Amendment means anything, it means that government may not distribute benefits or burdens on the basis of race. Isn't that what the Civil War was all about?

But in real life, history cuts hard against the fundamentalists' view. It strongly suggests that affirmative action policies were originally regarded as legitimate. Hence there is no historical warrant for the fundamentalist view that affirmative action is generally unconstitutional. On the contrary, history supports affirmative action. In the aftermath of the Civil War, Congress enacted programs that provided particular assistance to African-Americans, and this makes it extremely difficult to attack affirmative action on fundamentalist grounds.[5]

Consider a few details. The Reconstruction Congress that approved the Fourteenth Amendment simultaneously enacted a number of race-specific programs for African-Americans. In fact there was an eerily familiar debate about whether such programs were legitimate; and Congress concluded that they were. The most important examples involve the Freedman's Bureau, created in 1865 as a means of providing special benefits and assistance for African-Americans. The Freedman's Bureau Act authorized the secretary of war to provide "provisions, clothing, and fuel" for impoverished freedmen. Technically the statute allowed assistance for white refugees as well, but in practice the vast majority of its programs exclusively benefited African-Americans.

The act's opponents attacked it on precisely this ground—that it would apply only to members of one race. (Sound familiar?)

The response was that discrimination, of a sort, was justified in the interest of equality: "We need a freedman's bureau," said Senator Charles Sumner, quoting Secretary of War Edwin Stanton, "not because these people are negroes, but because they are men who have been for generations despoiled of their rights."[6] (Sound familiar?)

In 1866, a new Freedman's Bureau bill was proposed, with a still more elaborate discussion of the issue of special treatment. Opponents contended that the bill made "a distinction on account of color between the two races." Presaging the argument of contemporary opponents of affirmative action, they alleged that the bill amounted to "class legislation—legislation for a particular class of blacks to the exclusion of all whites."[7] They complained that the bill "undertakes to make the negro in some respects [the] superior [of whites] . . . and gives them favors the poor white boy in the North cannot get."[8] The educational programs of the Freedmen's Bureau, which excluded most whites, were especially targeted. Supporters of the bill spoke in terms highly reminiscent of modern arguments for affirmative action. Consider the words of Congressman Ignatius Donnelly: "We have liberated four million slaves in the South. It is proposed by some that we stop here and do nothing more. Such a course would be a cruel mockery."[9]

Against the charge of discrimination, one representative responded that the "very object of the bill is to break down the discrimination between whites and blacks. . . . Therefore I repeat that the true object of this bill is the amelioration of the condition of the colored people."[10] Representative Phelps explicitly justified, as legitimate, the "very discrimination [the law] makes between 'destitute and suffering' negroes and destitute and suffering white paupers."[11] President Andrew Johnson vetoed the resulting legislation—but a second bill, containing a number of race-conscious provisions, was enacted over his veto.

This was hardly all. In 1866, special legislation was enacted to assist African-American soldiers. This law, sharply attacked as discriminatory by its critics, was justified on the ground that African-American soldiers had special needs. Against this background, it is striking that there appears to be no significant evidence in the Fourteenth Amendment ratification debates that race-conscious programs benefiting African-Americans were believed to be constitutionally impermissible. One of the explicit goals of the Fourteenth Amendment, in fact, was to provide secure constitutional grounding for the Freedman's Bureau Acts. It seems peculiar, at best, to think that the Fourteenth Amendment prohibited the very types of legislation it was designed to legitimate. What is most remarkable is that fundamentalists have voted to strike down affirmative action programs without producing a hint of a reason to think that such programs are inconsistent with the original understanding of the ratifiers.

The most natural conclusion is that on fundamentalist grounds, the Equal Protection Clause does not ban affirmative action programs. Indeed, the history may be read to support a quite narrow reading of the clause, suggesting that it was designed in part to legitimate the Freedmen's Bureau Acts, but mostly to provide equal "protection" to the newly freed slaves by ensuring that they would be protected by the ordinary criminal and civil law on similar terms as white people. On historical grounds, it would not be at all implausible to say that the ratifiers of the clause understood it to permit racial segregation as well as affirmative action. On this view, the clause does not require color-blindness at all. It does include an antisubordination principle, but a modest one. The central point is that by invoking an ideal of color-blindness, fundamentalists are making up a principle, not following the original understanding.

I do not mean to say that clever fundamentalists could not try to attack affirmative action on fundamentalist grounds. Maybe there are relevant differences between the Freedman's Bureau Acts and the affirmative action programs that have recently been challenged in federal court. Maybe the Fourteenth Amendment is best read to set out a broad principle that forbids the Freedman's Bureau Acts. But at the very least, the history raises significant doubts about this view—and about whether fundamentalists are serious about the original understanding at all. As indirect evidence, consider Justice Thomas's powerful dissenting opinion in *Grutter v. Bollinger,* in which he argued that the Constitution forbids race-conscious programs in higher education.[12] Thomas, the Court's foremost fundamentalist, is usually concerned with the views of the Constitution's ratifiers, but here he offered not a single word about the views of those who framed and ratified the Fourteenth Amendment. Instead he emphasized the words of ex-slave Frederick Douglass, speaking to a group of abolitionists in 1865:

> [I]n regard to the colored people, there is always more that is benevolent, I perceive, than just, manifested toward us. What I ask for the negro is not benevolence, not pity, not sympathy, but simply *justice*. The American people have always been anxious to know what they shall do with us. . . . I have had but one answer from the beginning. Do nothing with us! Your doing with us has already played the mischief with us. Do nothing with us! If the apples will not remain on the tree of their own strength, if they are worm-eaten at the core, if they are early ripe and disposed to

fall, let them fall! . . . And if the negro cannot stand on his own
legs, let him fall also. All I ask is, give him a chance to stand on
his own legs! Leave him alone! . . . [Y]our interference is doing
him positive injury.

These are eloquent words, persuasive and perhaps wise. Certainly Justice Thomas endorses them. But it is not at all clear that
Douglass was speaking of affirmative action programs. More to
the point, Frederick Douglass did not help to draft the Fourteenth
Amendment. Is it sensible to suggest that he speaks authoritatively
for the meaning of the Equal Protection Clause? Is it even plausible to suggest that his views should control the judicial interpretation of that clause? Justice Thomas's opinion is full of
reasonable objections to affirmative action programs, but not one
is grounded in constitutional history.

If my claim here is wrong, why haven't fundamentalists bothered to investigate the history in order to find out? This is a most
serious embarrassment for fundamentalists in the context of race:
Their views are much closer to those of the most extreme right-
wing politicians of the twenty-first century than to those of the
ratifiers of the Fourteenth Amendment.

Beyond Text and History

Is there anything fundamentalists might say to legitimate their constitutional assault on affirmative action programs? In invalidating
these programs, the Supreme Court itself has raised several concerns.
It has pointed, for example, to the social divisiveness of affirmative
action, the fact that race is not chosen voluntarily, the moral irrele-
vance of racial differences, and the possibility that affirmative action
programs will harm or stigmatize their intended beneficiaries. All of
these points are reasonable, and they deserve to be discussed in pub-

lic debates. Maybe affirmative action should be scaled back or even abolished. But none of these points supports a convincing *constitutional* complaint about affirmative action. Many things government does are divisive, yet they may not necessarily be unconstitutional. The Iraq War was divisive; social security reform is divisive; President Johnson's War on Poverty was divisive. None of these initiatives raises the slightest constitutional question. Many human characteristics are morally irrelevant, and many are not voluntarily chosen. But a lot of them are used by government when it classifies people and even discriminates against them. Consider height, strength, and intelligence. The fact that these characteristics are not voluntarily chosen does not mean that the Constitution forbids their use.

It is certainly true that affirmative action programs can harm or stigmatize their intended beneficiaries, and this is a powerful argument against their use. But by itself, a harm or stigma does not create a constitutional objection. A harm or stigma might also be created by programs that benefit children of alumni or people from underrepresented regions—and those programs are not for that reason unconstitutional under the Fourteenth Amendment.

I am left wondering why fundamentalists are so confident that affirmative action plans are unconstitutional. Justice Thomas insists that affirmative action "can only weaken the principle of equality embodied in the Declaration of Independence and the Equal Protection Clause." Maybe so. But the Declaration of Independence has no legal status, and Thomas has said not a word to justify his claim that the Equal Protection Clause forbids affirmative action.

Doing What Minimalists Do

On affirmative action, many perfectionists want federal courts to follow a path of restraint. They believe that the legitimacy of such programs should be resolved democratically. They acknowledge that many citizens of good faith do not like affirmative action and would like to use race-neutral methods instead, but they believe these claims should be pressed in political processes. Here, at least, perfectionists think federal judges should stay their hand.

On these counts, perfectionists have exceedingly strong arguments, but the Supreme Court has proceeded quite differently. It has pursued an emphatically minimalist path. And that path is uniquely intriguing, because out of the Court's case-by-case decisions, narrowly focused on particular facts, has emerged a truly distinctive rule, at least for educational institutions: *Such institutions may engage in affirmative action, but only if they make case-by-case decisions, and do not create any rule.*

From the standpoint of the rule of law, the Court's minimalist decisions are nothing to celebrate, because from the start everything has turned on the details. In *Regents of the University of California v. Bakke,*[13] the first important affirmative action case, a badly divided Court could not produce a majority opinion. Four justices indicated that they would uphold any reasonable affirmative action program, even one that embodied a kind of quota; those justices embraced a form of perfectionism. Four others said that they would strike down any race-conscious program. What emerged as the "rule" of the case was that universities may use race "as a factor" in admissions but may not create quotas. But this rule represented the view of Justice Lewis Powell alone. The other eight justices explicitly rejected it. Ironically, the case stands for a proposition that only one justice thought sensible.

If *Bakke* was not an auspicious beginning for those seeking clear rules, the Court's second important affirmative action case, *Fullilove v. Klutznick,* compounded the problem.[14] A badly divided Court upheld a congressionally enacted program that allowed affirmative action in public contracting. The plurality said that Congress could create a "set-aside" program to ensure that 10 percent of federal funds for certain projects went to minority-owned business enterprises. But no majority spoke for the Court, and no standard of review was selected for affirmative action cases. By the plurality's own admission, its decision was highly dependent on the facts of the particular case, involving a program of limited duration and allowing a waiver from the 10-percent requirement in certain circumstances. The plurality made clear that in another case with slightly different facts, the outcome might be different.

These and other affirmative-action decisions seemed to turn on a large set of factors. In assessing these programs, the Court considered, among other things,

—whether official findings of past discrimination had been made, so that the affirmative action program was a specific response to identifiable discrimination;

—whether the program was rigid or flexible;

—whether it operated as a quota;

—whether it had been issued by Congress, by another politically accountable body, by a court, or by some other institution;

—whether innocent victims were injured, and if so in a severe way.

The use of so many factors led to unexpected decisions in particular cases, and outcomes were hard to predict in advance. Hence the constitutional position of affirmative action programs remained quite obscure. Not until 1989 did the Court finally settle on a standard of review for resolving affirmative action disputes.

In *City of Richmond v. J. A. Croson Co.,*[15] a plurality of the Court held that affirmative action programs would be subject to "strict scrutiny," meaning the highest form of judicial skepticism, at least if such programs had not been enacted by the federal government. But even while announcing a standard of review, the Court's opinion left the law obscure, and many decisions that preceded *Croson* remained in an uncertain state; it was not clear if they remained good law. In *Adarand Constructors Inc. v. Peña*,[16] in 1995, the Court finally announced that its strict standard of review applied to the national government as well as to the states. But it went out of its way to make clear that its standard would not lead to automatic invalidation, that outcomes would turn on particular facts, and thus that results in future cases would remain difficult to predict. Justice O'Connor wrote the crucial and characteristically minimalist passage for the Court:

> We wish to dispel the notion that strict scrutiny is "strict in theory, but fatal in fact." The unhappy persistence of both the practice and the lingering effects of racial discrimination against minority groups in this country is an unfortunate reality, and government is not disqualified from acting in response to it. . . . When race-based action is necessary to further a compelling interest, such action is within constitutional constraints if it satisfies the "narrow tailoring" test this Court has set out in previous cases.

The Court's two most recent decisions, in 2003, involved admissions programs at the University of Michigan. For undergraduate admissions, the Court invalidated a "point system" in which applicants received a specified set of points for various attributes: academic performance (up to 110 points), in-state residence (10 points), having alumni parents (4 points), athletic recruitment (20 points), and being a member of an underrepresented minority group (20 points). In striking down this system, the Court did not rule that the 20 points were too high; it ruled instead that any point system is invalid as such. The Court stressed "the importance of considering each particular applicant as an individual, assessing all of the qualities that the individual possesses, and in turn, evaluating that individual's ability to contribute to the unique setting of higher education."[17] The point system failed to "provide such individualized consideration" simply by its automatic nature, and was unconstitutional for this reason. (Apparently the practices of the University of Michigan's undergraduate admissions office were not minimalist enough!)

In its other decision, the Court permitted the University of Michigan Law School to continue its more flexible affirmative action program. That program did not assign points or impose quotas, but merely included race as a "plus" within a system of individualized judgment.[18] Such programs are acceptable if they remain "flexible enough to ensure that each applicant is evaluated as an individual." Hence the Court permits race-conscious admissions if there is "a highly individuated, holistic review of each applicant's file, giving serious consideration to all the ways an applicant might contribute to a diverse educational environment." (This may be the only time the word "holistic" appears as a word of approval in a Supreme Court opinion.) When no policy gives "automatic acceptance or rejection based on any single 'soft' variable," and when there are "no mechanical, predetermined diversity 'bonuses' based on race or ethnicity," affirmative action is permissible.

These decisions cleared much of the ground. The Court's minimalist path, carved out in small steps over nearly three decades, has led to a situation in which affirmative action programs are frequently unconstitutional in contracting, employment, education, and elsewhere. Educational institutions cannot impose quotas or use point systems, but they can consider race as a factor in a system of individual evaluation. In the military, it seems clear that race may be considered. Outside military and educational settings, race-conscious programs are not at all easy to defend. Still, some questions remain unsettled. We do not know, for example, whether a police department may engage in affirmative action to ensure that predominantly African-American communities are served by diverse police officers. The law is hardly a blank slate—quotas are out, while race "as a factor" may be in —but it is not simple and straightforward. We shall shortly see whether this state of affairs can be justified.

Democratic Debate and Affirmative Action

I have shown that with respect to affirmative action, the fundamentalist position is arrogant, hypocritical, and extremely hard to defend. Fundamentalists ought to approve of affirmative action as a matter of constitutional law, even if they disapprove of it as a matter of principle and politics. But I have not claimed that affirmative action programs are a good idea. The range of these programs is very wide, and to judge them on their merits it is necessary to have a sense of their variety and their consequences. This point is relevant, I believe, to a fair evaluation of minimalism.

Affirmative programs include relatively uncontroversial efforts to increase the pool of applicants by ensuring that the candidates are racially diverse; these efforts are certainly race-conscious, but at the stage of recruitment rather than actual appointment. Other affirmative action programs, like those approved by the Supreme Court in education, include race as a modest factor among many others. Other programs create an ugly system of racial spoils, as in the set-aside of a specified percentage of government contracts for minority-owned businesses. Some programs amount to rigid quota systems. Some programs give a minor boost to highly qualified candidates, while others allow people entry into programs for which they are ill-suited, and probably do not serve their interests. Still other programs seem designed to ensure that government can actually do its work well, as in efforts to ensure that police forces in African-American communities include a significant number of African-American officers. Members of the American military made exactly this argument in explaining to the Supreme Court why it has used race-conscious programs designed to place African-Americans in high positions. Without African-Americans in such positions, members of the military argued, it would be harder to recruit a wide range of people for military service, and harder too to maintain good morale.

This range of possibilities suggests a simple point. Affirmative action programs must be evaluated on the basis of their content and their consequences. Above all, we need to know how they are operating in the real world. Many are successful and widely perceived as such; others are disasters. The Supreme Court's refusal to invalidate all such programs has been influenced by the argument—pushed heavily on the Court by many businesses and by the military—that it would be harmful and perhaps even catastrophic for the Court to adopt the Scalia/Thomas position that affirmative action is unconstitutional as such.

In this light, the Court's minimalist approach is clearly preferable to the extraordinarily intrusive, and constitutionally shaky, position urged by fundamentalists. With respect to affirmative action, a general posture of judicial restraint would not be hard to defend. Fundamentalists, concerned with history, should certainly favor that posture. Still, minimalism has its appeal. Some affirmative action programs are a product of interest-group pressures and have nothing to do with legitimate public purposes. Some such programs have been adopted quietly, with little public scrutiny or review. Whatever the original understanding was, it is not implausible to generalize, from the Equal Protection Clause, a principle that requires government to explain itself whenever it attempts to use race as a basis for distributing benefits or burdens. One of the significant advantages of the Court's case-by-case approach is that it has signaled, to the public and its representatives, some of the considerable difficulties with race-consciousness in practice.

On affirmative action, fundamentalists have violated their own commitments, voting to strike down programs without making the slightest inquiry into history. Minimalist judges, on the other hand, have been a lot more aggressive than they should have been; they have struck down affimative actions programs, including the undergraduate program at the University of Michigan, in contexts in which they should have allowed public institutions to do as they chose. But even here, minimalism has considerable virtues, because it reflects a healthy appreciation of the diversity of programs that go by the label of "affirmative action"—and because it recognizes that some of these programs are much easier to defend, in principle, than others.

CHAPTER SIX

National Security

The Constitution has never greatly bothered any wartime President.

—Francis Biddle

We are now confronted by a profoundly disturbing trend in our national political life: the growing tendency of the judicial branch to inject itself into areas of executive action originally assigned to the discretion of the president. These encroachments include some of the most fundamental aspects of the president's conduct of the war on terrorism.

—John Ashcroft, November 12, 2004

T HE DISAGREEMENTS AMONG FUNDAMENTALISTS, perfectionists, and minimalists have become especially pressing in the face of conflicts between national security and constitutional freedom. None of us can predict the course of history. But it would not be a surprise if these conflicts ultimately became the most important in all of constitutional law.

It is easy to identify two opposing positions: National Security Fundamentalism and Liberty Perfectionism.[1] National Security Fundamentalists understand the Constitution to say that when national security is threatened, the President must be permitted to do whatever needs to be done to protect the country. If he cannot provide that protection, who will? Many people embrace this view and want the federal courts to accept it without qualification. If some fundamentalists have their way, it will be the wave of the future.

Liberty Perfectionists, by contrast, insist that in times of war, at least as much as in times of peace, federal judges must protect constitutional liberty.[2] Liberty Perfectionists believe that under circumstances of war, it is all the more important that federal judges take a strong stand on behalf of liberty.[3] If they do not, who will?

My purpose in this chapter is to challenge both Liberty Perfectionism and National Security Fundamentalism. In their different ways, both approaches are exceedingly dangerous. It is pretty easy to dispense with Liberty Perfectionism, for judges do not and should not accept it. National Security Fundamentalism has much more appeal to contemporary judges, but it has its own problems. Most important, its reading of the Constitution is implausible. Here, as with affirmative action, many fundamentalists do not follow their own creed. In addition, National Security Fundamentalism neglects the fact that under many circumstances, the executive branch is most unlikely to strike the right balance between security and liberty. In some circumstances the executive is likely to sacrifice liberty for no good reason. In a society that aspires to freedom, this is an extremely serious danger.

Liberty Perfectionism

In the abstract, Liberty Perfectionism has considerable attractiveness. Why should the government be permitted to restrict freedom during war if it cannot do so during peace? During World War II, many people objected to the detention and confinement of Japanese-Americans, arguing that the Constitution's most fundamental principles are not altered when national security is threatened. In the war on terror, many perfectionists have challenged initiatives from President Bush, including—to take just one example—his executive order authorizing the use of military commissions to try suspected terrorists. In their view, the rights to trial by jury and to fair procedures are not in the least affected by the attacks of September 11. For Liberty Perfectionists, the system of constitutional rights has a healthy kind of rigidity and firmness. It does not bend, let alone break, in the midst of war. For example, law professor David Cole writes, "[T]he fact that we are waging a 'war on terrorism' does not alter . . . basic constitutional principles."[4]

But if the nation is genuinely threatened, Liberty Perfectionism runs into big problems. First, it is unrealistic; judges simply will not protect liberty with the same aggressiveness when a country faces a serious threat to its survival.[5] After all, the Supreme Court did uphold the detention of Japanese-Americans during World War II, and it has long permitted restrictions on freedom, even on speech, in wartime.[6] Perhaps future courts might be expected to be more courageous; but even if so, they will not protect liberty as solicitously in war as in peace. By itself this is a large objection to Liberty Perfectionism. "Ought implies can," and it is unhelpful to urge courts to adopt a role that they will predictably refuse to assume.

The second and more fundamental problem with Liberty Perfectionism is that we shouldn't want it. Under our constitutional traditions, the government's power to intrude on liberty depends on the strength of the justifications it can muster on behalf of the intrusion. When security is at risk, government has greater justifications than when it is not. On airports and at train stations, officials may more legitimately compromise privacy when they have grounds to fear a terrorist attack. The argument for detention and even for coercive interrogation, at least if it falls short of torture, is much stronger if these measures are necessary to prevent devastating attacks on the nation. Hence it is correct to say, with Chief Justice William Rehnquist, that it "is neither desirable nor is it remotely likely that civil liberty will occupy as favored a position in wartime as it does in peacetime."[7]

None of this means that in times of war, the government may proceed however it wishes or act in blatant violation of constitutional commands. Restrictions on freedom of speech, for example, should be regarded with great skepticism, simply because they eliminate the principal method by which democracies correct themselves.[8] As we shall see in Chapter 7, courts do and should take steps to ensure against arbitrary detentions. In American law, it cannot be said that *inter arma silent leges* (amidst war laws are silent). But as a general approach for courts in wartime, Liberty Perfectionism is a nonstarter. It is too broad and too neglectful of legitimate government interests to have a serious claim to our attention.

National Security Fundamentalism

No one should be surprised to find that in the aftermath of 9/11, National Security Fundamentalism has obtained a great deal of support—and that many fundamentalists strongly endorse it. The rise of National Security Fundamentalism has been one of the noteworthy developments of the post–9/11 era.

So far, the Supreme Court has refused to accept the approach; and one has to struggle to find cases from before 9/11 in which

National Security Fundamentalism attracted strong support from federal judges. While the United States has a regrettably mixed record in the protection of freedom in wartime, it has not given the President the unilateral power to safeguard the nation's security as he sees fit. Recently, however, National Security Fundamentalism has seemed to enjoy growing appeal. Let us begin with the executive branch itself.

The Torture Memo

The most prominent expression of National Security Fundamentalism came from the Office of Legal Counsel of the Department of Justice, in its 2002 memorandum on the legality of coerced interrogation.[9] The most striking aspect of the memorandum is its suggestion that as Commander in Chief of the Armed Forces, the President of the United States has the inherent authority to torture suspected terrorists, making it constitutionally unacceptable for Congress to ban the practice of torture. The analysis is somewhat technical, but it is worth pausing over the basis of this extraordinary conclusion.

The Office of Legal Counsel emphasized that "the President enjoys complete discretion in the exercise of his Commander-in-Chief authority and in conducting operations against hostile forces." In addition, it insisted that a core function of the Commander in Chief includes interrogation of the enemy. Because of "the President's inherent constitutional authority to manage a military campaign against al Qaeda and its allies," congressional enactments "must be construed as not applying to" interrogations undertaken as part of the President's Commander in Chief authority. "Any effort by Congress to regulate the interrogation of battlefield combatants would violate the Constitution's sole vesting of the Commander-in-Chief authority in the President." Hence coercive interrogation, including torture, must be permitted if the President wants to engage in it.

The Office of Legal Counsel is part of the executive branch, and one of its major functions is to protect the constitutional prerogatives of the President—especially those associated with the Commander in Chief power. We wouldn't want the Department of Justice to be indifferent to the President's claims of constitutional authority. But in its endorsement of presidential power to torture, the memorandum on coerced interrogation went well beyond ordinary practice. To be sure, the President has inherent authority to oversee battlefield operations, and Congress has limited power to control such operations. The President also has the inherent authority to conduct interrogations amidst war. But at the least, it is unusual to say that this authority includes the power to torture people when Congress has expressly said otherwise. The power to command the armed forces is not easily taken to include torture of enemy combatants as an "inherent" authority. Even if it does include that authority, it is hard to contend that Congress cannot provide protection against torture.

The torture memorandum of the Office of Legal Counsel provides a dramatic example of National Security Fundamentalism— one that may be taken to presage future understandings if that approach ultimately prevails.

National Security Fundamentalism on the Supreme Court

In recent Supreme Court decisions involving the war on terrorism, National Security Fundamentalism has never attracted a majority opinion.[10] But it made a conspicuous appearance in a remarkable dissenting opinion by Justice Clarence Thomas in the *Hamdi* case.[11] Yosef Hamdi was an American citizen captured in Afghanistan and detained as an enemy combatant. I will turn to the particular facts of his case in Chapter 7. For the moment, note that Justice Thomas emphasized, very broadly, that any constitutional judgment in this domain should consider "basic principles of the constitutional structure as it relates to national security and foreign affairs." In his view, the Constitution accords to the President the "primary responsibility . . . to protect the national security and to conduct the nation's foreign relations." Hence judicial decisions should be made against the backdrop of the President's inherent and broadly discretionary power to protect national security.

With respect to the courts, Thomas contended, "it is crucial to recognize that *judicial* interference in these domains destroys the purpose of vesting primary responsibility in a unitary Executive." Judges "lack the relevant information and expertise to second-guess determinations made by the President." In fact congressional grants of power should be construed generously on the President's behalf, rather than narrowly, so as to fit with institutional limits on the power of the judiciary. Because the executive branch of the federal government "has an overriding interest in protecting the Nation," it can invoke that interest to justify depriving people of liberty. Thomas argued in favor of broad constructions of congressional grants of authority partly to avoid constitutional difficulties: "Although the President very well may have inherent authority to detain those arrayed against our troops, I agree with the plurality that we need not decide that question because Congress has authorized the President to do so."

Here is the ambitious breadth of National Security Fundamentalism at its most stark. Justice Thomas makes no effort to tailor his ruling to the facts of the particular case. On the contrary, he speaks expansively about the "primary responsibility" of the President in the domain of "national security." In addition, he adopts a kind of working presumption in favor of presidential authority, suggesting that statutes must be read in a way that does not conflict with the President's inherent power. But from the Constitution alone, it would not be entirely clear whether the President or the Congress has primary responsibility in the domain of national security—an issue to which I will return. The important point is that Justice Thomas offers a distinctive vision of the constitutional structure, a vision that accords principal authority to the President.

The President and "The War Power"

In the years since the September 11 attacks, National Security Fundamentalism has played a large role on the lower federal courts. Most of the cases involving a conflict between national security and individual liberty have been decided by the United States Courts of Appeals for the District of Columbia and for the Fourth Circuit. Both have shown a distinctive tendency toward National Security Fundamentalism. In nearly every case in which a serious challenge was mounted to the power of the President, the President has prevailed. This is an extremely revealing fact, because the lower courts are dominated by appointees of Presidents Reagan, George H. W. Bush, and George W. Bush. If National Security Fundamentalism is pervasive in the lower courts, it probably provides a harbinger of what is to come. Let us investigate the details.

One of the most strikingly fundamentalist lower court decision is *Al Odah v. United States*,[12] which was reversed by the

Supreme Court. In its exceedingly ambitious ruling, the lower court held that aliens captured outside the United States have no rights under the Due Process Clause. It ruled that the Guantanamo Bay detainees were, in law, analogous to German prisoners captured on the battlefield in World War II. While acknowledging that Guantanamo Bay is controlled by the United States military, the court insisted that this fact was irrelevant because Cuba has sovereignty over the general area. Broadly reading Supreme Court precedents, it ruled in favor of executive discretion.

A concurring opinion by Judge Ray Randolph went further still, resolving several issues that it was not necessary for him to discuss. Consider his opening sentence: "I write separately to add two other grounds for rejecting the detainee's non-habeas claims."[13] The motivation for his separate opinion seemed to be captured by his final sentence: "The level of threat a detainee poses to United States interests, the amount of intelligence a detainee might be able to provide, the conditions under which the detainee may be willing to cooperate, the disruption visits from family members and lawyers might cause—these types of judgments have traditionally been left to the exclusive discretion of the Executive Branch, and there they should remain." Here is an explicit endorsement of National Security Fundamentalism.

Other rulings in the lower courts fall in the same category. In *Center for National Security Studies v. Department of Justice*,[14] a divided court of appeals permitted an extraordinary level of secrecy from the executive branch. A number of public interest groups invoked the Freedom of Information Act (FOIA), the common law, and the First Amendment to require the government to release information about prisoners who had been detained in the aftermath of the September 11 attacks. The requested information included names, dates of arrest and release, and reasons for detention. The disclosure request had a strong democratic justification: the public could not easily evaluate the executive's behavior without this information. In ruling that disclosure was not required, the court relied on a broad interpretation of exemption 7(A) of FOIA, which exempts "records or information compiled for law enforcement purposes . . . to the extent that the production could reasonably be expected to interfere with enforcement proceedings."[15]

The court's interpretation of this exemption was exceptionally deferential to the government's vague statements about potential harms. To its credit, the court showed that it was entirely aware of this point. In language strongly reminiscent of Justice Thomas's dissenting opinion in *Hamdi*, it emphasized that "the judiciary owes some measure of deference to the executive in cases implicating national security, a uniquely executive purview. . . . We have consistently reiterated the principle of deference to the executive in the FOIA context when national security concerns are implicated. . . . [W]e have consistently deferred to executive affidavits predicting harm to the national security, and have found it unwise to undertake searching judicial review." The court even went so far as to comment on the distinctive nature of the current threat: "America faces an enemy just as real as its former Cold War foes, with capabilities far beyond the capacity of the judiciary to explore."

In the fashion of National Security Fundamentalism, the court insisted that deference was "mandated by the separation of powers," suggesting that disclosure under FOIA would raise constitutional problems. Its opinion left no doubt about the motivation for its action: "We are in accord with several federal courts that have wisely respected the executive's judgment in prosecuting the national response to terrorism." What is most noteworthy about the decision, then, is not the outcome, which is reasonable, but the remarkably broad pronouncements about the need to defer to the President.

Broad rulings in favor of executive authority can be found elsewhere.[16] Consider *Hamdi v. Rumsfeld*,[17] in which the court held that enemy combatants captured on the battlefield could be detained indefinitely and without trial, even if they were American citizens. The central question in the case was what procedural protection, if any, would accompany the exercise of the Commander in Chief power. The Court emphasized the need to defer to the President: "The Constitution's allocation of the war-making powers reflects not only the expertise and experience lodged within the executive, but also the more fundamental truth that those branches most accountable to the people should be the ones to undertake the ultimate protection and to ask the ultimate sacrifice from them." Hence deference to the executive would be the basic rule. The court was aware that in denying fair procedure, the President was doing something unusual. But this step was justified by the circumstances. "As the nature of threats to America evolves, along with the means of carrying those threats out, the nature of enemy combatants may change also. In the face of such change, separation of powers does not deny the executive branch the essential tool of adaptability."

Indeed the Court said that the source of the detention was not a statute, but "Article II, Section 2, of the Constitution, wherein the President is given the war power." (I will return to this statement in due course; it lies at the heart of National Security Fundamentalism.) Deference to the President stems from this explicit grant of authority. So long as a detention "is one legitimately made

pursuant to the war powers," it must be respected. A general statement on the part of the executive, supporting the claim that a citizen was detained in the course of war and qualified as an enemy
combatant, would be sufficient. The court left no doubt that this
conclusion stemmed from National Security Fundamentalism:
"The constitutional allocation of war powers affords the President
extraordinarily broad authority as Commander in Chief and com-
pels courts to assume a deferential posture."

That posture allowed Hamdi to be held indefinitely, even after
the end of the relevant hostilities. If National Security Fundamentalism prevails, this kind of reasoning will dominate the law.

The Appeal of National Security Fundamentalism

In the abstract, National Security Fundamentalism has considerable appeal. The President is far better placed than Congress to act
quickly and decisively to protect the citizenry. He is also more
likely to have relevant information about what must be done and
when to do it. Justice Thomas correctly emphasizes that Alexander Hamilton defended the creation of a "unitary executive" as a
means of ensuring energy, coordination, and dispatch in the presi-
dency. These qualities are crucial in time of war. The courts, by
contrast, lack good tools for assessing the President's claims of
military necessity. And whatever we may disagree about, we
should agree on this point: Because the President is Commander
in Chief of the Armed Forces, Congress cannot override the President's judgments about how to carry out a lawful war.

At least equally important, judicial overreaching in wartime
may turn out to be disastrous rather than merely harmful. To be
sure, American practice suggests that judges are most unlikely to
err by providing too much protection to civil liberties. It is hard
to find cases in which judicial protection of freedom seriously

damaged national security. But if Liberty Perfectionism were accepted, such errors would become far more probable. There is every reason for courts to avoid a decision that leads to freedom for terrorists, or to disclosure of information that helps those who want to kill Americans. In ordinary contexts, even in criminal justice, the stakes are not nearly so high. Simple prudence suggests that courts should respect presidential choices when national security is at risk.

These points provide important cautionary notes; they help explain the senselessness of Liberty Perfectionism. But there is another side to the problem.

Strike One: False Fundamentalism

If National Security Fundamentalism were mandated by the Constitution, judges would be bound to follow it. But far from requiring National Security Fundamentalism, the Constitution is best read to forbid it. Let us begin with the self-evident starting point for fundamentalists: the text of the document.

No one doubts that the President has considerable power in the domain of national security. Under Article II, he is explicitly authorized to be "Commander in Chief of the Army and Navy of the United States." He is allowed "to make Treaties," at least when two-thirds of the senators concur. He is authorized to "appoint Ambassadors" and "other public Ministers and Consuls." He "shall receive Ambassadors and other public Ministers." But none of this supports Justice Thomas's contention that the President has "primary responsibility—along with the necessary power—to protect the national security and to conduct the Nation's foreign relations." Nor does anything in the document support the lower court's suggestion that under Article II "the President is given the war power." On the contrary, that view is a tendentious reading of the legal materials. To see why, let us turn to Article I.

Perhaps most notably, Congress, not the President, has the power "to declare War." The Constitution also grants Congress, not the President, the power "to raise and support Armies." It authorizes Congress "to provide and maintain a Navy." In a formulation that bears on the President's supposedly "inherent" power to torture, and that much complicates any claims about the broad power of the Commander in Chief, the founding document permits Congress to "make Rules for the Government and Regulation of the land and naval Forces." It is Congress that is authorized to raise funds to "provide for the common Defense and general Welfare of the United States." Congress, not the President, is empowered to "regulate Commerce with foreign nations." Congress is also authorized to "define and punish Piracies and Felonies committed on the high Seas, and Offenses against the Law of Nations," as well as to "make Rules concerning Captures on Land and Water." It is under Article I, not Article II, that the Constitution allows suspension of habeas corpus "when in Cases of Rebellion or Invasion the public Safety may require it." That the Suspension Clause is found in Article I tends to suggest that Congress, not the President, is entitled to suspend the writ.

In this light, the Constitution does not repose in the President anything like a general authority "to protect the national security." National Security Fundamentalism neglects the most natural reading of the document, which is that protection of national security is divided between Congress and the President—and that if either has the dominant role, it is the national lawmaker. To be sure, the Commander in Chief Clause does give the President direction of the armed forces, an expansive authority; but even that authority is subject to legislative constraints, because Congress controls the budget and because Congress can choose not to declare war. And if Congress refuses either to authorize the use of force or to declare war, the President is usually not entitled to commence hostilities on his own.[18] The Commander in Chief Clause allows the President to manage wars; but it does not give him "the war power." All of this means that National Security Fundamentalism cannot claim a strong constitutional pedigree.

For many fundamentalists, this should be the end of the matter. And it is both unfortunate and noteworthy that recent judicial endorsements of National Security Fundamentalism, by Justice Thomas and others, have paid little attention to the constitutional text. Fundamentalists usually seek to understand that text in light of the understanding of the time. But an investigation of that understanding serves to confirm, rather than to undermine, the basic conclusion that the document contemplates a shared role between Congress and the President, and sharply constrains the President's authority to do as he likes.[19]

Of course, many people insist that the constitutional text is hardly all there is to our constitutional tradition. In the domain of separation of powers, historical practices and changes over time have been highly relevant to constitutional interpretation. As Justice Felix Frankfurter, a conservative and a minimalist, contended, "It is an inadmissibly narrow conception of American constitutional law to confine it to the words of the Constitution and to disregard the gloss which life has written upon them."[20] Here, an understanding of that "gloss" greatly favors the President. There can be no doubt that for questions of national security, the President has assumed authority that the text alone might not sanction. The power to make war is a leading example; Presidents have often engaged in military actions without the kind of legislative authorization that Article I appears to require.[21]

Historical "glosses" on constitutional text might well be taken to argue in the direction of National Security Fundamentalism. They make it plausible to contend that the President has more authority, in the domain of national security, than the document alone appears to contemplate. Undoubtedly the increasing power of the President is connected with the rise of the United States as an international power and the growing need for energy and dispatch. But even in the light of this history, it remains bizarre to contend that when the nation is at risk, the Constitution says that the President must be in charge of the apparatus of government. To say this is to reject a constitutional accommodation that, by tradition no less than text, unambiguously retains Congress's role as the nation's lawmaker.

Strike Two: The Incentives of the Executive Branch

The second problem with National Security Fundamentalism is that it understates the risks of unlimited presidential authority. The executive branch sees protection of the nation's security as one of its principal tasks—in part because political retribution will fall swiftly on any President who fails in that task. When the nation is under threat, the executive naturally takes precautionary steps to reduce the risks. So far, so good. But recall here Attorney General Francis Biddle's chilling observation: "The Constitution has never greatly bothered any wartime President."[22] The question is whether internal dynamics or external checks will help to ensure that the precautionary steps are reasonable rather than excessive. For two reasons, National Security Fundamentalism is far too optimistic on that count.

Internal dynamics and group polarization. Internal dynamics within the executive branch present a serious problem, precisely because that branch is designed so as to be neither diverse nor deliberative. As Justice Thomas notes, the executive branch is "unitary" in principle; it is run by a single person, who is constitutionally entitled to fill his branch with like-minded people. Here is the difficulty. One of the most robust findings in modern social science is that like-minded people go to extremes. More precisely: After deliberation, like-minded people usually end up thinking a more extreme version of what they thought before they started to talk.[23] Ordinary processes within the executive branch are all too likely to produce not careful investigation of alternatives, but a heightened version of what executive branch officials believed in advance.[24] Those heightened beliefs may put liberty at risk.

Of course a presidential disposition in favor of liberty over security can alter this dynamic. Suppose, for example, the President and his advisers believe that some national security risk is trivial and that liberty should not be compromised, while a small group within the administration disagrees. It is predictable that precautionary steps will not be taken even if they are justified. Deliberative processes among like-minded people can produce too much rather than too little concern for liberty. More fundamentally, a President can certainly take steps to ensure a diversity of views; it is possible to structure executive branch processes so as to create internal safeguards. A system of internal checks and balances within the executive branch can alter the dynamic by which groups end up amplifying their original tendencies. Different agencies and departments often have different agendas and interests. Consider the notoriously frequent disagreements between the Department of State and the Department of Defense.

But there can be no assurance that the executive branch, consisting of people who work under a single president and usually seek consensus, will consider the relevant factors in a way that produces sensible outcomes. If the President and his closest advisers are predisposed toward aggressive steps to counteract national security risks, even at the expense of liberty, the executive branch is likely to blunder. History offers countless illustrations.[25]

As a real-world example of a failure of deliberation within the executive branch, consider the account in the 2004 report of the Senate Select Committee on Intelligence, which explicitly accused the Central Intelligence Agency (CIA) of "groupthink." The agency's predisposition to find a serious threat from Iraq, said the committee, led it to ignore alternative possibilities and to neglect the information that it actually held.[26] In the committee's view, the CIA "demonstrated several aspects of group think: examining few alternatives, selective gathering of information, pressure to conform within the group or withhold criticism, and collective rationalization." Thus the agency showed a "tendency to reject information that contradicted the presumption" that Iraq had weapons of mass destruction. Because of that presumption, the agency failed to use its own formalized methods "to challenge assumptions and 'groupthink,' such as 'red teams,' 'devil's advocacy,' and other types of alternative or competitive analysis."

Above all, these conclusions emphasize the CIA's failure to elicit and aggregate information. Through failures of this sort it is easy to imagine that liberty could be sacrificed in favor of national security, with no adequate justification.

The finding of the Senate Select Committee is a remarkable and even uncanny echo of one that followed the 2003 investigation of failures at NASA, which also stressed the agency's failure to seek competing views, including those of agency employees.[27] The occasion this time was the crash of the Space Shuttle *Columbia*. The *Columbia* Accident Investigation Board explicitly attributed the accident to NASA's dysfunctional culture and an absence of "checks and balances." The agency pressured people to follow a "party line." At NASA it was "difficult for minority and dissenting opinions to percolate up through the agency's hierarchy"— even though, the board contended, effective safety programs required the encouragement of minority opinions and bad news. Here too the unitariness of the relevant agency was a central source of the problem.

These examples of executive branch failure reflect the process known to social scientists as "group polarization," through which like-minded people often go to unjustified extremes.[28] Suppose people within an executive agency believe that Iraq has weapons of mass destruction. If so, that very belief is likely to be heightened after members have started to talk. Now suppose that those within the executive branch think some abridgement of civil liberties is necessary as a precautionary measure. If so, internal deliberations are likely to produce more extremism in favor of abridging civil liberties.

Of course an outraged public is often able to discipline presidential choices. Sometimes political checks will ensure against unjustified intrusions on liberty. But to understand this point, we have to make a distinction.

Strike Three: Selective Restrictions

Some restrictions on liberty apply to all or most of us—for example, a general increase in security procedures at airports or a measure that subjects everyone, citizens and noncitizens alike, to special scrutiny when they are dealing with substances that might be used in bioterrorism. But other restrictions on liberty apply only to a few—for example, restrictions on Japanese-Americans during World War II, racial profiling, or the confinement of enemy aliens at Guantanamo Bay. When restrictions apply to all or most, political safeguards provide a pretty reliable check on unjustified government action. If the burden of the restriction is widely shared, it is unlikely to be accepted unless most people are convinced there is good reason for it. And for genuinely burdensome restrictions, people will not be easily convinced. But if the restriction is imposed on a small, identifiable group, the political check is weakened. Abridgements on liberty can be imposed even if they are difficult to justify. In these circumstances, political checks may provide an inadequate safeguard against unjustified presidential intrusions on liberty.

These claims can be illuminated by a glance at the views of Nobel Prize winner Frederick Hayek about the rule of law. Hayek writes, "how comparatively innocuous, even if irksome, are most such restrictions imposed on literally everybody, as . . . compared with those that are likely to be imposed only on some!"[29] Thus it is "significant that most restrictions on what we regard as private affairs . . . have usually been imposed only on selected groups of people or, as in the case of prohibition, were practicable only because the government reserved the right to grant exceptions." Hayek argues, in short, that the risk of unjustified burdens dramatically increases if they are selective and if most people have nothing to worry about.

The claim is especially noteworthy when the executive is imposing restrictions on civil liberties. People are likely to ask, with some seriousness, whether those restrictions are in fact justified *if* the result is to impose serious burdens on them. But if *other* people face the relevant burdens, then the mere fact of "risk," and the mere presence of fear, will seem like sufficient justification.

The danger of unjustified infringements is amplified when the victims are an identifiable group that is readily separable from "us." Stereotyping of groups significantly increases when people are fearful; when people are primed to think about their own death, they are more likely to think and act in accordance with group-based stereotypes.[30] Experimental findings of this kind support the intuitive idea that when people are afraid, they are far more likely to tolerate government action that abridges the freedom of members of some "out-group." And if this is the case, responses to social fear, in the form of infringements on liberties, will not receive the natural political checks that arise when majorities suffer as well as benefit from them.

Consider here the often-quoted remarks of the German Protestant minister Martin Niemöller, who wrote these words after his release from Dachau at the end of World War II:

> First they came for the Communists,
>   and I didn't speak up, because I wasn't a Communist.
> Then they came for the Jews,
>   and I didn't speak up, because I wasn't a Jew.
> Then they came for the Catholics,
>   and I didn't speak up, because I was a Protestant.
> Then they came for me,
>   and by that time there was no one left to speak
>   up for me.

These words are meant to make listeners identify with the "they" who are subject to unjustified infringements on freedom. As a matter of logic, the argument doesn't always follow. If "they" come for members of one group, it does not follow that "they" will eventually come for me. But the words make a great deal of psychological sense, and if taken seriously they will make people who are not really at risk start to identify with those who are—and thus decrease the likelihood of unjustified intrusions into the domain of liberty. Unfortunately, people do not identify with persecuted others so readily. Most of us are not greatly bothered by infringements that affect a group to which we don't belong.

In short, liberty-infringing action is most likely to be justified if those who support the action are also burdened by it. When this is so, the political process contains a built-in protection against unjustifiable restrictions. It follows that free societies need ways to ensure against unjustified intrusions on civil liberties. National Security Fundamentalism fails to come to terms with the problem.

Of course, these general propositions do not resolve concrete cases; everything turns on the specific legal challenge. But an appreciation of the risks of selective intrusions on freedom helps us to identify yet another serious problem with National Security Fundamentalism. Political processes are unlikely to provide an adequate check when government imposes burdens on people who cannot use those processes to protect themselves. The legislature has some advantages over the executive on this count, simply because it is both diverse and deliberative, in a way that ought to ensure a degree of representation for identifiable groups that are at risk.

These are the three strikes against National Security Fundamentalism. Most important, it can claim little support in the Constitution itself. The document does not give the President "the war power." Here, as in many other places, fundamentalists are failing to apply their own defining creed. In addition, National Security Fundamentalism reposes excessive confidence in the President. Deliberative processes within the executive branch are likely to amplify preexisting tendencies to protect security at the expense of liberty. Finally, when deprivations of liberty are limited to an identifiable few, external checks on the executive provide an insufficient safeguard of civil liberties.

But I have also said that Liberty Perfectionism is neither feasible nor desirable; it neglects the nation's needs when security is at risk. What then should constitutional law do to protect liberty amidst war? Past judicial practices, it turns out, provide some important clues.

CHAPTER SEVEN

Minimalism at War

Even more important than the method of selecting the people's rulers and their successors is the character of the constraints imposed on the Executive by the rule of law.

—John Paul Stevens[1]

I F NEITHER Liberty Perfectionism nor National Security Fundamentalism offers a sensible approach to individual rights in wartime, what does? It turns out that the most significant decisions of the Supreme Court show a consistent, and consistently minimalist, approach to deciding these issues.

That approach is built on three principles. First, Congress should be required to authorize any interference with constitutionally sensitive interests. As a general rule, the President should not be allowed to proceed on his own. Second, any deprivation of an individual's liberty should be accompanied by minimally fair procedures. Third, judicial decisions should be narrow and incompletely theorized. As we shall see, these three principles do a remarkably good job of explaining the practices of the American judiciary in wartime. The first principle is the most complex, and it provides the place to begin.

Clear Congressional Authorization

For many years, Israel's General Security Service has subjected suspected terrorists to certain forms of physical coercion. According to the General Security Service, this was done only in extreme cases and as a last resort, when deemed necessary to prevent significant loss of life. Nonetheless, practices worthy of the name "torture" did occur, and they were not rare. In a case brought by the Association for Civil Rights in Israel, these practices were challenged before the Supreme Court of Israel on the ground that they were inconsistent with the nation's fundamental law.

The government responded that abstractions about human rights should not take precedence over real-world necessities. Its use of coercion was justified, the government said, when the alternative was massive deaths in an area of the world that was often subject to terrorist activity. A judicial decision to the opposite effect would be a form of unjustified activism, even hubris.

In deciding the case, the Supreme Court of Israel refused to resolve the most fundamental questions.[2] But the Court nonetheless held those practices unlawful. Its main argument was that if such coercion was acceptable, it could not be because the General Security Service alone said so. At a minimum, the disputed practices must be endorsed by the national legislature, after a full democratic debate on the precise question. "[T]his is an issue that must be decided by the legislative branch which represents the people. We do not take any stand on this matter at this time. It is there that various considerations must be weighed."

It is worthwhile to pause over the central feature of this decision. The Supreme Court of Israel required clear legislative authorization for this particular intrusion on liberty; it insisted that an executive order, under a vague or ambiguous law, was not enough. Even when national security is threatened, the legislative branch of government must explicitly authorize infringements on civil liberty. The Court held that political safeguards, in the form of agreement from a diverse and deliberative branch of government, are a minimal precondition for such intrusions. The requirement of a clear legislative statement enlists the idea of checks and balances in the service of individual rights—not through flat bans on government action but by requiring approval from two branches of government rather than just one.

The 2002 torture memorandum of the Department of Justice's Office of Legal Counsel, sketched in the last chapter, provides a startling and ironic contrast. While the Supreme Court of Israel held that clear legislative *authorization* is required to permit torture, the United States Department of Justice concluded that even clear legislative *prohibition* is insufficient to forbid it. But we may doubt whether the Supreme Court of the United States, at least as currently constituted, would accept this reasoning. In a large number of cases, many involving national security, the Court has required a clear congressional statement before it would permit the executive to intrude on an interest that has a plausible claim to constitutional protection. This is a key part of the minimalist approach to the protection of liberty; it stands as a large contrast with National Security Fundamentalism.

To understand American law, perhaps the best place to begin is the 1958 case of *Kent v. Dulles*,[3] decided in the midst of the Cold War. In that case, the State Department denied a passport to the artist and writer Rockwell Kent, a member of the Communist Party, who sought to attend a meeting of the World Council of Peace in Helsinki, Finland. The State Department denied the passport on two grounds, both supported by its own regulations.

First, Kent was a Communist; second, he had "a consistent and prolonged adherence to the Communist Party line." The governing statute, enacted in 1926, authorized the Secretary of State "to grant and issue passports . . . under such rules as the President shall designate and prescribe for, and on behalf of, the United States." Kent sued the secretary of state, John Foster Dulles, arguing that the denial of his passport was unconstitutional.

The Supreme Court could have decided this case on any number of grounds. It could have said that Kent's First Amendment rights had been violated—that it was unconstitutional to deny someone a passport because of his political convictions. It could have said that the decision of the secretary of state violated Kent's right to travel—that the Due Process Clause includes a right to leave the country, and the government needs particularly strong grounds for interfering with that right. It could have said that the grant of open-ended discretion to the Secretary of State violated the nondelegation doctrine—that under Article I, Section 1, Congress must give the Secretary some guidelines by which to decide whether to grant or to deny passports. Most of these approaches would have reflected a form of Liberty Perfectionism. Or it could have ruled that the denial of the passport was lawful—authorized by the language of the relevant statute and, as authorized, within constitutional bounds.

The Court did none of these things. Instead it held that the denial of the passport was beyond the statutory authority of the secretary of state. Writing for the majority, Justice Douglas began his analysis with a bow in the direction of constitutional requirements: The "right to travel is a part of the 'liberty' of which the citizen cannot be deprived without due process of law under the Fifth Amendment." The question of statutory authority would be approached in this light. While the statute was phrased in broad terms, the secretary had "long exercised" his power "quite narrowly." Passports had been refused in only two kinds of cases: when the applicant's citizenship and allegiance to the United States were in doubt; and when the applicant was engaged in unlawful conduct. No one claimed that Kent fell in either of these categories. "We, therefore, hesitate to impute to Congress, when in 1952 it made a passport necessary for foreign travel and left its issuance to the discretion of the Secretary of State, a purpose to give him unbridled discretion to grant or withhold a passport from a citizen for any substantive reason he may choose." The Court was concerned that Congress had not particularly authorized the executive branch to do as it did. "No such showing of extremity, no such showing of joint action by the Chief Executive and the Congress to curtail a constitutional right of the citizen has been made here."

Justice Douglas left no doubt that the Court's decision was constitutionally inspired. He noted that the case involved "an exercise by an American citizen of an activity included in constitutional protection." For that reason, the Court would "not readily infer that Congress gave the Secretary of State unbridled discretion." The right to leave the country had constitutional foundations, and if it is "to be regulated, it must be pursuant to the law-making functions of the Congress." Douglas emphasized that the Court "would be faced with important constitutional questions" if Congress "had given the Secretary authority to withhold passports to citizens because of their beliefs or associations." But "Congress has made no such provision in explicit terms."

The Court's requirement of clear congressional permission was minimalist in the sense that it left undecided the larger questions about the meaning of the Constitution. The underlying idea—that Congress must speak unambiguously if it wants to compromise liberty—is known as a "clear statement" principle, and the body from which a clear statement is required is Congress. The advantage of the minimalist approach is that it reflects commendable uncertainty about difficult questions, enlisting political safeguards as the first line of defense against unjustified intrusions on freedom. Instead of making broad pronouncements about liberty, and providing final protection on their own, minimalist courts say that Congress must authorize the President to intrude on constitutionally sensitive interests.

Did *Kent v. Dulles* involve the Commander in Chief Clause, beloved of fundamentalists? That clause was not directly mentioned. But the Court's crucial citation involved an explicit reference to a case squarely involving the Commander in Chief power: *Youngstown Sheet & Tube Company v. Sawyer,* also known as the Steel Seizure case.[4] That case tells us a great deal about presidential power when national security is at risk. It is also one of the most dramatic and important in the entire history of American law.

In 1951, in response to a threatened strike that looked like it would jeopardize the nation's supply of steel, President Harry Truman directed his Secretary of Commerce, Charles Sawyer, to take possession of, and to operate, the majority of steel mills in the United States. According to President Truman, the strike put national defense at risk, because steel was an indispensable component in nearly all weapons and war materials. He defended his action as justified by his power as Commander in Chief of the Armed Forces. But the Supreme Court firmly rejected the argument. It emphasized that there "is no statute that expressly authorizes the President to take possession of the property as he did here. Nor is there any act of Congress to which our attention has been directed from which such a power can fairly be implied." Lawmaking power, it stressed, is vested in Congress, not the President: "The Founders of this Nation entrusted the lawmaking power to the Congress alone in both good and bad times. It would do no good to recall the historical events, the fears of power and the hopes for freedom that lay behind their choice."

The Court's leading minimalist, Justice Felix Frankfurter, wrote separately, also emphasizing the need for checks and balances. But Justice Frankfurter's opinion, and that of the Court itself, have come to be far less important than the concurring opinion of Justice Robert Jackson, who explored in some detail the central importance of a grant of authority from Congress.[5] Jackson famously offered a three-part division of presidential authority, suggesting that the President's power is at its maximum when he is acting under an authorization from Congress, in the middle when Congress has been silent, and at its lowest ebb when the President's exercise of power is "incompatible with the expressed or implied will of Congress." Less famously, Jackson offered a narrow interpretation of the Commander in Chief Clause that showed great skepticism about the idea of "inherent" presidential power. Jackson challenged the "loose and irresponsible use of adjectives," including words like *inherent, implied, incidental, war, plenary,* and *emergency*, which he believed amounted to an effort to "amend" the Constitution.

Minimalism in practice.

Jackson's three-part framework helps to organize a remarkable number of Supreme Court decisions involving civil liberty and war, many of them written before the Steel Seizure case. Time and again, the Court has emphasized the importance of congressional authorization for presidential action and refused to rule that the President has the power to act on his own. In these ways, the Court has refused to embrace National Security Fundamentalism and acted in good minimalist fashion, leaving many of the most fundamental questions undecided.

Consider, for example, *Ex Parte Endo*,[6] in which the Court struck down the detention of Japanese-Americans on the West Coast. The case involved a petition for a writ of habeas corpus sought on behalf of Mitsue Endo, a loyal American citizen who had been placed in a relocation center. In ruling that Endo had to be released, the Court relied on the absence of statutory authorization for her detention. It emphasized that even in the midst of war, the President needed clear statutory authorization for any such detention: "In interpreting a wartime measure we must assume that their purpose was to allow for the greatest possible accommodation between those liberties and the exigencies of war." The Court added that "if there is to be the greatest possible accommodation of the liberties of the citizen with this war measure, any such implied power [of the President] must be narrowly confined to the precise purpose of the evacuation program."

Duncan v. Kahanamoku,[7] involving the imposition of martial law in Hawaii during World War II, was decided in the same spirit. Civilians in Hawaii had been imprisoned after trial in military tribunals; the central question was whether those tribunals had the legal authority to try civilians. In a narrow ruling, the Court held that they did not. Although the Hawaii Organic Act, setting out rules for the governance of Hawaii, did allow the governor of the territory to declare martial law, the Court refused to agree that he could "close all the courts and supplant them with military tribunals"—even with presidential approval. Although the statutory language and history were unclear, the Court found guidance in "the birth, development, and growth of our political institutions. Courts and their procedural safeguards are indispensable to our system of government," it argued, and it would not construe an ambiguous statute to permit the displacement of ordinary courts with military tribunals.

The oldest example of a minimalist approach to civil liberties comes from the Civil War period. President Lincoln suspended the writ of habeas corpus, referring to Section 9, clause 2 of the Constitution, which says, "The Privilege of Writ of Habeas Corpus shall not be suspended, unless when in Cases of Rebellion or Invasion the public Safety may require it." The Suspension Clause is phrased in the passive voice; it does not say who may suspend the great writ. Chief Justice Roger Taney ruled that the President could not suspend the writ on his own but instead needed congressional authorization.[8] Taney pointed out that the Suspension Clause is found in Article I, which specifies the powers of Congress, rather than Article II, which deals with presidential authority. While this textual argument is certainly powerful, Taney's conclusion is also supported by a structural concern: Suspension of habeas corpus is a grave act that requires a judgment by a body that is both deliberative and diverse.

A clear statement principle, rather than the Constitution by itself, underlies one of the most celebrated free speech decisions in American history: Judge Learned Hand's ruling in *Masses Publishing Co. vs. Patten.*[9] At issue was an effort by the postmaster of New York, under the Espionage Act of 1917, to prevent the mailing of a revolutionary journal called *The Masses*. Judge Hand's opinion was animated by free speech principles, but he rested his decision on a narrow reading of the Espionage Act rather than on the First Amendment. He contended that under the act, speech would be protected unless it expressly advocated lawless action; it could not be regulated merely because it did so indirectly or by implication.

This interpretation was hardly inevitable. The Espionage Act banned any effort "to cause or attempt to cause insubordination, disloyalty, mutiny, or refusal of duty, in the military or naval forces of the United States"; it also banned any effort to "obstruct the recruiting or enlistment service of the United States." The relevant issue of *The Masses*, which praised and even glorified conscientious objectors to the draft, could easily have been held to violate these provisions. Judge Hand strained to argue instead that "One may admire and approve the course of a hero without feeling any duty to follow him. There is not the least implied intimation in these words that others are under a duty to follow." This narrow construction enabled Judge Hand to avoid resolution of a difficult constitutional problem.

Hand's minimalist approach is in line with some of the most famous dissenting opinions of the World War I era, by Justices Louis Brandeis and Oliver Wendell Holmes.[10] Both Brandeis and Holmes are now celebrated for their insistence on the constitutional protection of free speech. But their opinions have unmistakable minimalist features, arguing for narrow interpretation of authorization to the executive, not for invalidation on constitutional grounds. In one case, the Postmaster General revoked the mailing privileges of a newspaper because it published articles that criticized America's involvement in World War I and there-

fore might be taken to obstruct military recruitment and enlistment. Refusing to interpret the Espionage Act in this way, both
Brandeis and Holmes contended that the statute should not be
read to grant such open-ended power to the President.[11] As Justice
Douglas would later do in *Kent v. Dulles,* Brandeis sketched the
historical practices of Congress and the executive to suggest that
the Postmaster General lacked the authority to exclude materials
he deemed objectionable and even unlawful. Brandeis explicitly
invoked a clear statement principle on behalf of his narrow construction, suggesting that "even if the statutes were less clear in
this respect than they seem, I should be led to adopt that construction because of the familiar rule" that legislative enactments
should be read so as to avoid constitutional doubts.

A similar lesson emerges from the Court's decision in *Ex Parte
Quirin,*[12] in which it upheld the use of military commissions to try
German saboteurs captured during World War II. In that case,
President Roosevelt asked the Court to hold that as Commander
in Chief, he had inherent authority to create and to use military
tribunals. The Court refused to accept this argument: "It is unnecessary for present purposes to determine to what extent the President as Commander in Chief has constitutional power to create
military commissions without the support of Congressional legislation. For here Congress has authorized trial of offenses against
the law of war before such commissions." Thus the question
involved the unified position of Congress and the executive: "We
are concerned only with the question whether it is within the constitutional power of the *National Government* to place petitioners
upon trial before a military commission for the offenses with
which they are charged." But the congressional grant of authority
was far from unambiguous; the Court's interpretation may well

have been motivated, in part, by a desire to avoid confronting the President on his broad claims about his authority as Commander in Chief. The crucial point is that the Court's reliance on congressional authorization gives *Quirin* an unmistakable minimalist character.

Minimalism in surprising places.

The requirement of congressional authorization for intrusions on liberty thus unifies a remarkable variety of judicial decisions. But I have not discussed the Supreme Court's most notorious decisions in this domain, *Hirabayashi v. United States*[13] and *Korematsu v. United States,* both of which involved confinement of Japanese-Americans during World War II.[14] In *Hirabayashi,* the Court upheld a curfew order imposed by a military commander on an American citizen of Japanese ancestry. In *Korematsu,* the Court upheld a military order excluding Fred Korematsu, an American citizen of Japanese descent, from San Francisco. Korematsu, the son of Japanese immigrants, was born in Oakland, California, in 1919. In 1942, Korematsu was a welder in the San Francisco ship-yards. Under the government's detention order, his family was taken to Tanforan, a former racetrack south of San Francisco, for processing. Korematsu refused to relinquish his freedom and tried to remain in San Francisco unnoticed. On May 30, 1942, he was arrested and sent to Tanforan. Later, all the detainees were transferred to the Topaz internment camp in Utah.

It is tempting, and probably right, to see the Court's decisions as cowardly and deplorable capitulations to intrusions on liberty that had no justification in national security concerns. They might easily be read as vindications of National Security Fundamentalism. But the Court's overall approach also has an unmistakable minimalist feature, requiring executive action to be authorized by Congress, and deferring to it only if it has been so authorized.

Hirabayashi was decided largely on separation-of-powers grounds. The Court's initial claim was that "so far as it lawfully could, Congress authorized and implemented such curfew orders as the commanding officer should promulgate pursuant to the Executive Order of the President." Unilateral presidential action was not involved: "The question then is . . . whether, acting in cooperation, Congress and the President have constitutional authority to impose the curfew restriction here complained of." The Court ultimately concluded that "it was within the constitutional power of Congress and the executive arm of the Government to prescribe this curfew order for the period under consideration."

In *Korematsu*, the Court similarly emphasized that the exclusion order was based on a recent congressional enactment, making it a crime for any Japanese-American to "remain in . . . any military area or military zone" so prescribed by a competent official. The exclusion order, issued by General J. L. Dewitt, was specifically authorized by an Executive Order by the President, who was, in turn, acting under congressional authorization. The Court pointedly noted that it was dealing not with the executive alone, but with "the war power of Congress and the Executive."

If we consider *Hirabayashi* and *Korematsu* together with *Ex Parte Endo,* we can obtain a fresh perspective on how the Court was approaching the American government's acts of discrimination against Japanese-Americans. In short, the Court was rejecting National Security Fundamentalism and Liberty Perfectionism in favor of a distinctive form of minimalism. In none of these cases did the Court issue a broad ruling in favor of presidential authority.

When the executive acted without congressional authorization, it lost; its actions survived legal challenge only when Congress had specifically permitted them. In all three cases, the Court paid exceedingly careful attention to the role of legislation, and thus refused to rule that the Commander in Chief power allowed the President to act on his own. But in permitting the executive to implement a curfew and an exclusion order, the Court also rejected Liberty Perfectionism, indicating that it would yield to the shared judgments of the two democratically accountable branches.

Of course reasonable people object to these rulings. In my view, the Court should have required greater legislative clarity in *Hirabayashi*. It should have ruled, in the fashion of *Kent v. Dulles*, that if Japanese-Americans are going to be deprived of their liberty, the President must have clear and specific instructions from the national legislature. In *Korematsu*, the Court should have emphasized the absence of unmistakable authorization from Congress. Nonetheless, the three decisions reflect an emphatically minimalist approach to civil liberties in wartime—an approach that both defers to, and insists on, agreement from both of the democratically accountable branches.

Clear statements and terrorism.

In 2003 Supreme Court decisions involving terrorism, minimalist principles have played a central role. They were endorsed most explicitly by Justice David Souter, in his concurring opinion, joined by Justice Ginsburg, in the *Hamdi* case.[15] Yaser Esam Hamdi, an American citizen born in Louisiana, was seized by members of the Northern Alliance in Afghanistan and handed over to American forces. From Afghanistan he was transferred to Guantanamo Bay, then to a naval brig in Norfolk, Virginia, and then to a brig in Charleston, South Carolina. According to the United States government, Hamdi qualified as an "enemy combatant" and hence could be held indefinitely without formal proceedings of any kind. The government urged that Hamdi had become affiliated with a Taliban military unit, received weapons training, and had an assault rifle with him at the time that he surrendered to the Northern Alliance. Hamdi disputed these claims and said he had been unfairly charged. In this case and others, the President made the broad assertion that, as Commander in Chief, he had the inherent power to order military authorities to seize suspected terrorists without any judicial approval and to hold them indefinitely, incommunicado, with no access to a lawyer, a court, family, or friends, and without even informing their families what had been done with them. The President claimed this power even with respect to American citizens captured on American soil—a straightforward demand that the Court adopt National Security Fundamentalism.

Souter's central argument was that Congress had not authorized Hamdi's detention:

> In a government of separated powers, deciding finally on what is a reasonable degree of guaranteed liberty whether in peace or war (or some condition in between) is not well entrusted to the Executive Branch of Government, whose particular responsibility is to maintain security. For reasons of inescapable human nature, the branch of Government asked to counter a serious threat is not the branch on which to rest the Nation's entire reliance in striking the balance between the will to win and the cost in liberty on the way to victory. . . . a reasonable balance is more likely to be reached on the judgment of a different branch.[16]

Souter emphasized "the need for a clearly expressed congressional resolution of the competing claims." Not having found any such resolution, he concluded that the detention was unlawful. In an explicit rejection of the fundamentalist claim of inherent presidential power, Justice Souter went on "to note the weakness of the Government's claim of inherent, executive authority" to detain people. He acknowledged the possibility that the President could do this "in a moment of genuine emergency, when the Government must act with no time for deliberation." But that was not the case here.

The *Hamdi* plurality's own approach contains an endorsement of Souter's central idea. The plurality rejected the government's argument that because Congress had authorized the use of force in response to the 9/11 attacks, the executive was permitted to detain Hamdi indefinitely. In rejecting that argument, the plurality invoked a kind of clear statement principle, allowing detention only during active prosecution of the war in Afghanistan. The Court noted that a longstanding war on terror might mean that "Hamdi's detention could last for the rest of his life." Congress had said nothing to allow the President such latitude.

This approach is emphatically minimalist. It embodies a refusal to defer to the President's claims of need, requires authorization from Congress, and declines to read that authorization to allow the President to intrude to liberty as he sees fit.

Under the law as I have reconstructed it here, congressional authorization is ordinarily both a necessary and a sufficient condition for presidential intrusions into the domain of constitutionally sensitive interests. But in some areas, authorization is not necessary; sometimes the President can act on his own. For example, almost everyone agrees that the President can act to repel a sudden attack on the country, and he does not need specific congressional permission to confine people who have been captured on the battlefield.

In addition, Liberty Perfectionists will argue that in many areas, congressional authorization is not enough. They will fear that in times of genuine crisis, Congress is likely to capitulate to whatever the President wants. Here is the enduring appeal of Liberty Perfectionism. But without adopting that creed, we can approach the problem from another direction. Isn't it better to say that while congressional authorization is often sufficient, it should not always be, and that question must be resolved on a case-by-case basis rather than categorically?

A committed minimalist would be tempted to answer this question with an enthusiastic "Yes." In fact I have already suggested that congressional authorization is sometimes insufficient. We can imagine clear constitutional violations, even outrages, in which we should hope for a degree of judicial courage. Even if Congress and the President agree to silence political dissent during war, the First Amendment should stand in their way; and for reasons to be discussed shortly, fair hearings should generally be required even if the democratic branches want to dispense with them. But committed minimalists should also agree that outside of the worst cases, courts should be reluctant to rule against the combined will of Congress and the President. At the very least, American history attests to the likelihood that courts will follow this path when the stakes are high.

What I am emphasizing here is the minimalist plea: When national security is threatened, a requirement of congressional authorization is the first line of defense against intrusions on constitutionally sensitive interests.

Fair Procedures

In one of the wisest and most important pronouncements in the history of American law, Justice Felix Frankfurter wrote, "The history of liberty has largely been the history of the observance of procedural safeguards."[17] Here is the second component of the minimalist program.

Many of the cases explored thus far are centrally concerned with procedural safeguards. The clearest statement along these lines is found in *Duncan v. Kahanamoku,* in which the Court narrowly construed the law governing Hawaii so as to ensure that civilians would receive access to ordinary courts.[18] The Court offered a ringing endorsement of procedural safeguards, describing them as "indispensable to our system of government" and as ensuring checks on executive absolutism. The same concern animates Chief Justice Taney's rejection of President Lincoln's claim of authority to suspend the writ of habeas corpus.

The requirement of a hearing before government deprives people of their liberty deserves firm judicial support even when national security is at risk. Consider one of President George W. Bush's most unfortunate statements in the aftermath of the attacks of 9/11. Responding to criticisms of his executive order allowing the use of military tribunals to try suspected terrorists, President Bush suggested that the procedures we offer them will be more protective than those they gave us on September 11. This statement begs the very important question of whether suspected terrorists are in fact terrorists. The point of fair procedures is to ensure against conviction of the innocent. As a general rule, courts should insist on those procedures.

Of course minimalists will be the first to agree that a general proposition of this kind does not resolve all cases. If people have been captured on the battlefield and are held beyond the territorial jurisdiction of American courts, then judges are powerless to intervene.[19] But if the legal materials can fairly be interpreted to require procedural protection, they should be so interpreted. This idea has received ringing endorsement in recent Supreme Court decisions involving the war on terrorism. Of these the more elaborately reasoned was the plurality opinion of the Supreme Court in *Hamdi v. Rumsfeld*[20]; it is now time to explore that critical ruling in more detail.

The government contended that because Hamdi was seized in a combat zone, a fair procedure was not necessary. The plurality disagreed. Hamdi could not be lawfully detained unless he had been part of armed forces engaged in conflict against the United States— precisely the issue in dispute. The mere say-so of the executive would not be enough. The government also argued that no individual procedure was justified "in light of the extraordinary constitutional interests" in national security—or at most, that the court should ask whether "some evidence" supported the executive's determination that a citizen is an enemy combatant. The plurality disagreed here as well. In the key passage, the plurality said that an enemy combatant must be supplied with "notice of the factual basis for his classification, and a fair opportunity to rebut the Government's factual assertions before a neutral decisionmaker."

The plurality did not deny the possibility that the constitutional requirements could be met by a military tribunal. What was necessary was not any particular set of procedures, but a process that offers both notice and a fair hearing. "We anticipate that a District Court would proceed with the caution that we have indicated is necessary in this setting, engaging in a factfinding process that is both prudent and incremental."

I have lingered over some technical issues in order to cast light on the plurality's insistence on the right to a fair hearing before an American citizen may be deprived of freedom. Indeed, the plurality called this one of the "essential liberties that remain vibrant even in times of security concerns." Minimalists emphasize that

right above all others. Of all the opinions in the Court's terrorism cases, the clearest endorsement of this point can be found in
Justice Stevens's dissenting opinion in *Rumsfeld v. Padilla*,
where he wrote that "unconstrained Executive detention for the
purpose of investigating and preventing subversive activity is the
hallmark of the Star Chamber." The ability to retain "counsel
for the purpose of protecting the citizen from official mistakes
and mistreatment," he said, "is the hallmark of due process,"
even when the nation is attempting "to resist an assault by the
forces of tyranny."[21]

In times of war, minimalist judges are reluctant to impose
sharp constraints on the executive. But they are much less reluctant to intervene when the executive fails to ensure against arbitrary or mistaken deprivations of liberty.

Narrow and Incompletely Theorized Rulings

In rejecting National Security Fundamentalism, my emphasis has
been on the need to restrain executive power. But courts also need
to restrain themselves. In periods of war, minimalists endorse narrow, incompletely theorized rulings in order to promote two
goals. First, judges ought to avoid excessive intrusions into the
executive domain, and minimalist rulings help to ensure against
judicial overreaching. Second, judges ought to avoid setting precedents that, in retrospect, will seem to give excessive authority to
the President. Minimalist rulings help to ensure against that risk
as well.

Justice Frankfurter's concurring opinion in the Steel Seizure
case offers the most elaborate discussion of the basic point.[22] He
emphasized that when national security is at risk, "rigorous adherence to the narrow scope of the judicial function" is especially

important in the face of the national "eagerness to settle—preferably forever—a specific problem on the basis of the broadest possible constitutional pronouncement." In his view, the Court's duty "lies in the opposite direction," through judgments that make it unnecessary to consider "delicate problems of power under the Constitution." The Supreme Court has an obligation "to avoid putting fetters upon the future by needless pronouncements today." Thus he would have ruled, very narrowly, that Congress had never given the President the authority to seize steel mills—a ruling that would have said exceedingly little about the hard constitutional questions.

We have already encountered similar examples of judicial self-discipline. The ruling in *Kent v. Dulles* left the largest constitutional questions for another day. In protecting free speech in *Masses Publishing Co.,* Judge Hand did not hold that Congress lacked the constitutional power to punish the speech in question; he ruled more modestly that Congress had not seen fit to exercise whatever power it might have.

The same tendency toward minimalist rulings has been on excellent display in the Court's encounters with the war on terrorism. In *Rasul v. Bush*,[23] the Court was asked to say whether federal courts have jurisdiction to consider the detentions of foreign nationals captured and incarcerated at Guantanamo Bay. The Court chose to restrict itself to two exceedingly narrow questions. It held only that the federal habeas statute granted jurisdiction to federal courts to hear challenges by foreign nationals to their detentions, and that the Alien Tort Statute did not bar federal jurisdiction. Having reached these conclusions, the Court said almost nothing else: "Whether and what proceedings may become necessary after respondents make their response to the merits of petitioners' claims are matters that we need not address now. What is presently at stake is only whether the federal courts have jurisdiction to determine the legality of the Executive's potentially indefinite detention of individuals who claim to be wholly innocent of wrongdoing."

We might compare the majority's approach here with those of Justices Scalia and Thomas. Characteristically, Justice Scalia produced two opinions that were both deep and wide. In *Hamdi*, he argued that unless Congress has suspended the writ of habeas corpus, an American citizen is entitled to challenge his imprisonment and to obtain release unless and until criminal proceedings are brought.[24] The implication here is large: The President of the United States may not detain American citizens indefinitely, even if they are captured on the battlefield, unless the writ of habeas corpus has been suspended. "Many think it not only inevitable but entirely proper that liberty give way to security in times of national crisis . . . Whatever the general merits of the view that war silences law or modulates its voice, that view has no place in the interpretation and application of a Constitution designed precisely to confront war and, in a manner that accords with democratic principles, to accommodate it."[25] Unless habeas corpus is suspended by Congress, an ordinary trial-type hearing is the rule for American citizens.

Scalia's preference for an ambitious and broad ruling might be surprising to some, but it fits well with one of his strongest arguments on behalf of wide rather than narrow decisions: Width not only constrains judges but also emboldens them. "The chances that frail men and women will stand up to their unpleasant duty are greatly increased if they can stand behind the solid shield of a firm, clear principle enunciated in earlier cases."[26]

Scalia urges a different but similarly wide rule for foreign nationals detained overseas by the United States military.[27] Here his rule partakes of National Security Fundamentalism: The federal habeas corpus statute does not apply, and the President can detain people free from judicial oversight. Thus Justice Scalia rejects the Court's conclusion that some kind of hearing is necessary to support detention. "For this Court to create such a monstrous scheme in time of war, and in frustration of our military commanders' reliance upon clearly stated prior law, is judicial adventurism of the worst sort."

Justice Thomas joined Scalia on this point; and as we have seen, Justice Thomas also favors a broad rule that would permit the President to detain enemy combatants, even those who are American citizens, indefinitely. For present purposes, what is noteworthy about the Scalia and Thomas opinions is that they favor both width and depth. Thomas is quite explicit in his objections to the Court's use of a "balancing scheme": "I do not think that the Federal Government's war powers can be balanced away by this Court."

Of course Liberty Perfectionists are likely to approve of Justice Scalia's position in *Hamdi* and to reject those of Scalia and Thomas in *Rasul*. But as Thomas points out, Scalia's liberty-protecting position in *Hamdi* creates risks simply because of its breadth.[28] If either justice were clearly right on the law, then we might accept their pleas for depth and width. But when the law is not clear, and when a deep or wide ruling might be confounded by unanticipated circumstances, there is every reason for federal judges to refrain from freezing the law. If the underlying issues are extremely complex—as will often be true in connection with the war on terror—then the Court might well be reluctant to resolve them.

Skeptics will object that narrow decisions, stressing particular facts, are in a sense more intrusive than those that offer greater width and depth. Narrow decisions may leave the executive and other institutions uncertain about what they are supposed to do, and this uncertainty may itself create serious problems for the executive, the judiciary, and suspected terrorists alike. If judges can be confident about a wider ruling, then they should issue it. By doing so, they reduce uncertainty without compromising other important values. But when national security is threatened, judges often lack confidence, and for good reason.

To be sure, minimalist decisions will not wholly prevent unjustified intrusions into the domain of liberty. But such decisions have a major advantage: They carve out a role that is admirably well suited to the institutional strengths and weaknesses of the federal judiciary. At the very least, the minimalist approach is far preferable to National Security Fundamentalism, a constitutionally indefensible alternative that would permit the President to do essentially as he wishes whenever national security is threatened. Maybe Attorney General Biddle was right; maybe the Constitution has not greatly bothered wartime presidents. But under our founding document, the President cannot do however he likes, and it is a grave error to suppose that he has been given some general "war power."

CHAPTER EIGHT

Separation of Powers

T HOUGH DANGEROUS AND WRONG, National Security Fundamentalism isn't exactly radical. Fundamentalists do have a
radical idea, however, in the domain of separation of powers.
They believe, with great confidence, that the American Constitution contains an important doctrine specifically designed to ensure
far stricter separation of powers than the federal government now
observes.

According to this doctrine, called "the nondelegation doctrine,"
Congress is not permitted to "delegate" its lawmaking powers to
any other body. In defending the nondelegation doctrine, fundamentalists point to Article 1, Section 1, of the Constitution, which
says: "All legislative Powers herein granted shall be vested in a Congress of the United States, which shall consist of a Senate and a
House of Representatives." If legislative powers are vested in Congress, how can Congress pass them on to someone else?

Judge Douglas Ginsburg considers this a crucial part of the
separation of powers. In arguing for the Constitution in Exile, he
hopes to reinvigorate the nondelegation doctrine, which he thinks
central to the original constitutional structure. He is not alone.
When Antonin Scalia was a professor at the University of Chicago
Law School, he wrote, "Even with all its Frankenstein-like warts,

knobs, and (concededly) dangers, the unconstitutional delegation doctrine is worth hewing from the ice."[1] Many other fundamentalists agree. They argue that the grant of legislative power to Congress is the cornerstone of the Constitution, that many government agencies are now exercising that power, and that it is past time for courts to insist on constitutional essentials. Here is fundamentalism with a vengeance. While Justice Scalia no longer shows much enthusiasm for the nondelegation doctrine, Justice Thomas has explicitly embraced it and appeared to call for its revival.[2]

If the nondelegation doctrine were brought to life, Congress would be forbidden to let administrative agencies "make law." This view would raise grave doubts about important decisions of the Environmental Protection Agency, the Federal Communications Commission, and the Occupational Safety and Health Administration—for all of these agencies, and many others, issue regulations without clear guidance from Congress. The Environmental Protection Agency is told to issue air quality standards that are "requisite to protect the public health." The Federal Communications Commission is asked to regulate the airwaves as required by the "public convenience, interest, or necessity." The Occupational Safety and Health Administration is required to issue regulations that are "reasonably necessary or appropriate to provide safe or healthful employment and places of employment." Aren't they all being asked to legislate? Nor is this (even nearly) all. The National Labor Relations Board, the Food and Drug Administration, the National Highway Traffic Safety Administration, the Securities and Exchange Commission, and the Consumer Product Safety Commission are given the authority to protect the public, but without specific guidance from Congress. Are the decisions of these agencies unconstitutional?

Few questions are more important to the operation of modern government. If the nondelegation doctrine is really part of the American Constitution, then the Constitution is being violated every day. And if fundamentalists succeed in reviving that doctrine, then major changes are in store. Agencies that ensure clean air, safe workplaces, healthy food, and honesty in stock markets—among many others—could lack the power to do what they now do.

Separation of Powers Writ Large

According to many fundamentalists, the nondelegation doctrine was a central part of the original constitutional plan, but it fell into disuse in the aftermath of the New Deal. Here, then, is a narrative constitutional history, one in which the Court capitulated to the Roosevelt administration at the expense of a key commitment of the Constitution itself. The Supreme Court now says that the nondelegation doctrine exists and that Congress must supply an "intelligible principle" to limit agency discretion; but the Court always finds that such a principle exists, even if Congress appears to have given agencies a blank check.[3] Fundamentalists want the Court to revive the nondelegation doctrine by requiring Congress to provide a clear principle, not an open-ended grant of authority.

It is true that the Court referred to the nondelegation doctrine on a number of occasions in the pre–New Deal period.[4] Moreover, the Court invoked the doctrine to invalidate two acts of Congress in 1935, most famously in *Schechter Poultry Corp. v. U.S.*, decided in the early days of the New Deal.[5] There the Court struck down a provision of the National Industrial Recovery Act, which was designed by the Roosevelt administration to help pull the nation out of the Great Depression. The provision at issue was an open-ended grant of authority to the President to develop "codes of fair competition." A particular problem with this provision is that it combined a high degree of vagueness with a grant of power, in effect, to private groups to develop such codes as they chose.

Since 1935, however, the Court has not used the doctrine to invalidate any statute. It has said, on many occasions, that the nondelegation doctrine requires Congress to supply something like an "intelligible principle" to guide and limit executive discretion—but despite some golden opportunities, it has never found such a principle to be absent. Fundamentalists see this as a plain breach of constitutional requirements and argue for a large-scale revival of the nondelegation doctrine in its "conventional" (meaning pre-1935) form.

Those who are committed to the conventional doctrine have a number of underlying concerns.[6] The most basic ones are textual and historical. The Constitution's text acknowledges just one lawmaking authority, Congress; this seems to mean that Congress and no one else has the power to make law. It follows that a delegation of "legislative" power to any federal agency is inconsistent with the constitutional plan. In addition, the theory of checks and balances provides historical support for this view—suggesting that the original understanding would have condemned open-ended grants of power to the executive. Even if there is little direct evidence from the founding era that delegations were to be prohibited (a point to which I will return), the principle of nondelegation might seem such an inevitable implication of the division of powers that it went without saying.

To their textual and historical points, fundamentalists add a series of claims about constitutional purpose and structure. The most important is political accountability—in particular, the accountability that comes from the distinctive bicameral composition of Congress. The House and Senate, with their different compositions, represent different kinds of constituencies and thus different balances of interests. The House is more strictly dependent on the majority's will; the Senate is more protective of the views of small states and traditionally (though not lately) more conservative. To become law, a bill must be acceptable to both sets of interests. Fundamentalists believe that any "delegation" of lawmaking authority eliminates the special kind of accountability the Constitution created by thus dividing the legislature.

This point is closely related to another one, especially dear to fundamentalist hearts. The nondelegation doctrine requires legislators to agree on a relatively specific form of words. The simple need for agreement increases the burdens and costs of enacting national law. Fundamentalists think those burdens and costs are a crucial safeguard of individual liberty. They ensure that the power of the national government will not be brought to bear against individuals unless there is a real consensus, established by legislative agreement on relatively precise words, that this step is desirable. Fundamentalists insist that the original institutional design was founded largely on the belief that the central government was a threat to freedom. Open-ended delegations are thus a violation of a core constitutional commitment.[7]

The nondelegation principle also promotes values connected with the rule of law, above all because it ensures that government power will be constrained by clear limitations set out in advance. The ban on open-ended delegation is closely connected to the Constitution's "void for vagueness" doctrine, which requires laws to be clear rather than open-ended. The key purposes of the void for vagueness doctrine are to provide fair notice to affected citizens and also to limit the discretion of unelected administrators and bureaucrats. If laws are clear, people will know what they can and can't do, and bureaucrats and police offers will not be able to harass people at their whim. The nondelegation doctrine serves the same purposes, by ensuring that those asked to implement the law be bound by intelligible principles.

Finally, the requirement of legislative clarity is a check on the problems of interest-group power and self-interested representation, two of the problems most feared by the Constitution's framers. James Madison referred to both but spoke of the former as the more serious danger: "[I]n our Governments the real power lies in the majority of the Community, and the invasion of private rights is chiefly to be apprehended, not from acts of government contrary to the sense of its constituents, but from acts in which the Government is the mere instrument of the major number of the constituents."[8] Fundamentalists think the nondelegation doctrine is a way to reduce the risk that well-organized private groups will seize control of government to redistribute wealth or opportunities in their favor. The complex design of Congress was intended to limit the power of such groups over government. At the same time, the requirement of general approval from various legislators reduces the risk that self-interested representatives, with narrow agendas of their own, will use the lawmaking process to promote their parochial interests.

False Fundamentalism and More

Taken at face value, these claims are certainly plausible. But they run into three major problems. First and most important, the constitutional claims are much weaker than they seem. Here, as elsewhere, fundamentalists are far more confident about their view than history warrants. On its own premises, the fundamentalist project in this domain is hard to justify. Second, large-scale judicial revival of the nondelegation doctrine would do little to improve the operation of modern government. It might well make things worse, possibly much worse. Third, judicial enforcement of the nondelegation doctrine would raise serious problems of judicial competence, because it would transfer massive power to federal judges.

Text, history, precedent. Let's begin with the standard legal materials. In American law, does the conventional doctrine really have a clear constitutional pedigree? Fundamentalists think so, but they're wrong. In the devastating words of law professors Eric Posner and Adrian Vermeule: "The nondelegation position lacks any foundation in constitutional text and structure, in standard originalist sources, or in sound economic and political theory. Nondelegation is nothing more than a controversial theory that floated around the margins of nineteenth-century constitutionalism—a theory that wasn't clearly adopted by the Supreme Court until 1892."[9]

Fundamentalists like to point out, with some distress, that the Supreme Court last invalidated a statute on nondelegation grounds in 1935. They imply that this aspect of the Constitution in Exile was alive and well from the founding period until then. What goes conveniently unmentioned is that the Court *first* invalidated a statute on nondelegation grounds in exactly the same year—despite many previous opportunities. It is grossly misleading to suggest that the nondelegation doctrine was a well-entrenched one that the Supreme Court suddenly abandoned as part of some post–New Deal capitulation to Franklin Delano Roosevelt. The real anomaly is 1935. The conventional doctrine has had one good year and well over two hundred bad ones (and counting).

What about text and history? There is not much historical support for the conventional doctrine. Here is another case in which fundamentalists are spending too much time talking about the original meaning and too little time investigating it. Of course the Constitution grants legislative power to Congress; no one denies that. But the Constitution does not explicitly forbid Congress from giving discretion to the executive branch, and there are few indications in the founding era that such grants of discretion were originally thought to be banned. Fundamentalists have a hard time producing historical support for their position.[10]

Maybe we shouldn't draw big inferences from the general silence on this question. Maybe the ban on delegations was so obvious that it did not need to be discussed. But the practice of early Congresses strongly suggests otherwise: that broad grants of authority to the executive were thought to be just fine. The very first Congress granted military pensions, not pursuant to legislative guidelines but "under such regulations as the President of the United States may direct."[11] The second Congress gave the President the authority to grant licenses to trade with the Indian tribes, not with clear limitations but under "such rules and regulations as the President shall prescribe."[12] An early statute authorized the Attorney General and the Secretaries of State and War to issue patents "if they shall deem the invention or discovery sufficiently useful or important." In the second year of the young republic, Congress authorized presidential commissioners to "purchase or accept such quantity of land on the eastern side of the Potomac . . . as the President shall deem proper . . . and according to such plans as the President shall approve."

There is no serious evidence that members of Congress thought these or other grants of authority violated some general nondelegation principle. In fact there is overwhelming evidence that they did not. The strongest statement of concern with delegation, in the first fifteen years of the nation's existence, comes from James Madison, who worried that "if nothing more were required, in exercising a legislative trust, than a general conveyance of authority—without laying down any precise rules by which the authority conveyed should be carried into effect—it would follow that the whole power of legislation might be transferred by the legislature from itself."[13] But this isolated statement came in 1799, after Congress had made many grants of broad power to the executive without constitutional objection. If the historical material is taken as a whole, it would be reasonable to conclude that the nondelegation doctrine was a creation of the late nineteenth century, and that it lacks serious roots in the Constitution itself. At the very least, it can be seen that there was little talk of the nondelegation doctrine from the founding until decades after the Civil War—and that the nondelegation doctrine might well have started to have real appeal only as part of the political attack on the rise of the administrative state.

Perhaps fundamentalists can say that an investigation of the text and history does not definitely refute their position. But it is odd, to say the least, for fundamentalists to be asking courts to invalidate acts of Congress without being able to point to clear support in the Constitution itself.

Democracy, welfare, and more. Turn now from text and history to some broader issues. Despite initial appearances, considerations of democracy do not provide clear support for the nondelegation doctrine.[14] Any delegation to the President, or the

Environmental Protection Agency, must itself have come from a democratic exercise of lawmaking authority. If Congress has delegated such authority, maybe that is exactly what voters want. Congress may well face electoral punishment when it grants broad authority to the executive. This is a perfectly legitimate issue to raise in an election, and "passing the buck" to bureaucrats, or even to the President, will often be an unpopular strategy for reelection. In any case delegations are not made to General Motors or Ralph Nader or the University of Chicago. When Congress delegates power, it generally does so to the President, or to agencies that work under him and are accountable to him.[15]

I am not claiming that the nondelegation doctrine has absolutely nothing to do with democracy. Congress does have a distinctive form of accountability, through the mechanisms for representation and the system of bicameralism, and it is that form, not accountability in the abstract, that might justify a nondelegation doctrine. But the democratic argument for sharp limits on agency discretion is hardly clear-cut. In fact, when Congress does provide specific direction, things aren't always so wonderful. Legislative specificity often reflects the power of self-interested private groups—as, for example, when Congress gives special benefits to organizations that have the lobbying power to get them. And we should notice that delegations from Congress often stem from a simple lack of information—a pervasive and legitimate basis for delegation in law or even life. Congress may not know much about how to handle the problem of air pollution or workplace hazards; is it always terrible if it grants the President and his agents a great deal of power to decide how to do so?

I am not denying that Congress should usually try to provide some guidance. But it is hard to produce any abstract reason why decisions by agencies operating under specific instructions from Congress would necessarily be better than decisions by agencies under vaguer language. And in practice, there is no evidence that executive agencies operating under open-ended authority do worse, on any dimension, than agencies operating under stricter limits. The Department of Agriculture, whose discretion has been sharply limited by Congress, is hardly the most admired agency in American government. Agencies with little discretion don't do much better than agencies with a lot. Often they do worse.

Fundamentalists want to make it more burdensome to enact new law. But why? What precedes any new law is always some body of law, whether legislatively or judicially created. Why is there any reason to think that the preceding law is better? Suppose that we like freedom, and that we see freedom as immunity from law. (We might not see things that way; does a law that forbids discrimination or pollution or assault reduce freedom or increase it?) Even if this is so, many regulations, issued by agencies with broad discretion, eliminate the burdens of law, by deregulating or by increasing the flexibility of those in the private sector.

The most systematic and detailed analysis of congressional delegations of authority[16] is by political scientists David Epstein and Sharyn O'Halloran, who conclude that the whole idea of open-ended delegation is a myth. In many areas, "some of which, like the budget and tax policy, require considerable time and expertise—Congress takes a major role in specifying the details of policy."[17] Nor is Congress oblivious to executive performance. On the contrary, "legislators carefully adjust and readjust discretion over time and across issue areas." Most important for present purposes, Epstein and O'Halloran conclude that when Congress delegates power to the President or agencies, that step actually reduces the authority of legislative *committees,* where well-organized groups can often dominate. Delegation to the executive is "a necessary counterbalance to the concentration of power in the hands of committees" or to the surrender of "policy to a narrow subset" of members.[18] In these circumstances, the authors conclude that limits on delegation "would threaten the very individual liberties they purport to protect."

Judicial competence. In calling for a reinvigorated nondelegation doctrine, fundamentalists want to empower the courts. But why do they so trust the federal judiciary? Under the doctrine that they defend, the line between a permitted and a prohibited delegation is inevitably a matter of degree. The real question is: How much executive discretion is too much? It isn't easy to come up with a standard to answer. To his credit, Justice Scalia himself is troubled by this problem, and he now rejects the nondelegation doctrine on the ground that courts cannot enforce it in a way that leads to rule-bound law.[19]

Because we are dealing with a question of degree, judicial enforcement of the nondelegation doctrine would produce ad hoc, highly discretionary rulings, giving little guidance to lower courts or to Congress itself. The matter is even worse than that. Supreme Court decisions invalidating statutes as unduly open-ended would raise suspicions, perhaps justified, of judicial hostility to the particular program at issue. Without much exaggeration, and with tongue only slightly in cheek, we might say that judicial enforcement of the nondelegation doctrine would violate that very doctrine—since it could not be done without delegating a high degree of discretionary lawmaking authority to the judiciary. It is a simple fact that judicial enforcement of the doctrine would grant the federal courts massive new authority to second-guess legislative judgments about how much discretion is too much, without clear constitutional standards for answering that question.

Why are fundamentalists so enthusiastic about that?

Separation of Powers Writ Small

Minimalists do not want to reinvigorate the nondelegation doctrine. But they certainly believe in the separation of powers. They are eager to find modest and cautious ways to achieve the goals of those who support nondelegation. Minimalists want those paths to be administrable by federal courts. Instead of a general doctrine, minimalists favor specific *nondelegation principles* designed to enlist the separation of powers in the protection of individual rights. They contend that in order to protect important rights and interests, courts should not allow the executive branch to make certain choices unless Congress has specifically decided that those choices are appropriate. Minimalists believe these nondelegation principles are exceedingly important, and that federal judges can insist on them without compromising any important values. What I am saying, in short, is that American law already contains a set of particular nondelegation principles, and that they are far better than any general revival of the nondelegation doctrine could possibly be.

The nondelegation principles fall into three general categories. Some are inspired by the Constitution; others involve issues of sovereignty; still others have their foundations in public policy. The unifying theme—a generalization of the theme of Chapter 7— is that the executive branch should not be permitted to intrude on important rights or interests on its own. The national legislature, with its diverse membership and multiplicity of voices, must explicitly authorize any such intrusions. Here, then, is a situation in which the separation of powers can be enlisted for the benefit of individual rights.

Constitutionally inspired principles. Many nondelegation principles have constitutional origins. Consider the idea that executive agencies will not be permitted to construe statutes in such a way as to raise serious constitutional doubts. This means that constitutionally sensitive questions will not be permitted to arise unless Congress, the constitutionally designated lawmaker, has expressly chosen to raise them.

For example, a law will not ordinarily be taken to allow the executive branch to intrude on the right to travel, violate the right to free speech, interfere with religious liberty, or take private property without compensation. So long as the statute is unclear and the constitutional question is serious, Congress must decide to raise that question through explicit statement. Recall that even when national security is threatened, the President will not lightly be taken to have been authorized to intrude on constitutionally protected interests. A nondelegation principle broadens this point, saying that in general, the executive branch will not be presumed to be permitted to interfere with constitutionally sensitive rights.

Consider, as a second example, the exceptionally important "rule of lenity." This rule says that ambiguous criminal statutes will be construed favorably to criminal defendants. A key function of the lenity principle is to ensure against delegations, to courts or to anyone else. Criminal punishment must be a product of a clear judgment on Congress's part. Where no clear judgment has been made, the statute will not apply. The rule of lenity is a time-honored nondelegation principle.

As a third example, consider the notion that unless Congress has spoken with clarity, executive agencies are not to apply statutes retroactively.[20] Retroactivity is potentially unfair and hence disfavored in the law. For this reason, Congress is not taken to have delegated to administrative agencies the authority to surprise people by applying the law to them. The best way to understand this idea is as a pale echo of the notion that the Due Process Clause forbids retroactive application of law. The constitutional constraints on retroactivity are modest; while the Ex Post Facto Clause in the American Constitution forbids retroactive application of the criminal law, the clause is narrowly construed, and Congress is generally permitted to impose civil legislation retroactively if it chooses.[21] But Congress must make that choice explicitly and take the political heat if it does. It will not be taken to have attempted the same result via delegation, and regulatory agencies are not understood to have the authority to choose retroactivity on their own.

Also in this category is the idea that the executive agencies are not allowed to interpret ambiguous provisions so as to preempt state law.[22] The constitutional source of this principle is the commitment to a federal structure—a commitment that may not be compromised without a congressional decision to do so. This is an important requirement, because the Constitution creates various safeguards against cavalier disregard of state interests through the system of representation.[23] Notice that there is no constitutional obstacle to national preemption; Congress is usually entitled to preempt state law if it chooses. But the preemption decision must be made legislatively, not bureaucratically.

Sovereignty. The second category of nondelegation principles includes those that lack a clear constitutional source but are founded in widespread understandings about sovereignty. For example, the executive branch is not permitted to apply statutes outside of the territorial borders of the United States.[24] Our civil rights laws do not apply to American companies doing business in Iraq or Japan. If statutes are to receive extraterritorial application, it must be as a result of a deliberate congressional judgment to this effect. Because extraterritorial application calls for extremely sensitive judgments involving international relations, these judgments must be made through the ordinary lawmaking process (in which the President, of course, participates). The executive may not make this decision on its own.

For related reasons, executive agencies cannot interpret statutes and treaties unfavorably to Native Americans.[25] Where statutory provisions are ambiguous, the national government will not prevail. This idea is an outgrowth of the horrendous history of relations between the United States and Native American tribes, which have semi-sovereign status; it is an effort to ensure that any unfavorable outcome will be a product of an explicit judgment by the national legislature. The safeguards created by congressional structure must be navigated before a harmful decision may be made.

Consider, as a final illustration, the fact that federal agencies are not permitted to waive the sovereign immunity of the United States, and any such waiver must be explicit in legislation.[26] Sovereign immunity is a background structural principle, which can be eliminated only on the basis of a specific judgment to that effect by the national legislature.

Public policy. The final set of nondelegation principles is designed to implement public policy, by, among other things, giving sense and rationality the benefit of the doubt—and by requiring Congress itself to speak if it wants to compromise policy goals that are widely shared.

There are many examples. Exemptions from taxation are narrowly construed[27]; if Congress wants to exempt a group from federal income tax, it must express its will clearly. Such exemptions are often the product of lobbying efforts by well-organized private groups; hence agencies may not create them on their own. At the same time, there is a general federal policy against anticompetitive practices, and agencies are not permitted to seize on ambiguous statutory language so as to defeat that policy.[28] If Congress wants to make an exception to the policy in favor of competition, it is certainly permitted to do so. But agencies may not do so without congressional instruction. So too, it is presumed that statutes providing veterans' benefits will be construed generously for veterans, and agencies cannot conclude otherwise.[29]

Separation of Powers Minimalism

I have emphasized that there are serious problems with judicial enforcement of the nondelegation doctrine. With the nondelegation principles outlined here, those problems are much less severe. Courts need not address vague questions about whether the legislature has exceeded some permissible level of discretion. Instead they ask the far more manageable question of whether an agency has been asked to decide something Congress should decide instead. In other words, courts ask only whether certain areas are involved, and need not answer questions of degree.

Above all, the nondelegation principles ensure that certain important rights and interests will not be compromised unless Congress has expressly decided to compromise them. While there is no good reason to think that a reinvigorated nondelegation doctrine would improve modern regulation, it is entirely reasonable to think that for certain kinds of decisions, merely executive decisions are not enough. The nondelegation principles thus take their place as one of the most prominent domains in which protection of individual rights, and of other important interests, occurs not through blanket prohibitions on governmental action, but through channeling decisions to particular governmental institutions, in this case Congress itself.

The minimalist program for separation of powers, with nondelegation principles at its core, is far superior to the fundamentalist suggestion that courts should use the Constitution to ban Congress from giving discretionary power to regulatory agencies. In this context, the fundamentalist position is a partisan program lacking solid constitutional roots—and thus defies fundamentalism itself. Not incidentally, accepting that position would make American government work worse, not better.

CHAPTER NINE

Guns, God, and More

For us, and for Clarence Thomas, it's more important to get it right than to maintain continuity.

—Stephen Presser[1]

L EGAL FUNDAMENTALISTS HAVE A LONG WISH LIST. They want to interpret the Constitution to strike down gun control legislation; they want to weaken the separation between church and state; and they want to impose sharp limits on Congress's regulatory power. They would (and have) cast legal doubt on the Americans with Disabilities Act, the Violence Against Women Act, the Age Discrimination in Employment Act, and provisions of the Clean Water Act and the Endangered Species Act. They want the Supreme Court to interpret the Constitution so as to forbid government regulation of commercial advertising or expenditures on political campaigns. The Constitution, as they read it, requires government to pay property holders whenever environmental regulations diminish the value of their property.

Does any of this sound familiar? It should. On these counts, the constitutional judgments of fundamentalists are eerily close to the political judgments of conservative politicians. That alone should send up a red flag. If judges' opinions consistently fit with a partisan political agenda, we have reason to doubt whether they are interpreting the Constitution with anything like neutrality. And if "strict construction" requires judicial interpretations to fit the political preferences of particular politicians, then we should wonder what strict construction is really all about.

None of this means fundamentalists are wrong on all of these issues. On some of them, I believe that they are right. The problem is that too much of the time, their views line up with identifiable political commitments—sometimes radical ones.

Guns

Here is the entire text of the Second Amendment: "A well-regulated Militia, being necessary to the security of a free State, the right of the people to keep and bear Arms, shall not be infringed."

Fundamentalists believe that this provision means that many or most gun control laws are unconstitutional. The National Rifle Association has been so insistent on this claim that even Democratic politicians now contend that they strongly support "the Second Amendment right to have guns." Some judges are heading in the same direction. In an unusual pronouncement, Justice Scalia has suggested, in academic writing, that the Second Amendment does indeed confer an individual right to bear arms.[2] In an even more unusual and even astounding pronouncement, Justice Thomas went out of his way, in a judicial opinion on a related topic, to offer the same suggestion:

> This Court has not had recent occasion to consider the nature
> of the substantive right safeguarded by the Second Amendment.
> If, however, the Second Amendment is read to confer a personal
> right to "keep and bear arms," a colorable argument exists that
> the Federal Government's regulatory scheme, at least as it per-

tains to the purely intrastate sale or possession of firearms, runs afoul of that Amendment's protections. As the parties did not raise this argument, however, we need not consider it here. Perhaps, at some future date, this Court will have the opportunity to determine whether Justice Joseph Story was correct when he wrote that the right to bear arms "has justly been considered, as the palladium of the liberties of a republic.[3]

If fundamentalists have their way, we should expect a kind of constitutional revolution in which the Second Amendment results in judicial decisions striking down gun control laws. Those who favor gun control legislation are now on the constitutional defensive. In Judge Douglas Ginsburg's words: "And now let the litigation begin."

Should we really want that? Let's start, as fundamentalists rightly do, with the constitutional text. There is something unusual about the words of the Second Amendment. Uniquely among the provisions of the Bill of Rights, it has its own preamble, "A well-regulated Militia, being necessary to the security of a free State." Why does it begin this way? On the basis of the text alone, we might plausibly think that this amendment does not create an *individual* right to bear arms at all. Indeed the Second Amendment, which applies only to the national government, might really be about federalism. On one view, it was understood above all to prohibit the young government from banning state militias—which the amendment's supporters saw as "necessary to the security of a free State." On this view, the Second Amendment forbids Congress to ban state militias, but it does not stop the national government from regulating guns or controlling individual gun ownership, so long as militias are not implicated.

Does this interpretation seem implausible? In fact the major Supreme Court decision on the Second Amendment seemed to adopt it; and this has been the law for more than sixty years. In *United States v. Miller,* decided in 1939, the Supreme Court held that Congress could forbid the interstate transportation of sawed-off shotguns.[4] The Court said that the Second Amendment must be interpreted in light of the constitutional goal of recognizing and permitting militias. "With obvious purpose to assure the continuation and render possible the effectiveness of such forces the declaration and guarantee of the Second Amendment were made. It must be interpreted and applied with that end in view." The Court believed this point was enough to establish the legitimacy of the law in question. There was no evidence that sawed-off shotguns have "some reasonable relationship to the preservation or efficiency of a well regulated militia." Hence the Court could not "say that the Second Amendment guarantees the right to keep and bear such an instrument."

If this pronouncement is taken seriously, then almost all gun control legislation is constitutionally fine. And if the Court is right, then fundamentalism does not justify the view that the Second Amendment protects an individual right to bear arms. Those who contend that it does are arguing politics, not law.

Of course, the Supreme Court could have been wrong in the *Miller* case. But its reading of the text is reasonable, and the history is not without ambiguity. I am not insisting that there is no individual right to bear arms; the history can plausibly be read to support that right. But on the Constitution's text, fundamentalists should not be so confident in their enthusiasm for invalidating gun control legislation. In fact they face an additional obstacle. I have noted that the Second Amendment, like the rest of the Bill of

Rights, applies only to the national government. Many provisions of the Bill of Rights have been applied to state governments through a doctrine known as "incorporation." The Supreme Court has held that without doing so expressly, the Fourteenth Amendment actually "incorporates" parts of the original Bill of Rights. In a series of cases in the middle of the twentieth century, the Court established that states must respect central aspects of the Bill of Rights, such as the right to free speech and the right to be free from unreasonable searches and seizures.

Fundamentalists have resisted incorporation, and on purely textual and historical grounds they're right to raise questions.[5] (We'll skip the complexities that surround the general issue of incorporation. But it is worth asking fundamentalists this question: Under their approach, do states have to obey the Bill of Rights at all?) For gun ownership, however, there's a simple punchline: In 1886, the Supreme Court ruled that the Second Amendment is *not* incorporated in the Fourteenth Amendment and hence doesn't apply to the states at all.[6] In the Court's plain words, this "is one of the amendments that has no other effect than to restrict the powers of the National government." The Court has never questioned this conclusion.

Those who are enthusiastic about the right to bear arms might want the Court to change its mind and to apply the Second Amendment to the states. But if they believe the Second Amendment is incorporated, they have a great deal of work to do to justify any such change. They will have to explain why the Supreme Court should reject a rule that has been in place for over a century. They will be required, in effect, to reconstruct current law in two fundamental ways—first by asserting an individual right to bear arms, and second by asserting that this right applies against states as well as the national government. Both of these assertions would require dramatic and unprecedented revisions of constitutional doctrine. If the text and the historical evidence do not unambiguously justify those steps, why do fundamentalists favor them?

Perfectionists, with respect to the Second Amendment, fall into two camps. Some of them are committed in principle to the individual right to bear arms, and they want the Supreme Court to accept that right even if history does not call for it. Many gun control opponents purport to be fundamentalists but are really perfectionists. We shouldn't be fooled. Other perfectionists argue for judicial restraint, believing that the gun control question should be resolved democratically. They insist that the debate involves legitimate disagreements of both policy and principle, and they don't want federal judges to stand in the way of democratic resolution of those disagreements. They favor a degree of federalism on the gun control issue, allowing different states to come to different arrangements, free from constitutional limitations.

Minimalists are more cautious. They know that the text and history are complex and that a plausible argument can be made on behalf of an individual right to bear arms. They understand that the Supreme Court has long held otherwise—but they are not too sure that it, or they, are right. For the Second Amendment, minimalists have no program. They are willing to consider the possibility that a wholesale ban on individual gun ownership, such as exists in some other nations, would raise serious constitutional questions. They would not rule constitutional challenges out of bounds. But they believe that modest restrictions, of the sort now undertaken by both state and federal government, are well within the limits of what the Second Amendment might ban. Minimalists are puzzled by the fact that many fundamentalists have an agenda for the Second Amendment, especially because the text and history do not provide unambiguous support for that agenda.

God

The Bill of Rights contains two provisions that protect religious liberty. The first safeguards the "free exercise of religion." The second forbids the federal government from making laws "respecting an establishment of religion." For now, the debate over the Free Exercise Clause is reasonably quiet. Far more noise is being generated by the Establishment Clause, which is the source of the constitutional separation of church and state. Public schools are not permitted to require prayers, and government cannot endorse any religion. The Establishment Clause is the reason. Many fundamentalists want the Court to alter its understanding of that provision in a way that will make more space for government support of religion. Indeed, many fundamentalists believe that states can favor religion as such—and even that they can favor particular religions. With the rise of politically active citizens intensely concerned to protect religious institutions, the debate over the Establishment Clause has become one of the most heated in all of constitutional law.

Fundamentalists firmly reject the idea that the Establishment Clause requires the separation of church and state. In their view, the metaphor of "separation" is badly misleading.[7] If there is now a "wall" between church and state, they would like to tear it down. In fact the most extreme fundamentalists would allow states to have official, tax-supported state religions—the Mormon

Church of Utah, for example. And if we focus on text and history, we might be tempted to agree. Fundamentalism isn't obviously false in this domain—a striking contrast to the areas of affirmative action and separation of powers. As fundamentalists like to point out, the Constitution does not specifically decree a separation between church and state. It says, more narrowly, that the national government may not enact a law "respecting an establishment of religion."

What does this mean? At first glance, it seems to say, very simply, that Congress may not "establish" a national church of the sort that exists in Great Britain. If that is really what the clause means, then the national government can do a great deal, short of formal establishment, to assist religion. For example, it can certainly spend taxpayer funds on religious institutions.

Whether or not this argument is right—and history raises serious doubts — fundamentalists have another arrow in their quiver. Like the Second Amendment, the Establishment Clause applies to the federal government but not to the states. Hence a key question is whether the Establishment Clause is "incorporated" in the Fourteenth Amendment. The Court has long held that it is, so that states must respect the separation of church and state no less than the national government. Justice Thomas, among others, has argued that incorporation of the Establishment Clause is a big mistake: "The text and history of the Establishment Clause strongly suggest that it is a federalism provision intended to prevent Congress from interfering with state establishments. Thus, unlike the Free Exercise Clause, which does protect an individual right, it makes little sense to incorporate the Establishment Clause."[8] Thomas emphasizes that incorporation of any individual right against federal establishments would lead to "a peculiar outcome: It would prohibit precisely what the *Establishment Clause* was intended to protect—*state* establishments of religion."[9] In Thomas's view, states can favor particular religions, as they choose, without offense to the Establishment Clause.

This view is not implausible as a matter of history, but it would produce radical changes in American law and life. Consider how it would apply to a familiar controversy: The posting of the Ten Commandments on public buildings. Fundamentalists believe there is no problem with this practice at the federal or state level. Of course the Ten Commandments come from the Bible, but their posting does not literally establish a church. It follows that no constitutional problem is raised by the presence of the words "under God" in the Pledge of Allegiance, whether the Pledge is attributed to the federal government or the states. Many fundamentalists would go much further, permitting state governments, and possibly the nation as well, to favor religion over nonreligion or to use taxpayer funds to help religious institutions. Certainly they believe that the Constitution permits voucher programs, in which states allow parents to use taxpayer funds to pay for an education of their choice, religious or otherwise. On this count, the Supreme Court agrees with them.[10]

Justice Thomas's reading, however, would take things much further. It would essentially reverse the accepted meaning of the Establishment Clause. Far from prohibiting government sponsorship of religion, the clause would, at the state level, protect it from federal interference. Any state could freely recognize its own church, using taxpayer money to support its schools, places of worship, missionary work, and other religious activities. Illinois could have its own version of the Church of England: the Church of Illinois.

For their part, many perfectionists insist on a radical separation between church and state. They vehemently disagree with Justice Thomas's textual and historical arguments. They believe that properly read, the words "respecting an establishment of religion" go a long way toward separating church and state. The Constitution does not merely forbid the national government from "establishing" a church; more broadly, it forbids Congress from enacting any law "respecting" an establishment. Many perfectionists do not agree that public buildings may feature the Ten Commandments, which they see as a religious symbol. In their view, the use of the words "under God" in the Pledge of Allegiance is invalid, because the government is squarely endorsing a religious belief and imposing that belief on children participating in a public ceremony.

Many perfectionists believe that voucher programs are unconstitutional because they make taxpayer funds available to religious institutions. In the extreme, perfectionists would eliminate all preferential treatment of religious organizations—such as exemptions from taxes, zoning requirements, and equal-employment laws—as unconstitutional recognitions of religion by the state. They want to see religious groups treated no differently from secular nonprofit organizations.

Minimalists have no enthusiasm for perfectionism on these counts. In their view, perfectionists are advocating a program of their own—one with doubtful constitutional roots—that would use the Establishment Clause much as their fundamentalist adversaries use the Second Amendment and (as we shall shortly see) the free speech principle: as the basis for imposing a set of far-reaching principles that run counter to democratic judgments. Minimalists believe that no general agenda makes sense in this domain. Certainly they do not think a voucher program is intrinsically objectionable. If it is neutral between religious and nonreligious institutions, it is probably fine.

So long as students are not required to participate, minimalists are not greatly bothered by the phrase "under God" in the Pledge of Allegiance. The pledge is not a religious ceremony, and references to God have long played a role in civil life without endangering the respect and toleration for which the religion clauses have come to stand. As for the public posting of the Ten Commandments, a great deal depends on context. If the Ten Commandments are posted as a self-conscious effort to merge religious law and secular law, and to assert a public commitment to Christianity, minimalists will find a serious constitutional problem. It matters whether the posting as a religious purpose or an historical one. The Supreme Court has adopted just this kind of contextual approach.[11]

That approach offers a sensible orientation for the future— one that, for all its problems, is far better than that marked out by fundamentalism, which would throw out many decades of law on the basis of a speculative reading of history.

Speech

For most of the nation's history, fundamentalists took an exceedingly narrow view of the First Amendment. They believed that the government could regulate political dissent if it had a "tendency" to cause harm—and that government could "balance" the value of speech against the risks it created. In practice, they found that the balance often favored censorship. If speech was libelous or sexually explicit, fundamentalists tended to believe that it was unprotected. Dissenters and rebels had little to gain from the fundamentalist understanding of the free speech principle.

It is not widely known, in fact, that until the middle of the twentieth century, the First Amendment provided relatively little protection to speech, certainly by contemporary standards. Not until 1969 did the Supreme Court adopt a highly protective version of the "clear and present danger" test, in a decision forbidding government to regulate political dissent unless it could show that harm was both likely and imminent.[12] This standard was the culmination of a long set of minimalist rulings that ultimately protected political dissenters from the constraining arm of the state. By small steps, minimalists eventually ended up at a position long advocated by perfectionists.

In the last two decades, however, fundamentalists have become much more enthusiastic about aggressive judicial use of the First Amendment, at least as it relates to commercial advertising and campaign finance reform. In these areas, fundamentalists want the Supreme Court to strike down a lot of legislation. What is especially puzzling is that here, as with affirmative action, they have failed to investigate the original understanding of the text that they purport to be interpreting. Like perfectionists at their worst, fundamentalists are seizing on the text of the Constitution to strike down eminently reasonable legislation. What fundamentalists are doing, in short, is using the Constitution to promote a controversial and undemocratic program of deregulation. Many fundamentalists would certainly like to abolish the Federal Communications Commission, and some do not hesitate to invoke the First Amendment on their behalf.

Advertisements. For almost all of the nation's history, commercial advertising was thought not to be protected by the First Amendment. The "core" of the free speech principle has always been political speech. Above all, the First Amendment ensures that people are free to discuss political questions and to criticize their government. A company might use "speech" to advertise its soft drinks or its sneakers, but it is not protected for that reason. Much speech is far afield from the free speech principle; consider threats, bribes, or conspiracies to fix prices. The Constitution does not protect everything that comes out of someone's mouth, typewriter, television, or computer. And for nearly two centuries, commercial advertising lacked constitutional protection; the Court itself said that the First Amendment did not protect advertising.[13]

In 1976, however, the Supreme Court ruled that the government could not regulate commercial advertising, at least if it was true and not misleading.[14] In so ruling, the Court said that consumers should be permitted to evaluate advertising as they saw fit. This ruling was dramatic and in its own way revolutionary, but it had an unmistakable minimalist feature. The Court did not say that commercial advertising would be given the *same* protection as political speech, and indeed it made clear that such advertising could be subject to reasonable regulation.

Fundamentalists now seek to go much further. Here, as elsewhere, Justice Thomas is the most ambitious of all. Without any significant discussion of history or the founding period, he has said that he would rule that the First Amendment protects commercial advertising to the same degree that it protects political speech.[15] It would follow, for example, that restrictions on tobacco advertising are generally unconstitutional. Justice Scalia, normally a devotee of history, has indicated that he may be prepared to agree with Thomas.[16]

Minimalists are puzzled. On what theory should regulation of advertising be taken out of the hands of the American people and their elected representatives? The text and history of the Constitution need not be read to support Thomas's position. To be sure, minimalists believe it is too late to accept the suggestion, made by some perfectionists, that commercial speech does not deserve constitutional protection at all. But they prefer to operate within the framework of reasonable restrictions permitted by existing law. They would, for example, allow government to protect against false and deceptive advertising, advertising aimed at children, and advertising of products that cause demonstrable harm. They believe that in insisting on the protection of commercial advertising, fundamentalists are transforming the First Amendment into a species of laissez-faire economics.

And indeed, that does seem to be the fundamentalist program—to use the First Amendment to forbid government from regulating advertisements. Regardless of whether this is a sensible policy, it is a gross misreading of constitutional law.

Campaign finance. For campaign finance, fundamentalists self-consciously seek to promote deregulation. In principle, their arguments are not implausible. Money is, in a sense, speech. No one can stop you from using your printer to copy your writings, and it costs money to have a printer and make copies. But suppose money dominates political campaigns to the point of creating the appearance, or even the reality of, corruption. Suppose too that political candidates end up competing with one another to raise money—and that an unregulated system turns campaigns into a kind of fund-raising competition that obscures the character and policies of the candidates. Suppose finally that if regulations are not in place, wealthy people will have dispropor- tionate influence in the political process, drowning out less well- funded voices and compromising the important value of political equality.

In these circumstances, the free speech principle might be seen to permit reasonable regulation, not to forbid it—at least if that principle is understood in terms of the requirements of a well- functioning democracy.

Fundamentalists are skeptical about this claim, but history, their self-proclaimed lodestar, does not help them much. True, campaign finance regulation was not in place in the founding period—not because it was considered unacceptable but because the young country did not have the fund-raising issues we have today. It would be ludicrous to argue that the original understand- ing of the First Amendment plainly dooms campaign finance laws. If fundamentalists believe that a practice is constitutional unless it specifically runs afoul of a judgment in the founding era, they can- not disapprove of campaign finance regulation. Perhaps they can argue that the founding generation would have disapproved of it if it had occurred to them, but this is speculative in the extreme. It involves an extrapolation—it certainly is not a matter of find- ing anything—and fundamentalists are supposed to despise extrapolations.

Many people believe that judicial restraint is the appropriate path here, but minimalists are not so sure. In practice, campaign finance laws can operate as incumbent-protection legislation; and they can exclude unpopular or minority voices. In light of the evi- dent dangers that arise when incumbent legislators are enacting campaign finance regulation, minimalists believe government should be required to justify its regulation in terms that are compatible with democratic goals. This belief does not lead to rigid rules; it leaves room for continuing debate and argument. But the minimalist approach is broadly compatible with the Court's current approach to campaign finance reform, which allows reasonable restrictions aimed at reducing corruption and promoting democratic principles.[17]

Property

The Fifth Amendment requires government to pay "just compensation" for any "taking of private property." But what counts as a "taking"? Of course government must pay if it is literally taking your land—if it is saying that it owns today what you owned yesterday. There is also a "taking" if the government physically invades your property by saying that a certain percentage of it must be used by the public or by public officials. Physical invasions are the defining instances of "takings." Thus far everyone is in agreement. Fundamentalists, minimalists, perfectionists, and most majoritarians are entirely comfortable with these conclusions.

But what if the government diminishes the value of your property? Suppose it enacts a zoning law that prevents you from building as you had planned, or reduces the value of your property by relocating a highway, or enacts an environmental regulation that makes your property worth only 80 percent of its previous value. Must the government compensate you? Many fundamentalists think so. They argue that the constitutional protection against "takings" is a barrier to many steps that diminish the value of property.

If this argument is accepted, it would have extraordinary implications. Among other things, it would create a new barrier to many valuable projects, including those in the environmental area. If government has to identify everyone who loses as a result of an environmental initiative, calculate the losses, and award compensation, it might not go forward at all.

Some fundamentalists are even more extreme. Isn't the tax system unconstitutional as a "taking"? Why is government allowed to "take" the income of rich people for the benefit of less rich people? Almost no one argues that taxes are unconstitutional as such. But for those who believe that regulatory takings are a violation of the Fifth Amendment, it isn't easy to explain why a progressive income tax, taking more from the rich than the poor, is constitutionally acceptable. If regulation isn't permitted to "take" resources from some for the benefit of others, why are taxes allowed to accomplish the same end? As far as I am aware, no federal judge is yet willing to press this question. But many fundamentalists, including some on the bench, would like a massive expansion in the limited protection the Court now gives to those whose property declines in value as a result of regulation.

Can fundamentalists invoke some original understanding on behalf of their argument? Here's the worst part: They don't even try. The leading academic commentators spend little time with the historical materials; the Supreme Court justices who show some sympathy with them—Scalia, Thomas, and Rehnquist—spend even less. An understanding of the founding period raises serious doubts about the pro-property position of purported fundamentalists. The most careful survey, by legal historian John Hart, concludes that "the Takings Clause was originally intended and understood to refer only to the appropriation of property"—and that it did not apply to regulation at all.[18] In the area of property rights, we find a clear and particularly sad example of false fundamentalism.

Hart demonstrates that regulation was extensive in the founding period and that it was not thought to raise a constitutional question. Buildings were regulated on purely aesthetic grounds, and no one argued that compensation was required. States asked farmers who owned wetlands to drain their lands and to contribute to the costs of drainage—without any complaints about "taking." Some landowners were forbidden to sell their interests in land, and compensation was not required. In numerous cases, the public interest took precedence over property rights. Of course government was not permitted literally to "take" land. But regulation was pervasive, and it was not considered troublesome from the constitutional point of view. Invoking no less an authority than James Madison, the author of the Takings Clause, Hart contends that the Court has already gone much too far in its occasional decisions requiring just compensation for regulatory takings.

Many perfectionists, not normally interested in original meaning, would be pleased to seize on Hart's analysis to abandon judicial protection of property when there is no literal "taking." But minimalists have a better idea. They are sympathetic to the claim, elaborated by Justice Scalia, that government should be required to compensate people when regulation has eliminated 100 percent of a property's value.[19] If people's land is rendered valueless, isn't the injury identical to that imposed when government takes their land away? Minimalists are also open to the possibility that some regulations, eliminating (say) 90 percent of the value of property, trigger the compensation requirement.

What minimalists resist is any ambitious agenda for the Takings Clause. They believe that the fundamentalist agenda lacks solid constitutional roots and is an unjustifiable intrusion into democratic processes. But despite anything history says, fundamentalists continue to press their claims, seeking to enlist the Constitution to block regulations that they believe unfair, even while they argue elsewhere that history should be the foundation of the Constitution's meaning.

Federalism

Everyone agrees that under the Constitution, the national government is one of the "enumerated" powers—that government cannot act whenever and wherever it likes. The framers of the Constitution created a system of dual sovereignty, in which both states and nation can govern—and under good conditions can check one another, to the ultimate benefit of We the People. Under this system, Congress is permitted to do a great deal. It can "lay and collect Taxes"; it may "pay Debts and provide for the common Defense and general Welfare of the United States"; it can "regulate Commerce with foreign Nations, and among the several States." It can do a lot more too. But whatever it does, it must be able to show that the Constitution authorizes it to act.

Commerce. Between 1937 and 1995, the Supreme Court gave a great deal of deference to Congress's authority over interstate commerce. In those decades the Court *never* struck down a legislative enactment under the Commerce Clause. This posture of restraint was based on both a practical point and a theoretical one.

The practical point is that our economy is now interdependent in the extreme. If a large company in New York goes bankrupt, many people will be affected even if they never visit New York. The Supreme Court has been highly attentive to the simple fact of national interdependence. Consider here the Court's 1937 decision in *NLRB v. Jones & Laughlin Steel Corp.*, upholding the National Labor Relations Act[20]—a ruling that Judge Ginsburg singles out for criticism. But the decision makes a lot of sense. As the Court said, a workplace stoppage in Pennsylvania "by industrial strife would have a most serious effect upon interstate commerce." Jones & Laughlin was the fourth largest steel producer in the United States, shipping its products to warehouses in Chicago, Detroit, Cincinnati, and Memphis. The impact of a strike in its manufacturing operation "would be immediate and might be catastrophic. We are asked to shut our eyes to the plainest facts of our national life."

For this reason, *Jones & Laughlin* was an exceedingly easy case. But the Court has also upheld congressional enactments whose connection to interstate commerce was not quite so clear. For example, it allowed Congress to forbid extortion in credit transactions, deferring to Congress's judgment that this kind of crime had interstate effects.[21] The Court also said that Congress could regulate strip-mining in Virginia, accepting Congress's finding that by destroying wildlife habitats and polluting the water, strip-mining affected many states, not only the state in which it occurred.[22] The Court has allowed Congress to impose minimum-wage laws on the manufacturing of goods destined for interstate shipment.[23] It explained that Congress was attempting to ensure that "interstate commerce should not be made the instrument of competition in the distribution of goods under substandard labor conditions, which competition is injurious to the commerce and to the states from and to which commerce flows." Time and again, the Court deferred to Congress's judgments about interstate effects so long as they were "rational"—and because our economy is so interdependent, rational judgments were easy to find.[24]

A theory, and not just common sense, lies behind this posture of restraint. In refusing to strike down acts of Congress, the Court was responding to the "political safeguards of federalism."[25] As the Constitution is constructed, the states have a strong role in the national government. The Senate is composed so as to ensure that each state has no more than two representatives, making it most unlikely that state interests will be ignored. Because of the filibuster and the system of seniority, minority representatives are in a good position to invoke the interests of their own states to constrain the national government. All this is by deliberate design. For these reasons, many people believe the Supreme Court should be exceptionally reluctant to disturb a congressional judgment that commerce is involved. Some people have even argued that the Court should get out of the federalism business altogether; and in the 1980s, it looked like the Court might be doing exactly that.

Under the Rehnquist Court, all this has changed dramatically. The opening salvo came in 1995, when the Supreme Court struck down the Gun-Free School Zones Act in *United States v. Lopez*.[26] The Gun-Free School Zones Act made it a federal crime to possess a firearm within a school zone. It was defended on the grounds that the possession of guns is the result of commercial activity, that the interstate market for possession of handguns by school-age children is substantial, and that guns can be used to restrict interstate commerce. As Justice Stephen Breyer argued, Congress could rationally conclude that there is a significant connection between gun-related school violence and interstate commerce. But in an opinion by Chief Justice Rehnquist, the Court disagreed, in a way that suggested at least some degree of sympathy for the Constitution in Exile. The Court went so far as to cast doubt on the "broad language" in its own previous opinions. Justice Thomas, writing separately, went much further, casting much doubt on decades of previous decisions.

But the more far-reaching decision came in *United States v. Morrison*,[27] decided in 2000. There the Court struck down a provision of the Violence Against Women Act that gave victims of sex-related violence a right of access to federal court to sue the perpetrators. Congress had found that sex-related violence has harmful effects on interstate commerce, not least because women are less likely to travel to places that have high levels of such violence. It is intuitively plausible that such violence has major effects on commercial activity. But going well beyond its decision in *Lopez*, the Supreme Court rejected the argument, signaling that it would give careful scrutiny to congressional efforts to regulate activities that were not themselves commercial. Here too, Justice Thomas suggested that he would welcome a large-scale rethinking of the Court's longstanding willingness to defer to congressional judgments that interstate commerce is involved.

The *Morrison* decision has been much celebrated by supporters of the Lost Constitution or the Constitution in Exile, who hope that the Court will move a lot further in the direction of limiting congressional power. And there are strong signals that some federal judges are interested in doing exactly that. Some prominent judges have argued that in some applications, the Endangered Species Act should be struck down as beyond congressional powers.[28] The Supreme Court has raised the possibility that the Clean Water Act may not be applied to bodies of water that do not cross state lines,[29] though it has refused to extend *Morrison*.[30]

Minimalists think these views are implausible. The loss of endangered species has unambiguous interstate effects insofar as it can affect scientific research and recreation. Water pollution within a single state is highly likely to affect interstate commerce, and Congress should be permitted to generalize from the many cases in which such effects occur. To be sure, minimalists agree that there are limits on congressional power. They reject the position, offered by some perfectionists, that the Supreme Court should allow Congress to use the Commerce Clause however it wishes. Minimalists demand a demonstration of some link between national action and interstate commerce. For this reason, they are comfortable with *Lopez,* where Congress did not seem to take constitutional constraints seriously at all. But they are not at all comfortable with *Morrison,* where Congress paid a great deal of attention to the constitutional question, and where the link with interstate commerce was hardly obscure.

What minimalists like least, and what no one ought to approve, is the fundamentalist idea that the Court should adopt a self-conscious agenda to limit congressional power of a sort that has long been considered legitimate.

Rights. Under the Constitution, Congress is explicitly given the power to "enforce" the provisions of the Fourteenth Amendment. What does this mean? For many years, the Supreme Court said that Congress had a great deal of discretion to remedy violations of this amendment.[31] It could, for example, invalidate all literacy tests for voting on the ground that some such tests were imposed for racially discriminatory reasons. Even more, Congress had some power to depart from the Court's own understanding of what the Constitution required. It could, for example, conclude that literacy tests are racially discriminatory even if the Court were reluctant to do so. In this way, the Court seemed to suggest that Congress was permitted to interpret the Fourteenth Amendment to embody a kind of antisubordination principle (see Chapter 5), even if the Court itself did not adopt that theory.

For a long time, fundamentalists have insisted on a much narrower understanding of Congress's power. They believe that Congress must follow the Court's reading of the Constitution and may not enlarge on what the Court has said. Accepting this argument, the Court struck down the Religious Freedom Restoration Act, an effort to protect religious liberty more broadly than the Court had been willing to do.[32] Even more ambitiously, the Court struck down provisions of the Americans with Disabilities Act, the Age Discrimination in Employment Act, and the Violence Against Women Act.[33] In these decisions, the Court rejected bipartisan congressional judgments about the need for measures to prevent violations of the Constitution's equality principle.

Perfectionists believe these decisions are badly misconceived—an abuse not only of history but also of the proper role of the Supreme Court. On this count, minimalists think that perfectionists are pointing in the right direction. Of course, Congress cannot use its enforcement power to do whatever it likes. But if the national legislature is acting to remedy an admitted constitutional violation, or if it is understanding the Fourteenth Amendment to protect rights somewhat more expansively than the Supreme Court has, the justices ought not to stand in its way. Minimalists do not have an agenda here, but they would be inclined to give Congress the benefit of reasonable doubt. What is most disturbing is that fundamentalists are willing to insist on an

exceedingly aggressive judicial role, and doing so without even a
short glance at the historical materials.

And More

These are only some of the most important areas in which fundamentalists want to move the law. There is a great deal more. Some
fundamentalists want to use the Due Process Clause to protect
companies from punitive damage awards. Others want to interpret the Constitution to limit Congress's power to allow people to
bring suit to enforce environmental law. Still others want to
reduce the use of the Constitution to protect those accused of
crime.

On some of these issues, their arguments are quite plausible,
and sensible minimalists are willing to make common cause with
them. But there is reason to be extremely uncomfortable when
judges are part of a movement—and above all when that movement is hard to distinguish from an ideological one.

CHAPTER TEN

Fundamentals

IN THE ABSTRACT, FUNDAMENTALISM APPEARS both principled and neutral. But too much of the time, fundamentalists offer an unmistakably partisan vision of the Constitution. Their Constitution casts serious doubts on affirmative action programs, gun control laws, restrictions on commercial advertising, environmental regulations, campaign finance reform, and laws that permit citizens to sue to enforce federal law. As many fundamentalists understand America's founding document, it raises doubts about the Environmental Protection Agency, the Occupational Safety and Health Administration, the Securities and Exchange Commission, the Federal Communications Commission, and many other federal agencies. It allows the President extraordinarily wide authority to wage war even at the expense of the most basic liberties. It contains no right of privacy. It allows the national government to discriminate on the basis of race. It permits states to benefit religious believers and perhaps even to establish churches. It imposes sharp limits on Congress's power to regulate interstate commerce and to enforce the guarantees of the Fourteenth Amendment. Most ambitiously, fundamentalists want to move in the direction of some Lost Constitution or the Constitution in Exile—the document as it was understood in the distant past.

Fundamentalists claim to embrace originalism, and to their credit, some of their conclusions do fit well with the original understanding of the Constitution. But they write as if their approach is the only legitimate approach to interpretation—as if those who reject the original understanding, and refuse to be bound by the views of those long dead, are refusing to do law at all. This is a myth. The Constitution doesn't call for fundamentalism. Nor have fundamentalists confronted the serious conceptual difficulties with following the "original understanding" of a document that was written centuries ago. And they have been evasive rather than candid about the radicalism of their approach, which would threaten to undo much of the fabric of our democracy and our rights.

Fundamentalists assert their approach more consistently than they follow it. For several of their positions, the historical evidence is exceedingly thin. Fundamentalists use the Constitution to attack affirmative action—even though history appears to suggest that affirmative action is entirely acceptable. Most fundamentalists show no interest in the history of the Takings Clause, which indicates that regulation is constitutionally unobjectionable. They insist that the Second Amendment protects the individual right to bear arms; this is far from implausible, but the question is complex and the Supreme Court has long ruled otherwise. Fundamentalists claim that the Constitution imposes sharp restrictions on Congress's power to allow people to sue to enforce the law. But here too, they fail to investigate whether their position has historical support. Too much of the time, fundamentalists read the Constitution not to fit the original understanding but the views of the extreme wing of Republican Party.

In the last two decades, fundamentalism has had a large influence on the Supreme Court. Often speaking in fundamentalist terms, the Rehnquist Court invalidated about three dozen congressional enactments from 1985 to 2005. In terms of sheer numbers, this is a record of activism unparalleled in the nation's history. The decisions of the Rehnquist Court have made the contemporary Constitution very different from the Constitution of 1980. In some ways it is better, but on many questions, it has moved in the direction sought by fundamentalists. To date, the movements have been far less radical than they might have been—partly because Justice Scalia pays attention to precedent, but mostly because Justices O'Connor and Kennedy give the Court a strong minimalist presence.

Fundamentalists want a lot more. It is ironic but true that some fundamentalists, having gained a stunning series of victories in Republican-dominated courts over the last two decades, are now mounting an assault on the very idea of judicial independence—and are seeking to produce a federal judiciary that operates as an arm of the political branches. Some activists are asking for radicals in robes.

Embracing Imperfection

Fundamentalists regard perfectionists as their major antagonists. Perfectionists agree that the Constitution's text is binding, but they have little interest in the specific views of the ratifiers. Perfectionists are comfortable with a Supreme Court that does not much hesitate to engage directly with the deepest issues in moral and political theory. The Court, they believe, properly serves as a kind of forum of principle in American politics, where the inquiry into principle is not constrained by the views of people long dead.[1] Many people think that the majestic generalities of the Constitution should be taken as a gift to posterity—as an invitation to subsequent generations to infuse the document with their own best understanding of how government should exercise its powers and understand its citizens' freedoms.

Perfectionists thus find it entirely appropriate for the Supreme Court to use the Constitution's broad phrases as a basis for protecting the right to choose abortion or physician-assisted suicide. Many perfectionists are sympathetic to the claim that as a matter of principle, the Constitution is best understood to require states to permit same-sex marriages—or even to require the national government to ensure that all citizens have food, housing, and medical care. If reasonable people can show, in principle, that the idea of "equal protection" supports a constitutional claim, and if the claim is not foreclosed by precedents (or even sometimes when it is), perfectionists tend to advise the Court: *Go for it.*

In the abstract, there is no decisive argument against either fundamentalism or perfectionism. We can imagine times and places in which judges might properly pursue one or the other. I have emphasized that Chief Justice John Marshall, the most celebrated figure in the history of American law, was a perfectionist of the nationalist kind. Many Americans celebrate some of the Warren Court's perfectionist decisions—for example, its embrace of the principle of one person, one vote. A little science fiction: If judges were infallible and our democracy were incurably flawed, it wouldn't be impossible to defend perfectionism as a way of ensuring that Americans have the rights that they deserve. Some more science fiction: If the ratifiers of the Constitution were infallible, and if judges who reject fundamentalism would almost always be wrong, we might all be fundamentalists.

But in general, neither fundamentalism nor perfectionism makes much sense for the United States at the present time. I hope I have said enough to show that fundamentalism would make us much less free and the American constitutional system much less democratic. Liberals have long liked aggressive courts, and so they have been attracted to perfectionism, most recently in hoping that federal judges will require states to recognize same-sex marriage; but their approach too has fatal defects. If perfectionists succeeded in giving federal courts the authority to interpret ambiguous constitutional provisions however they see fit, liberals might end up extremely unhappy with the results. To pull a few examples (not) out of the air, judges might invalidate minimum-wage laws, strike down campaign finance reform, and disable states from adopting affirmative action programs. So empowered, federal judges might even rule that restrictions on abortion are not constitutionally forbidden but actually required (as the Constitutional Court of Germany has in fact done).

But the objection to perfectionism doesn't rest only on the possibility of (what some would consider) bad results. Self-government is one of the rights to which people are entitled, and perfectionism can compromise that right. Suppose judges are correct about morality and justice; suppose they can be trusted to come up with the best understandings of equality and liberty. Even if so, their rulings could be futile or counterproductive. They would still amount to an imposition, by federal judges, on an unwilling society.

Consider, as a cautionary note, *Brown v. Board of Education,* a decision perfectionists frequently regard as exemplary. In *Brown,* the Court ruled that racial segregation in the public schools is unconstitutional, and it did so without being able to claim the authority of those who originally ratified the Fourteenth

Amendment. In fact the Court said, plainly, that it could not and would not "turn the clock back to 1868 when the Amendment was adopted. . . . We must consider public education in the light of its full development and present role in American life throughout the Nation." In 1955, the Court ruled that desegregation must occur "with all deliberate speed."[2]

A quiz: In 1960, on the sixth anniversary of the original *Brown* decision, how many of the 1.4 million African-American children in Alabama, Georgia, Louisiana, Mississippi, and South Carolina attended racially mixed schools? Answer: Zero. Even in 1964, a decade after *Brown*, more than 98 percent of African-American children in the South attended segregated schools. As Michael Klarman has shown, the Court, on its own, brought about little desegregation, above all because it lacked the power to overcome local resistance.[3] Real desegregation began only after the Department of Justice, empowered by the Civil Rights Act of 1964, started to bring pressure on segregated schools. Martin Luther King, Jr., helped to energize political processes in a way that produced large-scale change. It is hard to show that the Supreme Court did the same.

My point is not to reject *Brown*, which was the culmination of a long line of cases and for that reason can be defended on minimalist grounds. But we should hesitate in endorsing an aggressive judicial role even if we believe that courts will do what is right. The public might resist, and the judges' judgments might do far less than their defenders hope; they might even undermine the very goals they attempt to promote.

Roe v. Wade provides an additional reason for caution.[4] Before the Court's decision, the nation was moving steadily in the direction of permitting freedom of choice. State practices varied, perhaps fitting the diversity of moral views within a heterogeneous nation; but the movement toward the pro-choice position was unmistakable. Consider a remarkable fact: In the three years *before Roe*, there was a larger increase in the number of lawful abortions than in the three years *after Roe* (a pretty impressive statistic in light of the fact that after *Roe*, practically all abortions were lawful). Consider also the fact that *Roe* has had a massive and extraordinarily divisive effect on national politics. None of this demonstrates that *Roe* was wrong. But it is certainly reasonable to think that the Court would have done far better to proceed in minimalist fashion and with more respect for democratic prerogatives—and for the many millions of citizens who believe, on principle, that abortion is a serious moral wrong.

One Cheer for Perfectionism?

Many perfectionists will respond that with their cautious methods, minimalists could not have produced the very results they now attempt to safeguard—the right of privacy, freedom from sex discrimination, the ban on segregation, the broad protection of political dissent, and much more. In the perfectionist view, minimalists would have been stuck with the Constitution as it existed in, say, 1953, before the revolutionary decisions of the Warren Court. (Is 1953 the year of the minimalists' Constitution in Exile?) And if minimalism would produce a weaker system of constitutional rights, perhaps perfectionism is more supportable than it seems.

Perfectionists might challenge minimalism on the same grounds that I have used to challenge fundamentalism: that it is a partisan program masquerading as law. Perfectionists might say to minimalists: Sure, you're against perfectionism, but only because we've already given you most of what you want. For their part, fundamentalists might say to minimalists: Sure, you favor minimalism, but only because you're happy with the status quo.

Neither of these challenges is convincing. To a greater extent than we appreciate, our most basic rights are a product not of perfectionism but of minimalism itself.[5] The ban on racial segregation did not come as a bolt from the blue; it was the culmination of a long series of cautious, narrow rulings from the Supreme Court. The same is true of freedom of speech and even the right of privacy. To be sure, the nation accepts and even celebrates some judicial rulings that are harder to defend in minimalist terms. The right to freedom from sex discrimination was not made up out of whole cloth, but the case-by-case developments that led to it occurred over less than a decade. Suppose perfectionists really can show that their approach produced a number of decisions that are desirable and that no other approach could have generated. The principled minimalist responds: So what? If the Court had not acted, the democratic process might have done so instead. The Court's prohibition on sex discrimination played a significant role in stopping the Equal Rights Amendment, which seemed unnecessary in light of the Court's decisions. If you favor gender equality, the amendment might well have been a better option.

In any event, we cannot make the case for perfectionist judging simply by pointing to some apparent success stories. If perfectionist judges are unleashed, we are likely to have as many failures as successes. With this point, minimalists can turn perfectionism against itself. Judges seeking perfection are likely to make American democracy less perfect. Perfectionists are right to say, against fundamentalism, that no one should choose any approach that would make our system much worse. But they are wrong to say, against minimalism, that our system works best if judges feel free to read the Constitution in a way that fits with their own moral and political commitments. Democratic self-government has its claims, and many perfectionists do not take democracy seriously enough.

Liberty's Spirit

Seen in this light, nonpartisan restraint has real attractions, even a kind of nobility. Oliver Wendell Holmes, history's greatest advocate of nonpartisan restraint, offered a distinctly majoritarian vision of the Constitution, seeing it as a flexible instrument that recognizes the diversity of values within a large nation and across time. Fundamentalists have no enthusiasm for Holmes, whose vision cannot be attributed to the Constitution's ratifiers. But nothing in the text of the Constitution forecloses a general attitude of restraint. It is unfortunate and even amazing that in the last half-century, not one member of the Supreme Court has consistently adopted that attitude. We have lacked justices who are willing to say, for example, that the Constitution does not forbid affirmative action programs while also saying that the Constitution permits laws restricting both abortion and sodomy. Nonpartisan restraint deserves more defenders than it now has.

But the Court has had many minimalists, who insist that judges should not be part of any movement, and who seek outcomes on which people with varying views can agree. Minimalists come in different stripes. In my view, majoritarianism is too extreme, but the best versions of minimalism show a keen interest in it, and a willingness to uphold reasonable measures even when many people intensely object on moral grounds. I believe the Supreme Court should be more willing than it now is to uphold democratic judgments in favor of campaign finance laws, affirmative action programs, assistance for religious organizations, and limits on personal privacy. For the next decades, the Court would do well to refuse to entrench highly controversial positions about liberty and equality.

Of course there is a "core" of rights into which government cannot intrude. This core includes freedom of speech, the franchise, and (perhaps above all) a right to procedural protection against unjustified imprisonment. Outside of the core, the best brand of minimalism tends to be respectful of democratic prerogatives. But the most important point is much broader. By their very nature, minimalists are not too sure that they are right. In a free society, this lack of certainty is an excellent place for judges to start.

Fundamentalists stand at the opposite pole. Proclaiming their devotion to history and their fidelity to the law, they are all too willing to dress up a partisan program in legal garb. Purporting to value democratic processes and judicial restraint, they are all too willing to read the founding document as if it embodied a party platform, one that would endanger both our rights and our democratic institutions. The irony is that this platform has been pressed most aggressively by those who contend, and even seem to believe, that they are speaking neutrally for the Constitution.

Notes

Introduction

1. This speech has been published as Douglas Ginsburg, On Constitutionalism, *Cato Supreme Court Review* 7 (Washington, DC: Cato Institute, 2003).

2. Douglas H. Ginsburg, Delegation Running Riot, 18 *Regulation* 84 (1995).

3. See Randy Barnett, *Restoring the Lost Constitution: The Presumption of Liberty* (Princeton, NJ: Princeton University Press, 2003).

4. Mona Charen, *Do-Gooders: How Liberals Hurt Those They Claim to Help (and the Rest of Us)* (New York: Sentinel, 2004).

Chapter One

1. See Cass R. Sunstein, David Schkade, and Lisa Ellman, Ideological Judging on Federal Courts of Appeals; A Preliminary Investigation, 90 *Va. L. Rev.* 301 (2004).

2. See Antonin Scalia, *A Matter of Interpretation* 23 (Princeton, NJ: Princeton University Press, 1998).

3. Id.

4. Id.

5. For an argument in favor of width, see Antonin Scalia, The Rule of Law As a Law of Rules, 56 *U. Chi. L. Rev.* 115 (1989); the best general treatment is Adrian Vermeule, Interpretive Choice, 75 *NYU. L. Rev.* 74 (2000).

6. Scalia, supra note 2, at 119.

7. Minimalism is discussed in general terms in Cass R. Sunstein, *One Case at a Time: Judicial Minimalism on the Supreme Court* (Cambridge, MA: Harvard University Press, 1999).

8. See Richard A. Posner, *Law, Pragmatism, and Democracy* 80 (Cambridge, MA: Harvard University Press, 2003): "The pragmatic judge tends to favor narrow over broad grounds of decision in the early stages in the development of a legal doctrine. . . . What the judge has before him is the facts of the particular case, not the facts of future cases. He can try to imagine what those cases will be like, but the likelihood of error in such an imaginative projection is great. Working outward, in stages, from the facts before him to future cases with new facts that may suggest the desirability of altering the contours of the applicable rules, the judge avoids premature generalization."

9. The perfectionist approach to constitutional law should not be confused with perfectionism in political philosophy. For discussion, see John Rawls, *Political Liberalism* (New York: Columbia University Press, 1993).

10. See Ronald Dworkin, *Law's Empire* 229 (Cambridge, MA: Harvard University Press, 1985).

11. Christopher Hitchens, *The New York Times,* Book Review, Nov. 7, 2004, Book Review, p. 8.

12. See Leonard Levy, *Emergence of a Free Press* (New York: Oxford University Press, 1985).

13. Learned Hand, *The Spirit of Liberty* 190 (Irving Dilliard, ed.) (New York: Knopf, 1953).

14. See John Hart Ely, *Democracy and Distrust* (Cambridge, MA: Harvard University Press, 1981), for the classic defense of this position.

15. See James Bradley Thayer, The Origin and Scope of the American Doctrine of Constitutional Law, 7 *Harv. L. Rev.* 129 (1893).

16. 198 U.S. 45 (1905).

17. The major exception is freedom of speech. Holmes was a strong

advocate of the free speech principle, and he invoked that principle in order to invalidate, rather than to uphold, the outcomes of political processes. See *Abrams v. United States*, 250 U.S. 616, 630 (1919) (Holmes, J., dissenting). Holmes's enthusiasm for free speech can be seen as part and parcel of his majoritarianism. Without free speech, the system of majority rule cannot really work, simply because people are not able to exchange ideas. We can see Holmes as allowing a small bit of perfectionism to accompany his majoritarianism—perfecting the democratic process, or at least improving it, in the interest of genuine self-rule.

18. *Buck v. Bell*, 274 U.S. 200 (1927). For an extensive discussion, see Stephen Jay Gould, *The Mismeasure of Man* (New York: W. N. Norton, 1993).

19. See Mark Tushnet, *Taking the Constitution Away from the Courts* (Princeton, NJ: Princeton University Press, 1999).

20. See Robert Bork, *The Tempting of America* (New York: The Free Press, 1989).

21. See Larry Kramer, *The People Themselves: Popular Constitutionalism and Judicial Review* (New York: Oxford University Press, 2004).

Chapter Two

1. Originalism: The Lesser Evil, 57 *U. Cin. L. Rev.* 849, 862 (1989).

2. Letter from Thomas Jefferson to Samuel Kercheval (July 12, 1816), reprinted in *The Portable Thomas Jefferson* 552, 559 (M. Peterson, ed.) (New York: Viking, 1977).

3. Robert Bork, *The Tempting of America* 2 (New York: The Free Press, 1989).

4. Oliver Wendell Holmes to Harold Laski, March 4, 1920, *Holmes-Laski Letters*, vol. 1, 249 (Cambridge, Mass.: Harvard University Press, 1953).

5. Antonin Scalia, *A Matter of Interpretation* 47 (Princeton, NJ: Princeton University Press, 1998).

6. Id. at 38.

7. Id. at 43.

8. Id. at 45.

9. Bork, supra note, at 265.

10. Id. at 252–53.

11. Id. at 258–59.

12. William H. Rehnquist, The Notion of a Living Constitution, 54 *Tex. L. Rev.* 693 (1976).

13. Id. at 704.

14. O. W. Holmes, Natural Law, in *Collected Legal Papers* 310–11 (New York: Peter Smith, 1990; originally published 1920).

15. The strongest defense of the desegregation decision on fundamentalist grounds is Michael McConnell, Originalism and the Desegregation Decisions, 81 *Va. L. Rev.* 947 (1987).

16. See *Elk Grove Unified School District v. Newdow,* 124 S. Ct. 2301 (2004).

17. See Caleb Nelson, Originalism and Interpretive Conventions, 70 *U. Chi. L. Rev.* 519 (2003); H. Jefferson Powell, *The Original Understanding of Original Intent*, 99 *Harv. L. Rev.* 885 (1985).

18. Bork, supra note.

19. See Richard A. Posner, Bork and Beethoven, 42 *Stan. L. Rev.* 1365 (1990).

20. Quoted in Stephen Presser, Touting Thomas, *Legal Affairs* (Jan./Feb. 2005).

21. Id.

Chapter Three

1. *Lawrence v. Texas*, 539 U.S. 558, 592 (2003) (Scalia, J., dissenting).

2. 410 U.S. 113 (1973).

3. 381 U.S. 479 (1965).

4. *Eisenstadt v. Baird*, 405 U.S. 438 (1972); *Carey v. Population Services*, 431 U.S. 678 (1977).

5. 262 U.S. 390 (1923).

6. *Pierce v. Society of Sisters*, 265 U.S. 510 (1925).

7. 198 U.S. 45 (1905).

8. 60 U.S. 393 (1857).

9. See Samuel Warren, The New "Liberty" under the Fourteenth Amendment, 39 *Harv. L. Rev.* 431 (1926).

10. See Lawrence Tribe, The Puzzling Persistence of Process-Based Constitutional Theories, 89 *Yale L J* 1063, 1066 (1980).

11. For details, including support for the claims in this paragraph, see Geoffrey R. Stone et al., *Constitutional Law* ch. 6 (Boston: Aspen, 2005).

12. *Lochner v. New York*, 198 U.S. 45, 55 (1905) (Holmes, J., dissenting).

13. 478 U.S. 186 (1986).

14. *Michael H. v. Gerald D.*, 491 U.S. 110, 127–128 (1989).

15. See *Cruzan v. Director*, 497 U.S. 261 (1990); *Washington v. Glucksberg*, 521 U.S. 707 (1997).

16. See, e.g., *Stenberg v. Carhart*, 530 U.S. 914 (2000).

17. See *Washington v. Glucksberg*, 521 U.S. 707 (1997).

18. See Laurence Tribe, *Lawrence v. Texas:* The Fundamental Right That Dare Not Speak Its Name, 117 *Harv. L. Rev.* 1893, 1955 (2004).

19. See, e.g., J. R. Philip, Some Reflections on Desuetude, 43 *Jurid Rev* 260 (1931); Linda Rogers and William Rogers, Desuetude as a Defense, 52 *Iowa L. Rev.* 1 (1966).

20. See Gerald Rosenberg, *The Hollow Hope* (Chicago: University of Chicago Press, 1988).

21. See *Marcum v. MacWharter*, 308 U.S. 635 (2002).

22. See Rosenberg, supra note 20.

23. *Planned Parenthood v. Casey*, 505 U.S. 833 (1992).

24. See Ruth Bader Ginsburg, Some Thoughts on Autonomy and Equality in Relation to *Roe v. Wade*, 63 *N. Carolina L. Rev.* 375 (1985).

Chapter Four

1. 381 U.S. 479 (1965).

2. Patricia A. Cain, Imagine There's No Marriage, 16 *Quinnipiac L. Rev.* 27 (1996).

3. *Maynard v. Hill,* 125 U.S. 190, 205 (1888).

4. 262 U.S. 390 (1923).

5. 316 U.S. 535 (1942).

6. 381 U.S. 479 (1965).

7. 388 U.S. 1 (1968).

8. 434 U.S. 374 (1978).

9. 482 U.S. 78 (1987).

10. I draw here on David L. Chambers, What If? The Legal Consequences of Marriage and the Legal Needs of Lesbian and Gay Male Couples, 95 *Mich. L. Rev.* 447 (1996).

11. See *Califano v. Jobst,* 434 U.S. 47 (1977).

12. See, e.g., *Harper v. Virginia State Board of Elections,* 383 U.S. 663 (1966); *Reynolds v. Simms,* 377 U.S. 533 (1964).

13. See, e.g., *Dandridge v. Williams,* 397 U.S. 471 (1970); *Lindsey v. Normet,* 405 U.S. 56 (1972).

14. I try to defend this view in Cass R. Sunstein, Sexual Orientation and the Constitution: A Note on the Relationship Between Due Process and Equal Protection, 55 *U Chi L Rev* 1161 (1988).

15. *Lochner v. New York,* 198 U.S. 45, 57 (1905) (Holmes, J., dissenting).

16. See Edmund Burke, *Reflections on the Revolution in France* (Oxford: Oxford University Press, 1999).

17. See Jack Balkin, Tradition, Betrayal, and the Politics of Deconstruction, 11 *Cardozo L. Rev.* 1613 (1994); Lawrence Tribe and Michael Dorf, *On Reading the Constitution* (Cambridge, MA: Harvard University Press, 1991).

18. See *Michael H. v. Gerald D.,* 491 U.S. 505 (1989) (plurality opinion of Scalia, J.).

19. Henry B. Biller, *Fathers and Families: Paternal Factors in Child Development*, 1–3 (New York: Auburn House, 1993); Lynne Marie Kohm, *The Homosexual "Union": Should Gay and Lesbian Partnerships be Granted the Same Status as Marriage?*, 22 J. Contemp. L. 51, 61 & nn.53, 54 (1996); Cameron, *Homosexual Parents*, 31 *Adolescence* 757, 770–774 (1996).

20. Patterson, *Family Relationships of Lesbians and Gay Men*, 62 J. Marriage & Family, 1052, 1060, 1064–1065 (2000).

21. Cf. Lawrence G. Sager, The Legal Status of Underenforced Constitutional Norms, 91 *Harv. L. Rev.* 1212 (1978).

22. *Goodridge v. Department of Public Health*, 440 Mass. 309, 798 N.E. 2d 941 (2003).

Chapter Five

1. *Grutter v. Bollinger*, 539 U.S. 306, 373 (2003) (Thomas, J., dissenting).

2. A more modest ban, not specifically involving racial discrimination, can be found in the Privileges and Immunities Clause.

3. Ruth Colker, Anti-Subordination Above All, 61 *NYU L Rev* 1003 (1986).

4. *City of Richmond v. Croson*, 488 U.S. 469 (1989).

5. The best discussion, from which I borrow here, is Eric Schnapper, Affirmative Action and the Legislative History of the Fourteenth Amendment, 71 *Va. L. Rev.* 753 (1985).

6. Cong. Globe, 38th Cong., 1st Sess. App. at 2800 (1864).

7. Cong. Globe, 36th Cong., 1st Sess., app at 544 (statement of Rep. Taylor).

8. Id. at 401 (statement of Sen. MacDougall).

9. Id. at 588 (Statement of Rep. Donnelly).

10. Id. at 631–632 (Statement of Rep. Moulton).

11. Id. app. at 75 (statement of Rep. Phelps).

12. *Grutter v. Bollinger*, 539 U.S. 306 (2003).

13. 437 U.S. 265 (1978).

14. 448 U.S. 448 (1980).

15. 488 U.S. 469 (1989).

16. 515 U.S. 200 (1995).

17. *Gratz v. Bollinger,* 539 U.S. 244 (2003).

18. *Grutter v. Bollinger,* 539 U.S. 306 (2003).

Chapter Six

1. For excellent and related discussions from which I have learned a great deal, see Eric A. Posner and Adrian Vermeule, Accommodating Emergencies, 56 *Stan. L. Rev.* 605 (2003); Richard Pildes and Samuel Issacharoff, Between Civil Libertarianism and Executive Unilateralism: An Institutional Process Approach to Right During Wartime, 5 *Theoretical Inquiries in Law* (Online Edition) No. 1, Article 1 (Jan 2004), online at http://www.bepress.com/til/default/vol5/iss1/art1 (visited Dec. 1, 2004).

2. See generally David Cole, *Enemy Aliens: Double Standards and Constitutional Freedoms in the War on Terrorism* (New York: W. W. Norton, 2003).

3. This is one reading of Geoffrey R. Stone, *Perilous Times: Free Speech in Wartime, from the Sedition Act of 1798 to the War on Terrorism* (New York: W. W. Norton, 2004).

4. David Cole, Enemy Aliens, 54 *Stan. L. Rev.* 953, 958 (2002).

5. See Lee Epstein et al., The Supreme Silence During War (unpublished manuscript 2003) (offering quantitative study of judicial deference during war); William Rehnquist, *All the Laws But One* (New York: Knopf, 1998).

6. See Stone, supra note.

7. Id. at 224–225.

8. See Stone, *Perilous Times*, supra note; see also Aharon Barak, A Judge on Judging: The Role of a Supreme Court in a Democracy, 116 *Harv. L. Rev.* 16, 149 (2002): "[M]atters of daily life constantly test judges' ability to protect democracy, but judges meet their supreme test

in situations of war and terrorism. The protection of every individual's human rights is a much more formidable duty in times of war and terrorism than in times of peace and security. . . . As a Justice of the Israeli Supreme Court, how should I view my role in protecting human rights given this situation? I must take human rights seriously during times of both peace and conflict."

9. See Office of Legal Counsel, *Memorandum for Alberto Gonzales, Counsel to the President, Re: Standards of Conduct for Interrogation under 18 U.S.C 2340–2340A* (August 1, 2002) (copy on file with author).

10. See *Rasul,* 124 S Ct 2686 (2004); *Rumsfeld v. Padilla,* 124 S Ct 2711 (2004); *Hamdi v. Rumsfeld,* 124 S Ct 2633 (2004).

11. *Hamdi,* 124 S Ct 2633, 2674 (2004).

12. 321 F3d 1134 (DC Cir 2003).

13. Id. at 1145.

14. 331 F3d 918 (DC Cir 2003).

15. 5 U.S.C §552 (2000).

16. See, for example, *United States v. Moussaoui,* 382 F3d 453 (4th Cir 2004).

17. 316 F3d 450 (4th Cir 2003), revd, *Hamdi v. Rumsfeld,* 124 U.S. 2633 (2004).

18. The principal exception is that the President is always permitted to repel sudden attacks—a category that is not self-defining. See John Hart Ely, Suppose Congress Wanted a War Powers Act That Worked, 88 *Colum. L. Rev.* 1379, 1388 (1988); Note, Congress, the President, and the Power to Commit Forces to Combat, 81 *Harv. L. Rev.* 1771, 1782 (1968).

19. See John Hart Ely, *War and Responsibility* (Princeton, NJ: Princeton University Press, 1995).

20. See *Youngstown Sheet and Tube Co. v. Sawyer,* 343 U.S. at 610–611. For general discussion, see Curtis Bradley and Jack Goldsmith, Congressional Authorization and the War on Terrorism, *Harv. L. Rev.* 2047 (2005).

21. For relevant discussion, see Harold Koh, *The National Security Constitution: Sharing Power after the Iran-Contra Affair* 38–41 (New Haven, CT: Yale University Press, 1990); John Hart Ely, The American War in Indochina, Part I: The (Troubled) Constitutionality of the War They Told Us About, 42 *Stan. L. Rev.* 877 (1989); Gregory Sidak, To Declare War, 41 *Duke L. J.* 29 (1991).

22. Francis Biddle, *In Brief Authority* 219 (New York: Doubleday 1962).

23. See Cass R. Sunstein, *Why Societies Need Dissent* (Cambridge, MA: Harvard University Press, 2003).

24. See Irving Janis, *Groupthink* (New York: Houghton Mifflin 1983), for many examples.

25. For illustrations, see Stone, *Perilous Times.*

26. Available at *ht://intelligence.senate.gov/* (visited Dec. 1, 2004).

27. NASA, 1 *Report of The Columbia Accident Investigation Board,* available at http://www.nasa.gov/columbia/home/CAIB_Vol1.html (visited Dec. 1, 2004).

28. See S. Moscovici, and M. Zavalloni, The Group As A Polarizer of Attitudes, 12 *J. of Pers. and Soc. Psych.* 125 (1969).

29. Friedrich A. von Hayek, *The Constitution of Liberty* 155 (Chicago: University of Chicago Press, 1960).

30. See William von Hippel et al., Attitudinal Process Versus Context: The Role of Information Processing Biases in Social Judgment and Behavior, in Joseph P. Forgas et al., eds., *Social Judgments* 251, 263 (Cambridge: Cambridge University Press, 2003).

Chapter Seven

1. *Rumsfeld v. Padilla,* 124 S Ct 2711, 2735 (2004) (Stevens, J., dissenting).

2. *Association for Civil Rights in Israel v. The General Security Service.* Supreme Court of Israel: Judgment Concerning the Legality of the General Security Service's Interrogation Methods, 38 I.L.M. 1471 (1999).

3. 357 U.S. 116 (1958).

4. 343 U.S. 579 (1952).

5. Id. at 634 (Jackson concurring).

6. 320 U.S. 81 (1943).

7. 327 U.S. 304 (1946).

8. See William H. Rehnquist, *All the Laws But One: Civil Liberties in Wartime* 36–38 (New York: Vintage, 2000).

9. See *Masses Publishing Co. v. Patten,* 244 F 535 (SDNY 1917); see generally Stone, *Perilous Times* at 164–70, for a detailed discussion.

10. *United States v. Bureleson,* 255 U.S. 407 (1921); *Abrams v. United States,* 250 U.S. 622 (1919).

11. 255 U.S. at 417 (Brandeis, J., dissenting); id. at 436 (Holmes, J., dissenting).

12. 317 U.S. 1 (1942).

13. 320 U.S. 81 (1943).

14. 323 U.S. 214 (1944).

15. *Hamdi v. Rumsfeld,* 124 U.S. 2633 (2004).

16. Id. at 2655.

17. *McNabb v. United States,* 318 U.S. 332, 347 (1943).

18. 327 U.S. 304 (1945).

19. See *Johnson v. Eisentrager,* 339 U.S. 763 (1950).

20. 124 S Ct 2633 (2004).

21. *Rumsfeld v. Padilla,* 124 S Ct 2711, 2735 (2004) (Stevens, J., dissenting).

22. 343 U.S. at 594–597.

23. 124 S Ct 2686 (2004).

24. 124 S Ct 2633, 2671 (Scalia, J., dissenting).

25. Id. at 2674.

26. See Antonin Scalia, The Rule of Law as a Law of Rules, 56 U. Chi. L. Rev. 1165, 1181 (1989).

27. *Rasul v. Bush,* 124 S Ct 2686 (2004).

28. The difficulty is that it is easy to imagine cases of emergency in which the writ may not be suspended, because "Cases of Rebellion or Invasion" are not involved. 124 S Ct 2682–2683. If the writ may not be suspended, then the President must hold formal trials and may not detain people—perhaps a plausible conclusion, but not what Justice Scalia intended.

Chapter Eight

1. Antonin Scalia, A Note on the Benzene Case, 4 *Regulation,* July/August 1980, at 28.

2. See *Whitman v. American Trucking Associations,* U.S. (2002).

3. Id.

4. See, e.g., *J. W. Hampton v. U.S.,* 376 U.S. 394, 409 (1928).

5. *A. L. A. Schechter Poultry Corp v. U.S.,* 295 U.S. 495 (1935). The only other decision invalidating agency action on nondelegation grounds is *Panama Refining Co. v. Ryan,* 293 U.S. 388 (1935).

6. See David Schoenbrod, *Power Without Responsibility* (New York: Oxford University Press, 2000); Gary Lawson, The Rise and Rise of the Administrative State, 107 *Harv L Rev* 1231, 1240–1241 (1994).

7. The Nazi experience might provide an instructive lesson here. One of the earlier decisions by the German legislature, under Hitler, was to authorize Hitler to rule "by decree," and the resulting experience helped inspire an explicit nondelegation principle in the German Constitution. See David P. Currie, *The Constitution of the Federal Republic of Germany* 125–126 (Chicago: University of Chicago Press, 1994). See also German Const Art 80, § 1, requiring that the content, purpose, and extent of the legislative authorization be specified in the statute itself. Note also that the Constitutional Court of South Africa has embarked on enforcement of a nondelegation principle, at least in extreme cases. See Executive Council, *Western Cape Legislature v. President of the Republic South Africa* 1995 (4) SA 877, 898–906, 918–919 (Const Ct).

8. Letter from Madison to Jefferson (Oct 17, 1788), in R. Rutland and C. Hobson, eds., 11 *The Papers of James Madison* 298 (Charlottesville, VA: 1977).

9. Eric Posner and Adrian Vermeule, Interring the Nondelegation Doctrine, 69 *U. Chi. L. Rev.* 1721 (2002).

10. In the Constitutional Convention, James Madison did move that the President be given power "to execute such other powers, not Legislative nor Judiciary in their nature, as may from time to time be delegated by the national Legislature." But his motion was defeated, with many people suggesting that it was believed to be unnecessary, because the Constitution already conferred that power implicitly. See Eric Posner and Adrian Vermeule, Interring the Nondelegation Doctrine, 69 *U Chi L Rev* 1721, 1734 (2002).

11. 1 Stat 95 (1789).

12. 1 Stat 137 (1790).

13. 4 The Debates of the Several State Conventions on the Adoption of the Federal Constitution 560 (Jonathan Elliot, ed.) (Burt Franklin, 1888).

14. See the excellent treatment in Jerry L. Mashaw, *Greed, Chaos, and Governance: Using Public Choice to Improve Public Law* 131–157 (New Haven, CT: Yale University Press, 1997).

15. As a technical matter, some agencies, such as the Federal Communications Commission, are "independent" of the President in the sense that their heads cannot be fired at the President's whim. But even independent agencies are subject to a measure of presidential control, and usually tend to follow his policies, at least after any particular president has been in office for a year or more.

16. See David Epstein and Sharyn O'Halloran, *Delegating Powers* (Cambridge: Cambridge University Press, 1999).

17. Id at 237.

18. Id.

19. See *Mistretta v. United States,* 488 U.S. 361 (1989) (Scalia, J., dissenting).

20. *Bowen v. Georgetown University Hospital,* 488 U.S. 204, 208 (1988).

21. See, for example, *Usery v. Turner Elkhorn Mining,* 438 U.S. 1, 14–20 (1976).

22. See *National Association of Regulatory Utility Commissioners v. FCC,* 880 F2d 422 (D.C. Cir 1989).

23. See Herbert Wechsler, The Political Safeguards of Federalism, 54 *Colum L Rev* 543 (1954), for the classic discussion of these safeguards.

24. *EEOC v. Arabian American Oil Co.,* 499 U.S. 244, 248 (1991).

25. See *Ramah Navajo Chapter v. Lujan,* 112 F3d 1455, 1461–1462 (10th Cir 1997).

26. *United States Department of Energy v. Ohio,* 503 U.S. 607, 615 (1992).

27. *United States v. Wells Fargo Bank,* 485 U.S. 351, 354 (1988).

28. *Michigan Citizens for an Independent Press v. Thornburgh,* 868 F2d 1285, 1299 (D.C. Cir 1989) (Ginsburg, J., dissenting) (noting the "accepted rule" that antitrust exemptions must be narrowly construed); *Group Life & Health Insurance v. Royal Drug Co,* 440 U.S. 205, 231 (1979) (noting the "well settled" rule that antitrust exceptions "are to be narrowly construed").

29. *King v. St. Vincent's Hospital,* 502 U.S. 215, 220 n. 9 (1991).

Chapter Nine

1. Stephen Presser, Touting Thomas, *Legal Affairs* (Jan./Feb. 2005).

2. See Antonin Scalia, *A Matter of Interpretation* 43 (Princeton, NJ: Princeton University Press, 1998).

3. *Printz v. United States,* 521 U.S. 898, 938 (1997) (Thomas, J., concurring).

4. 307 U.S. 174 (1939).

5. See Geoffrey Stone et al., *Constitutional Law* (Boston, MA: Aspen, 2005) 734–741 for an overview.

6. *Presser v. Illinois,* 116 U.S. 252 (1886).

7. The best discussion is Michael McConnell, Accommodation of Religion, 1985 *Sup. Ct. Rev.* 1562.

8. *Elk Grove Unified School District v. Newdow,* 542 U.S. 1, 80 (2004)(Thomas, J., concurring in the judgment).

9. See id.

10. *Zelman v. Simmons-Harris,* 536 U.S. 639 (2002).

11. *See McCreary County v. ACLU,* 2005 U.S. Lexis § 211 (2005), *Van Orden v. Perry,* 2005 U.S. Lexis § 215 (2005).

12. *Brandenburg v. Ohio,* 395 U.S. 444 (1969).

13. Valentine v. Christensen, 316 U.S. 52 (1942).

14. *Virginia State Bd. of Pharmacy v. Virginia Citizens Consumer Council,* 425 U.S. 748 (1976).

15. See *44 Liquormart v. Rhode Island,* 517 U.S. 484, 518 (1996) (Thomas, J., concurring in the judgment).

16. See id at 517 (Scalia, J., concurring in the judgment).

17. See *McConnell v. FEC,* 540 U.S. 93 (2003).

18. John F. Hart, Land Use Law in The Early Republic and the Original Meaning of the Takings Clause, 94 *Nw. U. L. Rev.* 1099 (2000).

19. See *Lucas v. South Carolina Coastal Council,* 505 U.S. 1003 (1992).

20. 301 U.S. 1 (1937).

21. *Perez v. U.S.,* 402 U.S. 146 (1971).

22. *Hodel v. Virginia Surface Mining Assn.,* 452 U.S. 264 (1981).

23. *U.S. v. Darby,* 312 U.S. 100 (1941).

24. 317 U.S. 111 (1942).

25. See Herbert Wechsler, The Political Safeguards of Federalism, 54 *Colum. L. Rev.* 543 (1954); Jesse Choper, *Judicial Review and the National Political Process* (Chicago: University of Chicago Press, 1980).

26. *United States v. Lopez,* 514 U.S. 549 (1995).

27. 529 U.S. 598 (2000).

28. See *GDF Realty Investments v. Norton,* 362 F.2d 285, 287 (5th Cir. 2004) (Jones, J., dissenting from the denial of rehearing en banc).

29. *Solid Waste Agency v. U.S. Army Corps of Engineers*, 531 U.S. 159 (2001).

30. *Gonzales v. Raich*, 125 S. Ct. 2195 (2005).

31. See, e.g., *Katzenbach v. Morgan*, 384 U.S. 641 (1966).

32. *Employment Division, Department of Human Resources v. Smith*, 494 U.S. 872 (1990).

33. *Board of Trustees v. Garrett*, 531 U.S. 356 (2001); *Kimel v. Florida Board of Regents*, 528 U.S. 62 (2000); *U.S. v. Morrison*, 529 U.S. 598 (2000).

Chapter Ten

1. See Ronald Dworkin, The Forum of Principle, 56 *NYU L. Rev.* 469 (1981).

2. *Brown v. Bd. of Educ. of Topeka*, 349 U.S. 294 (1955).

3. See Michael Klarman, *From Jim Crow to Civil Rights* (New York: Oxford University Press, 2003).

4. See the powerful discussion in Mary Ann Glendon, *Abortion and Divorce in Western Law* (Cambridge, MA: Harvard University Press, 1989).

5. For an excellent extended treatment, see David Strauss, Common Law Constitutional Interpretation, 63 *U. Chi. L. Rev.* 877 (1996).

Index